SERVING THEIR COMMUNITIES

50 *Years of the New York State Broadcasters Association*

SERVING THEIR COMMUNITIES

50 *Years of the New York State Broadcasters Association*

Stephen Warley

New York State Broadcasters Association
Albany, New York

Copyright © 2005 The New York State Broadcasters Association

Published by The New York State Broadcasters Association

Distributed for The New York State Broadcasters Association by

Fordham University Press
University Box L
Bronx, New York 10458
www.fordhampress.com

Tel 1 (718) 817-4795

Fax 1 (718) 817-4785

ISBN: 0-9776117-0-1

Library of Congress Cataloguing-in-Publication
Data is available from the Library of Congress

Design and Production: A Good Thing, Inc.
Copyediting and proofreading: Milton Horowitz

Printed in the United States of America

DEDICATION

To those great broadcasters of NYSBA's first 50 years. Their example and dedication continue to inspire and instruct those who serve today.

TABLE OF CONTENTS

PHOTOGRAPHS

Photographs 1 to 34 follow page 52

Photographs 35 to 72 follow page 148

Photographs 73 to 90 follow page 196

FOREWORD

"The strongest and sweetest songs remain yet to be sung."
—Walt Whitman, New York poet

It has been an exciting journey and a rare privilege to research and assemble the remarkable story of the New York State Broadcasters Association. It is not merely a commercial trade organization as much as it is a brotherhood and sisterhood of dedicated public servants.

In recording its history, I found it difficult not to appreciate NYSBA as a microcosm of the entire American broadcasting industry from coast to coast. Unlocking its respect and admiration for the past provides keys to its future and the industry its members serve so nobly.

In an attempt to map the cavernous history of NYSBA, this 50th anniversary book provides a mosaic drawn from the amazing individual stories of over 100 New York broadcasters and industry insiders, spoken in their own words. They share their experiences as members of NYSBA, how they served their own disparate communities, and the unique challenges they overcame to build and develop radio and television broadcasting in the Empire State.

It would be impossible to record each and every story mined from the archives of this great association or the collective memories of its founders and participants. There are too many to count, one better than the next. It has been our intention, then, only to hold up a mirror to the Association, reflecting the work and dedication of these enlightened broadcasters and to chronicle their contributions in markets large and small, from radio and television, as well as to offer perspectives from both owners and corporate executives.

The stories found within these pages are not unlike the ones overheard at the NYSBA Annual Meetings or Executive Conferences over the last 50 years, when Empire State broadcasters gathered together to share ideas and offer support to their colleagues. Hopefully their triumphs and trials will unlock your own personal memories to be shared with a colleague or better yet, to inspire the next generation of New York broadcasters.

Stephen Warley

ACKNOWLEDGMENTS

When I was first approached by Joe Reilly and invited to be among those being considered to write a history to celebrate NYSBA's 50th anniversary, I held few expectations and was in fact quite naive of the daunting task that might lay before me. My two greatest passions in life are history and media. I have always been most attracted to projects that tug at my creative instincts in these two important fields. While I have recently retreated to my New England roots, New York will *always* by my favorite city. Its relentless energy chiseled away at me for almost a decade, shaping me as a media professional, shaping me as an adult. It gave me ideas, inspiration and guts. Accepting the privilege of writing the history of the New York State Broadcasters Association was an honor for me.

Much of NYSBA's dynamic and colorful history is owed to the 25-year tenure of its president, Joseph Reilly, praise he would be quick to dismiss. He has been the engine, the tour de force of the Association. He is the "author" and "editor" of many of the stories that lie within the pages of this book. To his credit, he helped me understand that NYSBA was never about any one individual or their accomplishments, but rather it was about the diversity of its voices, united in the service of New York's communities. It is true, it would have been very easy to gravitate toward the titans of broadcasting in the telling of NYSBA's history, but that would only represent a few patches in the quilt that represents the full range of broadcasters in New York State from television and radio, upstate and downstate, and individual owners and corporate executives. Joe Reilly made sure no voice was left unheard as he served NYSBA over the last 25 years, as well as in the preparation of this book. I thank him for his remarkable energy, persistence, and attention to detail as he spent hours on end sorting through mountains of old photos and editing innumerable drafts, leaving no stone unturned. Not only did he give me this chance of a lifetime, he taught me that broadcasting is all about "serving the community."

I owe much gratitude to my other "editor" and consultor William O'Shaughnessy. His electrifying passion for his "profession" breathed life into the "characters" of this book in ways my youthful years have left me unable to do. His institutional memory within the Association is virtually unmatched, helping to sharpen the tints, tones, and shades of the scenes that will play out in the mind's eye of the readers of this book. As one of the last independent broadcast owners, he provided me with a living link to the past, helping me capture the texture and feel of what it was like to be a broadcaster 20, 30, 40, and even 50 years ago. Observing him at work as a local broadcaster has not only offered me a window to a time that has now passed us by, but also a glimpse into the future direction of the broadcasting profession.

Special thanks to Aaron Richman, Shoshana Feinstein, Howard Petlack, Milton Horowitz, and Sandi Schroeder from A Good Thing, Inc., for the many long hours of hard work they put into designing the cover and laying out the entire book. Their flexibility and talent to incorporate our most challenging of requests took the aesthetics of this book to even greater heights. Their attention to detail was impeccable.

I would like to thank two of my former Fordham colleagues as well: Dr. Everette Dennis, distinguished Felix E. Larkin professor and chairman of Fordham Business School's Center for Communications, for having the confidence to send so many wonderful opportunities my way, especially for suggesting me for this project. I would also like to thank my long-time friend and colleague James Sheridan, who also earned his MBA from Fordham Business School, for always making time to bounce around ideas to help clarify my thoughts.

The success of a project like this is completely dependent on sound and reliable communications as countless documents are whirred around in cyberspace, and never-ending decisions have to be made to keep the momentum moving forward. Thus I am grateful to Mary Anne Jacon, Sandy Messineo, and Barbara Munderville at NYSBA for accommodating my deluge of requests, phone calls, e-mails, and for coordinating photo submissions. I should also like to extend special thanks to Cindy Gallagher and Don Stevens of Whitney Radio for keeping all the balls in the air when it seemed impossible to do so.

During the first half of this project I was employed as general manager of TVSpy.com and ShopTalk, both owned by Vault, Inc. I would like to thank Vault for giving me the opportunity to devote the necessary time required for a project of this magnitude, with special thanks to its CEO, Samer Hamadeh.

Special thanks also to former U.S. Senator Alfonse D'Amato and former Governor Mario M. Cuomo for taking the time to share their perspective as public servants and their thoughts on the impact of broadcasting on New York's communities. Thank you as well to Governor George Pataki for his help with the development of this book.

I also acknowledge the kindness of Eddie Fritts, president of the National Association of Broadcasters, and Gary Fries, president of the Radio Advertising Bureau, for finding the time to be interviewed for this special anniversary in New York broadcasting and for lending their experiences and national viewpoint to appropriately identify New York's place in broadcast history.

Much of the research for this book was derived from NYSBA's own voluminous archives and from direct first-person interviews with New York broadcasters. Several organizations were very helpful with "filling in the gaps" to help tell a fuller story about New York broadcasting. Special thanks to Sharon Wolin for sharing all her research, interviews, and photos from the production of NYSBA's video tribute to its first class of Hall of Fame inductees in 2005. Thanks to Don Angelo of the Buffalo Broadcast Pioneers, the Radio Advertising Bureau, the National Association of Broadcasters, Artbitron, Nielsen Media, the U.S. Census Bureau, the Library of American Broadcasting, the Broadcasters Foundation, and the Museum of Television and Radio. Special thanks to those organizations who submitted photos, including WPIX-TV in New York, WNBC-TV in New York, WTEN-TV in Albany, WOR Radio in New York, WIXT-TV in Syracuse, WKBW-TV in Buffalo, and Whitney Radio in Westchester.

As previously noted, the driving force behind this book are the original interviews with New York broadcasters, who conveyed in vivid detail what it was like to broadcast in the Empire State over the last 50 years. In no particular order then, I should properly thank the following for taking time out of their busy schedules and in many cases, going through old, almost forgotten files for additional research and photos: Alan Chartock, John Kelly, Bob Ausfeld, Jim Morrell, the late Phil Spencer, Bill Brown Jr., Bill Brown III, Amos Finch, Myra Youmans, Al Anscombe, Don Angelo, Jim Arcara, Larry Levite, Frank Lorenz, Bill McKibben, John Zach, Richard Novik, Merrill Rosen, Dennis Webster, Jim Roselli, Ramblin' Lou Shriver, Richard Beesemyer, Phil Beuth, Bob King, Wally Schwartz, Larry Taishoff, Don West, Martin Beck, Arty Angstreich, Jim Champlin, Ernie Anastos, Bob Bruno, Ralph Guild, Leavitt Pope, Al Primo, Jim Greenwald, David Hinckley, Nick Verbitsky, Roger King, David Feinblatt, Pat Tocatlian, Andrew Langston, Bud Wertheimer, Paul Sidney, Jim Rodgers, Keela Rodgers, Jim Delmonico, Joel Delmonico, Randy Bongarten, Frank Boyle, Dick Foreman, Gordon Hastings, Ed McLaughlin, Ed Levine, Shell Storrier, Paul Dunn, R. Peter Straus, Eric Straus, Tony Malara, Walter Maxwell, Michael Collins, Tom Murphy, Stu Subotnick, Maire Mason, Erica Farber, Jane Barton, Bill Grimes, Jim Duffy, Jack Ellsworth, Warren Bodow, Dennis Swanson, Dean David Rubin, Steve Baboulis, Jerry Gillman, Sasha Gillman, Adrienne Gaines, Bill Jaker, Nancy Widmann, and Stephanie McNamara.

Thank you especially to John Tabner, NYSBA's long-time legal counsel, and Matthew Mataraso, NYSBA's current counsel, for their insights into the many different policy stands the Association developed in response to New York State and federal legislation affecting broadcasters through the years.

On a personal note, I would be remiss if I did not thank my family, my parents in particular. What I admire most about my parents has been their ability to guide me to make my own decisions. They never directly told me what course of action to take, merely the options I should consider. It is a rare gift. That process has helped me balance the competing views of so many deserving broadcasters who were an important part of this book. I can only hope this history is judged not by the amount of copy devoted to individual achievements, but rather by the accuracy with which the complete mosaic of broadcasting has been represented in its united, consistent, and becoming mission to serve the people of New York State.

Stephen Warley

Introduction

"New York State has been richly blessed by a bounteous and generous Creator with magnificent mountains and unrivaled seashores, beautiful lakes, majestic rivers, and fertile agricultural land. But New York's greatest asset is its 18 million men, women, and children. We know these people —where they live—in New York's 62 counties and 62 cities, including the greatest city in the world, and in our 556 villages and 931 towns."

—Malcolm Wilson, 50th governor of New York

On July 27, 1788, after months of fierce debate and careful consideration, the State of New York became one of the last of the 13th original colonies to ratify the U.S. Constitution, making it the 11th state to be admitted to the new union. Much like New York's late entrance into the union of the United States, it would also be one of the last states to form a broadcasters association. Despite its early reluctance to subjugate itself to a powerful federal government, New York quickly took hold of its destiny as the leading voice in the political, economic, and cultural development of the new American republic, a role it possesses to this day as host to the country's largest and most influential city. The same would surely be true of the New York State Broadcasters Association's (NYSBA) dynamic and enlightened leadership in broadcasting.

The creation of the New York Stock Exchange, along with the visionary economic policies of the young New Yorker Alexander Hamilton, the nation's first secretary of the treasury, established a vibrant capitalist system that made America the mighty nation it is today, with New York at the very heart of that economic vitality. New York's prestige grew dramatically, spreading westward with the building of the Erie Canal in the early 19th century. Goods from all over the world passed through New York harbor, traveling up the Hudson River, along the Erie Canal to its western terminus in Buffalo, to be shipped throughout the burgeoning western frontier. This economic lifeline also helped make Buffalo one of America's largest and most important cities. The same would actually be true of its place in broadcast history.

It is often said that visiting New York City isn't like visiting anywhere else in the United States. It is everything the rest of the country is not: fast-paced, dynamic, welcoming of change, a blending of cultures, and a place that truly never sleeps. Yet it represents everything America stands for: innovation, creativity, free markets, democratic discourse, and the freedom to pursue one's loftiest dreams. There is little wonder why the major broadcast networks made their home in New York, where the confluence of ideas and sheer willpower to create and succeed are unmatched.

New York Firsts in Broadcasting

Early on, New York demonstrated its ability to be worthy of bearing the mantle as the unquestioned center of mass communications. The landmark trial of John Peter Zenger in 1735 would provide the foundation for common law protection of free speech. For the first time in Western civilization, a jury handed down a verdict of "not guilty," determining that the *words* printed in Zenger's paper did not amount to seditious libel. The British practice until that time permitted only a jury to determine whether the publisher *printed* the allegedly seditious libel. Thus, New York established a long, enviable history as a voracious defender of free speech, and that example would become crucial in the development of broadcast journalism.

It should be no surprise that the very first radio commercial was broadcast in New York City, the commercial mecca of the United States. The Queensboro Corporation of New York paid $50 for sponsorship of five programs over as many days on WEAF to sell real estate in 1922.

President Franklin Delano Roosevelt, who had served as the 44th governor of New York, was the nation's first chief executive to regularly use radio to communicate with the American people, familiarly known as his "fireside chats." In his 31 radio addresses as president, FDR frequently invited the American people to "tell me your troubles." Roosevelt understood the power of this new medium to help unite his people into a nation of active citizens. He and his speech writers used language that was plain and simple, crafting anecdotes to help the average American understand complex issues. To maximize his audience, the chats were broadcast at 10 p.m. Eastern Standard Time, early enough for Easterners getting ready for bed, and late enough for those on the West Coast coming home from work. By the end of the Roosevelt administration, almost 90% of all Americans owned a radio. It's worth noting that New York has produced eight presidents, more than any other state, another indication of its sweeping influence as a national leader.

As the Golden Age of radio was in full swing during the Roosevelt years, a brilliant and eccentric New York inventor named Edwin Armstrong developed a new radio technology that would one day turn radio on its head. In 1934, Armstrong completed his first field test for FM (frequency modulation), using an RCA tower atop the Empire State Building. The frequency was sent to a friend's receiver in Long Island, reportedly coming through "loud and clear," something the AM signal was unable to do.

Armstrong's research demonstrated that FM eliminated the "static" plaguing AM signals and produced sound superior to AM. He also discovered multiplexing, the ability of an FM signal to carry two radio programs at once. His expanded FM research in World War II led to the development of radar, using FM, which, unlike AM waves, could not be jammed. His work also laid the groundwork for space communications, bouncing an FM signal to the moon and back again. While aware of the far reaching impact FM would have on radio, Armstrong unfortunately never saw the full potential of his discoveries. FM as a technology was stifled by the radio industry, especially by David Sarnoff's Radio Corporation of America, for several years. Believing he was a failure, Armstrong committed suicide in 1954, approximately two decades before his invention was to rule the airwaves.

Television was not invented by a New Yorker, but the pioneering efforts of General Electric (GE) engineers in Schenectady helped make it a commercial reality. America's first television station, WRGB, aired its first public broadcast in 1928. Later that year, the station aired its first newscast, with Kolin Hager broadcasting farm and weather reports three times each week. The federal government originally gave WRGB the call letters "W2XB," but they were changed in honor of Dr. Walter R. G. Baker, a GE vice president and pioneer in television and radio. In 1939, the station became NBC's very first television affiliate.

Upstate and Downstate

"New York is unique because it is the capital of the world. Broadcasters have the best pool of talent to draw from in New York City. We are competing for the same talent as all the other performing arts. I think New York talent set the stage for what radio and television in America is really all about," comments Warren Bodow, former president and general manager of WQXR. Not only is New York the de facto capital of the world, accommodating the permanent seat of the United Nations, but it is also the center for mass communications in America and around the globe. New York City serves as the headquarters of nearly all major radio and television networks. Its famed "Madison Avenue," home to the most prestigious advertising agencies, acts as arbiter of marketing trends. As the most populous city, New York is the largest "local" community in America.

However, let there be no mistake, the grandeur and prominence of New York City does not make it the sole representative of New York State broadcasting. "Obviously a great deal of New York's clout in broadcasting is attributed to the fact that all the major broadcasters are headquartered in New York City. But another reason is that New York State is so diverse. NYSBA encompasses broadcasters from both the smallest and the largest markets," explains John Kelly, the popular former president of Albany Broadcasting, now overseeing radio activities at Siena College.

"As far as comparing 'upstate' and 'downstate' broadcasters, it's really just a multiplication of numbers, but everything else is the same," says NYSBA senior vice president Dick Novik. "If you can run a good station in a small market, you can run one in a larger market." Tony Malara, perhaps, more than any other New York broadcaster can attest to that. Malara's implausible career began in Watertown, before he vaulted to the top of broadcasting as president of the CBS Television Network. "You cannot put down small towns. There's an assumption in our profession that if you're from a big town, you must be really bright. In fact, some of the biggest phonies I've ever met in this business are from big towns. I used to say to people in New York City, when you come from a small town, you cannot hide. Everything about you is out there for everybody to see, and it's a little different from being in New York City or Buffalo. If you screw up in Watertown, the world knows about it, and that gives you a whole different perspective on broadcasting," notes Malara. New York's smallest television market happens to be Watertown, from whence Malara began, with a demographic market area (DMA) ranking of just 175 out of 210 markets in the entire country!

There are many broadcasters in out-of-the-way places—like Plattsburgh, Saranac Lake, Ogdensburg, Deposit, and Montauk—along with the larger cities—Buffalo, Albany, Syracuse, and Rochester—who shine brightly in the shadow of New York City. It is the sum of these communities and many more that reflect the rich and storied history of broadcasting in the Empire State over the last 50 years.

North Country

The vast open spaces of the "North Country" are blanketed by a patchwork of small family farms, Native American reservations, and the pristine forest preserves of the Adirondacks, touched by a bit of a Canadian influence. Its slow pace of life and appreciation of nature couldn't be more opposite from the "go-go-go" world of the Big Apple. Radio still plays a more prominent role in local communities like Malone, Saranac Lake, and Ogdensburg. Watertown and Plattsburgh are the only two rated television markets in these parts, and even then, Plattsburgh shares its DMA designation with neighboring Burlington, Vermont.

Buffalo

Former Governor Mario M. Cuomo once described Buffalo not as a New England city or even a Northeastern city; he suggested it can be more appropriately described as a vibrant Midwest town. Buffalo's rich broadcasting history is second only to New York City, even when considering every other American city. At the time NYSBA was founded, Buffalo was the ninth largest city in America. Once the country's first radio station, KDKA, went on the air in nearby Pittsburgh, it was only natural for Buffalo to grab on to the rising star of broadcasting. Its first radio license was granted to WWT in 1922.

Buffalo produced more than its fair share of broadcast icons, including Buffalo Bob Smith, Jack Paar, long-time WVIB-TV general manager Les Arries, Tim Russert, St. Bonaventure basketball broadcaster Don McLean, former WUTC-TV operations director Lois Ringle, George "Hound Dog" Lorenz, former WKBW-TV personality and later CBS News producer Liz Dribben, former WBEN-AM owner Larry Levite, newsman Jim Fagan, WEBR newsman Jack Eno, Buffalo's first female TV newscaster Doris Jones, public television humorist Mark Russell, newscaster Ralph Hubbell, broadcast innovator Bill McKibben, and WBEN-AM legend Clint Buehlman. Programs like "The Lone Ranger" and "The Howdy Doody Show" also attribute their roots to Buffalo.

Rochester

If Buffalo was once the gateway to the American West, Rochester was one of the gleaming jewels in the crown of American industry. Great corporate icons like Kodak, Xerox, and Bausch & Lomb call the "Flower City" home. And great broadcasters like Andrew Langston, owner of WDKX, C. Glover Delaney, former president of WHEC-TV, Arnold Klinsky, general manager of WHEC-TV, and rising stars like Tim Busch, senior vice president and regional manager at Nexstar Broadcasting have been proud to call Rochester home.

Media conglomerate Gannett also traces its origins to western New York. Its first newspaper holdings were located in Elmira, Ithaca, and Rochester. In fact, *The Star-Gazette* of Elmira in the southern tier was the very first daily under the Gannett banner. With the success of its flagship newspaper, *USA Today*, the company moved its headquarters from Rochester to Virginia in 1986. Gannett owns 21 television stations today. WGRZ-TV in Buffalo is one of those TV outlets in the Gannett stable. Both Buffalo and Rochester are among America's most wintry cities, situated along the Great Lakes in New York's relentless "snow belt."

The famous Blizzard of 1977 has unfairly saddled both cities with the reputation for being perpetually buried in the white stuff. Also nestled in the snow belt are smaller communities like Jamestown, Batavia, Elmira, Olean, Geneva, and Ithaca, where broadcasters have also left a lasting impression on New York radio and television, certain never to melt away with the passage of time. Bill Brown Jr. was the voice of Batavia, doubling as an announcer at Batavia Downs. The civic voices of Howard Green in Elmira, Si Goldman in Jamestown, John Hensel in Olean, and Louis O. Schwartz in Geneva (also current president of the American Sportscasters Association) may have disappeared from the airwaves, but their inspiration and example live on in the civic awareness and activities of the citizens they once served, and their example instructs us still.

Bill Parker in Binghamton is still going strong, after more than 50 years in broadcasting at WNBF Radio and WNBF-TV, now WBNG, Channel 12. Recently honored for his lifelong dedication to Binghamton, Mayor Richard Bucci remarked: "Bill Parker embodies what it means to be a good community citizen . . . in addition to his many talents as a broadcaster, Bill has also used his abilities to educate our community about a number of vital issues."

Syracuse

Further northeast along Interstate 90 (the New York State Thruway) in central New York lies Syracuse, home of the Newhouse School of Public Communications, one of the world's preeminent academic institutions for mass communications. Some famous alumni include Len Berman, sportscaster at WNBC-TV; John Sykes, the former chief executive officer of Infinity Broadcasting; ABC's Ted Koppel; former CBS Sports announcer Sean McDonough; Steve Kroft of "60 Minutes"; Bob Costas, the voice of the Olympics; and Marty Glickman of the Knicks and New York Giants. Also sports announcer Marv Albert and Dick Clark. Many of these famous faces and voices would go on from Syracuse to carve out illustrious careers in network broadcasting.

Some of the neighboring communities around Syracuse—like Rome, Oneida, and Utica—fielded broadcasters who were equally dedicated to their craft: Shell Storrier, with more than 40 years of service as general manager of WKTV-TV in Utica; Paul Dunn with over 35 years as a radio station owner in Utica and now a public broadcaster; and Bill and Vivian Warren with their astounding 60-plus years at WMCR in Oneida. And, indeed, the local broadcasters who tirelessly served Syracuse itself should also not be forgotten. The likes of E. R. "Curly" Vadeboncoeur, founder of WSYR-TV; the entrepreneurially gifted Ed Levine, founder of Galaxy Communications; and the 62 WHEN "Basebreakers" come immediately to mind. This fabled WHEN softball team, which took on all comers to benefit charity for good causes, raised thousands of dollars traveling around, playing the central New York charity circuit.

The Capital District

Situated along the mighty Hudson River at the crossroads of New York's major interstate highways, Albany is the heart of New York in many ways. As the state capital, it is the political seat of power in the Empire State. Prior to becoming the capital of New York, Albany served as the meeting place of the Albany congress in 1754, in which Benjamin Franklin presented the first formal proposal to unite the colonies. It is little wonder, then, 200 years later, New York's broadcasters chose Albany as the permanent location for its executive offices, balancing the interests of upstate and downstate broadcasters.

One of the finest broadcasting companies ever built would also be born in Albany: Capital Cities Broadcasting. It would grow to become a leader in the industry, eventually acquiring the ABC Television Network, which was later merged with the mighty Walt Disney Company. CapCities legendary chief Thomas S. Murphy is widely admired in corporate and financial circles all over the globe.

As previously noted, Schenectady, just 11 miles west of Albany, witnessed the establishment of America's very first television station. WRGB alone produced many notable broadcasters: Jim Delmonico, general manager of the station and an exemplar of what a broadcast executive should be; long-time anchor Ernie Tetrault; news director Don Decker, who also spent time at WGY and WTEN; and anchor Ed Dague, whose career included stints at each of Albany's three network television stations.

The Albany market also saw the first radio station power up to 50,000 watts. It was the legendary powerhouse WGY, in 1925. The wide spectrum of broadcasters who left their mark on Albany radio include WPTR DJ "Boom Boom" Brannigan; WGY personality Harry Downie; John Kelly, former president of Albany Broadcasting; WTRY-FM on-air personality Kerry James of WTRY-FM (formerly WDKC); and the late Carol Reilly, executive vice president of the Merv Griffin stations. Also, popular Albany radio executive Robert Ausfeld.

Hudson River Valley

The majestic Hudson River once served as the major artery for the flow of trade and travelers from New York harbor to Albany. Historic communities perched along its banks offer vivid details of New York's greatness: Hudson, named for the adventurer Henry Hudson, the first European to explore the Hudson Valley; Kingston, the state's original capital; Poughkeepsie, once called home by Samuel Morse, inventor of the telegraph, which ushered in a new age of electronic communications; Newburgh, which served as George Washington's headquarters in 1782–1783, where he rejected a proposal to become "king" of a new American monarchy; West Point, home of America's oldest and most distinguished military academy; and Yonkers, where resident Edwin Howard Armstrong transmitted the first FM radio broadcast on station W2XCR.

Many broadcasters found the Hudson Valley the ideal place to practice their craft. Sandwiched in between the natural splendor of the North Country and the orbit of New York City, they had the best of both worlds. "You've got folks who are trying to make it big in New York City radio and television. Then you've got folks who've already experienced that world and are seeking a slower pace of life," comments Binghamton television producer and broadcast history buff Bill Jaker. Much like the North Country, this area is dominated by radio, serving the smaller communities in between the larger markets of Albany, Poughkeepsie, and New York. The region was indeed a launching pad for many broadcast careers, as well as a place where many broadcasters were content to dedicate their lives to these tranquil communities.

There was James O'Grady, owner of WALL in Middletown and several other stations; Dick Novik, owner of stations in Brewster and Poughkeepsie; Campbell Thompson, manager of WGNY in Newburgh; Gene Blabey, a former UPI executive who owned WSUL at the foothills of the Catskills in Sullivan County; and Al and Bob Lessner of Beacon.

The Golden Apple

As one drifts into the lower Hudson Valley, Rockland County sits on the right bank and Westchester County on the left just before passing into New York City. Westchester is a symbol of American social upward mobility, aptly nicknamed the "Golden Apple." It is a hop, skip, and jump away for commuters who work in New York City but prefer to escape to the elusive luxury of a relaxed life in the suburbs each evening. Its close proximity to the Big Apple and the prominence of its citizens have made broadcasting here more influential than in other New York communities of comparable size. No broadcaster has better called attention to the unique influence of this well-endowed community than the "voice of Westchester," William O'Shaughnessy, long-time owner of Whitney Radio's WVOX-AM and WRTN-FM.

Westchester also gave birth to the careers of several nationally known broadcasters, including Howard Cosell, Martin Stone, Ted Koppel, Jackie Gleason, Dennis Elsas, Peter Fornatale, Bob Bruno, Jean Ensign, Rod Calarco, Ken Harris, John Winkel, and Morton Dean. And less one forget, Howard Stern got his start in the Golden Apple at WRNW, a tiny, obscure FM station in Briarcliff Manor. And Francis Lough and his brother-in-law Irv Cottrell were owners of WLNA-AM and WHUD-FM, which proudly served Peekskill (the birthplace of Governor George E. Pataki). Lough, now in his 80s, resides in Maine, where he has become the largest egg producer in the Northeast!

Long Island

Over the last three decades, Long Island, once dotted with farms and regarded as a summer getaway by dwellers in Manhattan, has quickly become New York State's most densely populated region. It now boasts a population of 3 million people, and its suburban wealth rivals that of Westchester. Broadcasting in Long Island was characterized by "mom and pop" radio stations for many years, until many of them were acquired by major corporations in the consolidation of the 1990s. Martin Beck is undoubtedly one of Long Island's most well-known broadcast owners, possessing the attributes of what it means to be a great community broadcaster.

It would be impossible to imagine listening to Long Island radio without hearing the mellifluous voices of Jack Ellsworth in Nassau County or Paul Sidney farther out in Suffolk County. These hardy perennials have each been on the air in Long Island for over 40 years! Paul Godofsky, owner of WHLI in Hempsted, and Dick Scholem, manager of the potent combination of WGSM and WGLI, were also influential in the development of radio on Long Island. While the island has a sizable population, it has no definitive center. Long Island is an Arbitron-rated market for radio, but it is counted as part of the New York City market for television. Its only commercial television station is WLNY-TV.

New York City

"We have a city called New York City, and it changes the complexity of our association. Rather than fight it, we took advantage of it. It's like having another country inside your state. It's so unique and so different. Having a world-class city in our state gave us entrée to a lot of things we might not have been able to do. It's the same for NYSBA. People listen to us because we're the *New York* State broadcasters," proudly remarks Lev Pope, the legendary chief of WPIX-TV in New York City. New York is not merely a city, it's an idea, a unique way of life. It is a confluence of creative energies, ideas, passions, and wealth that no other mass of humanity has been able to command. It is the Rome of its day. And in broadcasting, it is the standard by which the rest of its peers all across America measure themselves.

It would be harder to name those iconic broadcasters whose careers never passed through New York than to name those who owe their tremendous success to the city. While many New York broadcasters must be shared with the rest of America, New York has been able to keep many talented and creative practitioners all to itself. Some include Mel Allen, the fabled voice of the New York Yankees; Dick Beesemyer, former WABC-TV executive; Stan Z. Burns, WINS newsman; cult deejay Al "Jazzbeaux" Collins; radio personality Dan Daniels; the cutting-edge deejay Dennis Elsas at WNEW-FM; Barry Farber of WMCA; rock deejay Peter Fornatale; the great interpreter of Frank Sinatra, Jonathan Schwartz; WOR iconoclastic humorist and master storyteller Jean Shepard; WNEW legend Art Ford; Bob Grant, the original conservative talk show host; Walter Neiman, former WQXR president; Allison Steele, "Night Bird" of WNEW-FM; popular former WABC executive George Williams; the veteran WNBC-TV reporter Gabe Pressman; even His Honor Michael Bloomberg, the first broadcaster to become mayor of New York; and countless other disparate and dedicated broadcasters who have loyally served the people of New York City.

Among those presently writing their own chapter of achievements and contributions to be recorded in the next 50 years are Barry Mayo, senior vice president of WQCD, WQHT, and WRKS; Scott Herman, executive vice president of Infinity Broadcasting; Betty Ellen Berlamino, vice president and general manager of WPIX-TV; Tim McCarthy, general manager of WABC-AM and WPLJ-FM; Lew Leone, vice president and general manager of WCBS-TV; Maire Mason, vice president and general manager of WNEW; Frank Comerford, president of WNBC-TV; Andrew Rosen, head of all Clear Channel stations in New York City; and Joe Bilotta, chief operating officer of Buckley Broadcasting and his WOR colleague Bob Bruno.

Serving Their Communities

Landing a job at one of the networks in New York City is often the pinnacle of a broadcaster's career. It is an achievement that validates the years spent fine-tuning his or her craft to become one of the best in the business. However, broadcasting for the most part was never about glitz and glamour in most other New York cities and towns; rather it has been about serving local communities. Like most Empire State broadcasters, New York State Broadcasters Association President Joseph Reilly got into the business to serve the public: "I grew up in the industry believing I was serving my community. I thought of myself as a public servant. It wasn't about Henny Youngman or Arthur Godfrey . . . it was about serving your local community."

The manner in which Reilly, his colleagues, and constituents served their communities ranged from promoting Red Cross blood drives to joining the board of a local charity to attending dinners at the chamber of commerce. By ingratiating themselves within the community they could truly understand the needs and desires of their fellow citizens. Just as important as their responsibility as trustees of the public's airwaves, they understood the importance of connecting with their community and involving listeners and viewers in the overall broadcast process. Whether it was as playful as letting a child hear their voice on the air or throwing the full promotional power of broadcasting behind local charities, it is the countless stories these pioneering broadcasters told and the events they covered over the last five decades that held up a mirror to the unique characteristics and local flavor of each New York community.

Uniting together under the banner of the New York State Broadcasters Association has enabled broadcasters from both upstate and downstate to better address the multitude of challenges they faced over the last 50 years. Regardless of technological innovations, boom-and-bust economic cycles, government regulations, and the evolving tastes of the audience, New York broadcasters always remained fixed on their mission to serve the public.

Excelsior

In his soaring Inaugural Address in 1993, Governor Mario M. Cuomo, the 52nd governor of New York, quoted E. B. White, the great essayist: "New York is to the nation what the white church spire is to the village . . . the visual symbol of aspiration and faith, the white plume saying the way is up!"

The governor closed his address in Albany on that winter day with the famous motto of New York State—"Excelsior!" Translated from Latin, it means "Ever Upward!", which also almost perfectly describes the mantra and modus operandi by which NYSBA's colorful and dedicated members served the people of New York—and their profession—during the Association's first 50 years. This then is their story . . .

1

Making New York Broadcasting Even Better

> "NYSBA is head and shoulders above virtually every other state organization in the country. It is professional in every sense of the word and provides actionable information and services to its members."
> — Robert Bruno, vice president and general manager, WOR-AM, New York City

There comes a time when individual businesses or organizations within a given industry find it necessary to band together to strengthen their voice in government, to better share their hopes and aspirations with the public, or to simply improve their business practices through the exchange of ideas. The broadcasters of New York came together five decades ago for many of these same reasons. At its core, the New York State Broadcasters Association (NYSBA) is an association of broadcast licensees. To describe NYSBA as merely a lobby or a trade organization would be telling only half the story of its support for the broadcasters serving New York's local communities. It is not simply an association of "broadcasters" as much as it is a fraternity of dedicated "public servants." Throughout the last five decades, NYSBA members have been united in their calling not only to facilitate local commerce but also to guide democratic discourse and to help communities realize their full potential.

In an NYSBA newsletter published in 1968, Bob King, a former NYSBA president, articulated the Association's special place in the pantheon of American broadcasting: "In the Empire State, we enjoy a unique and sometimes envied position. No state capital in America is more closely watched; no city in the world enjoys a greater importance in terms of the world's economy than New York City. Our state is the home of the radio and television networks; some of America's greatest radio and television stations are here. Nearly all that happens in advertising and marketing happens here—first! It is a responsible position one holds to be a broadcaster in this state." King was vice president and general manager of Capital Cities' WKBW-TV in Buffalo at the time. The Association would evolve to become a national force as an arbiter of advertising and marketing trends, as well as setting the standard for excellence in the broadcast industry on the national level. Ralph Guild, chairman and chief executive officer of Interep, reflects on the impact of NYSBA locally: "Overall NYSBA has helped raise the professionalism of New York State broadcasters and made them more attuned to the needs of their communities." Despite its impressive footprint in the national arena, it is the multitude of individual fingerprints NYSBA has left in the cities, towns, and villages of New York that touch upon the true spirit of broadcasting.

Regardless of New York's relative importance in the broadcast industry, it was one of the last states to establish a broadcast association. By the time 1955 rolled around, 42 states had already created their own state associations. Arriving fashionably late, as only New Yorkers can, NYSBA quickly became a powerful lobby for broadcasters in New York and across America. In one of the Association's first newsletters in 1962, its influential role as a lobbyist is clearly staked out: " . . . with the retention of legal counsel, the Association seeks to serve every broadcaster in New York by monitoring legislative bills that would have a direct effect on the industry and to inform each local lawmaker about the content of each bill and its potential effect." Through the years, the Association would establish a myriad of special committees, host workshops and organize its members to sharpen their lobbying efforts in their hometowns.

Beyond being given a voice in Albany and Washington, most broadcasters in New York looked to NYSBA as a source of guidance, support, and contact with fellow colleagues. Nancy Widmann, former president of CBS Radio, regarded the Association as both an important mechanism in the development of her career and in the evolution of the industry: "It was so necessary for me to get out of the CBS building and interact with other broadcasters. The first, critically important contribution I believe I made to the Association was being a woman with that kind of responsibility, sitting side by side with all the guys from different kinds of broadcast properties." Widmann was one of the first women to sell advertising for a radio station in New York City and the first at CBS. The legendary Bernice "Tudie" Judis built a formidable reputation selling ads on Madison Avenue when she presided at the helm of WNEW-AM in the late 1950s.

The broadcast industry has always been famous for its competitiveness. Well-known and beloved Long Island broadcaster Martin Beck, founder of Beck-Ross Communications, cites NYSBA's unique ability to bring broadcasters together to work toward common goals: "I believe the broadcasters in New York have engendered a spirit of cooperation here that is very unusual." The genius of the Association was its ability to address the concerns of both small and large broadcasters. Much of that credit is owed to Joseph Reilly, the Association's first full-time executive director. It provided a forum not only for small broadcasters to learn from the big boys, but also to enable larger broadcasters to receive feedback from smaller operators serving on the front lines. Maire Mason, a seasoned New York City broadcaster, holds considerable admiration for broadcasters who toil in smaller markets: "Since my involvement with NYSBA, I find those upstate and rural broadcasters outside the metro New York area to be enormously more involved and more knowledgeable about the business, because they have to be." Mason worked at CBS-FM for over 20 years, rising through the ranks to become vice president and general manager. Currently, she is general manager of WNEW-FM in New York City. Although the Big Apple serves as the "nerve center" for the industry, the sharing of knowledge and ideas between NYSBA members in all the far-flung regions has been a productive two-way street.

Not only would the Association connect broadcasters with each other but also with strategic advice and timely information to guide them in their day-to-day decisionmaking. Simply put, many broadcasters like Jim Champlin view the Association as a repository of advice: "It has always been a source for technical information. You could call and get some good advice." A son-in-law of Martin Beck, Champlin joined Beck-Ross Communications in the early 1970s and helped launch WBLI-FM in Long Island. As the company expanded, he eventually became president.

NYSBA also produced booklets and workshops to arm broadcasters with the latest information on a wide range of issues from beer and wine advertising to sexual harassment to lottery advertising to the federally mandated digital upgrade.

During the consolidation of media properties in the 1990s, Joe Reilly would guide the Association to adapt to the changing needs of broadcasters as ownership changed from single owners to corporate owners. "One of the things about NYSBA is that it has continued to garner respect and work on behalf of not only the large markets, but the medium and small markets. That's becoming more and more of a challenge with consolidation today. Many times when you have one or two very large markets in the state, it's the smaller companies in remote, out of the mainstream markets, that tend to continue to support the state association. I think Joe has done a great job soliciting the support of not only the number-one market but all the disparate and diverse markets in New York," observes Erica Farber, publisher and CEO of *Radio and Records* Magazine. Farber worked as a vice president and general manager for WXLO, now KISS Radio, in New York during the 1970s and spent over a decade working for Interep before heading back to her roots in Los Angeles to build an enviable career at the helm of *Radio and Records*.

The Early Years

In the fall of 1954, mythical Syracuse broadcaster, E. R. "Curly" Vadeboncoeur organized a committee at Lake Placid to investigate the establishment of a state broadcasters association. Joe Bernard and Ham Shea served as co-chairman of that committee. On a cold winter day the following January, 62 broadcasters from around the state met in Parlor D at the Hotel Syracuse in Syracuse to incorporate "The New York State Radio and Television Broadcasters Association." The name of the organization would be changed to "The New York State Broadcasters Association" in 1958. Already counting 44 members in its ranks, the Association stated its mission at that historic inaugural meeting: "General purposes are to foster and promote the arts of aural and visual broadcasting and to promote these arts to better serve the public." The first year's dues were set at $25 for each station and $50 for "associate" members.

Serving as temporary chairman, Bill Fay of WHAM in Rochester, called for the election of the first slate of officers. Mike Hanna of WHCU in Ithaca served as the Association's very first president, Bill Doerr of WEBR in Buffalo as first vice president, Gordon Gray of WOR in New York City as second vice president, George Dunham of WNBF in Binghamton as treasurer, and Elliott Stewart of WIBX in Utica as secretary. The first board members were Ham Shea, WRCA, New York; Sam Cook Digges, WCBS, New York; Fred Keesee, WMBO, Auburn; Joe Bernard, WGR, Buffalo; Morris Novik, WLIB, New York; William Fay, WHAM, Rochester; Joel Scheier, WIRY, Plattsburg; and E. R. Vadeboncoeur, WSYR, Syracuse.

Mike Hanna opened the floor to discussion, so members could express their thoughts as to the direction their new organization should take. Some broadcasters pressed for lobbying efforts to protect them from unfair legislation, while others suggested the formation of a group insurance plan. Vadeboncoeur requested support for a plan to secure "immunity" for radio newsmen, as well as their newspaper colleagues in regard to protecting their sources of news information.

Later that month a second meeting was held at CBS in New York. Another seven members had joined since the first meeting. Total revenue from dues thus far was reported at $1,420. John Titus would serve as the Association's first legal counsel and was retained at an annual fee of $600.

Mike Hanna served two terms as president. As a sign of the times, he was given a Zenith radio as a gift for his service to the Association when his second term expired in 1956. He was vice president and general manager of WHCU in Ithaca for many years and would continue to serve the Association for almost 15 years on its Legislative Committee and as an elected member of the board during the 1960s. Hanna was a true visionary and pioneer. He was later named the Association's first "Life Time Honorary Member."

NYSBA would further establish itself as a powerhouse in broadcasting with a series of "firsts" for the organization in 1961. "This first issue of your Association's newsletter marks the beginning of a new era in the life of our organization," wrote Paul Adanti, in the Association's inaugural newsletter, volume 1, number 1. Adanti, vice president of WHEN AM-TV in Syracuse, served as president of NYSBA in 1961–1962. Permanent executive offices were also established in the State Bank Building in Albany that same year. To coordinate all the activities of the Association, Hal Van de Car would be hired as a part-time executive director on May 1, 1961.

Van de Car had been a news commentator on WSNY Radio in Schenectady since 1951 and served as a director and officer of the station. In 1952, he started a full-time public relations counseling agency. By 1959 it was known as the Van de Car, Deporte & Johnson Advertising Agency when it expanded into advertising and fundraising. Essentially, NYSBA was a part-time client of Van de Car's agency. In the late 1960s, he became ill and was forced to disband his agency in 1970. He also retired from his position as executive director of the Association.

For a brief period, NYSBA installed John Van Buren Sullivan as acting executive director. Sullivan was a colorful, dashing figure of great articulation and style, who had run the mighty WNEW-AM in New York City. He also served as president of Metromedia Radio and Playbill, the theater publication. After NYSBA split from Van de Car's agency, it set up shop on 9 Herbert Drive in Latham. Joe Reilly describes the building: "NYSBA was in this old, rickety, three-story house in a backroom on the second floor. There wasn't even a sign outside." The dedicated Ellen Cody, an employee of the Van de Car Agency, would continue to serve NYSBA, overseeing day-to-day administrative operations. She would also organize NYSBA's Legislative Dinners, the Annual Meeting, and Executive Conference.

"Every time you saw her at some meeting she would ask you, 'How is your room? I hope it's OK,'" remembers Shell Storrier. Having begun his career in local sales at WKTV-TV in Utica in 1951, Storrier would stay with that station for almost 40 years, rising to become vice president and general manager. Ellen Cody was a demure southern woman, darting around in her white gloves, fussing over everyone at all the meetings. "Ellen Cody was the glue that held the whole thing together," according to Wally Schwartz, former president of ABC Television, expressing how members felt about their "mother hen." She was a dear woman, beloved by everyone. After 25 years of service and afflicted by failing eyesight, Mrs. Cody would retire in 1983.

The Reilly Revolution

In 1979 the Association put together a search committee to hire a full-time executive director to "zoom the organization up," as Jack Thayer, a former vice president and general manager of WNEW-AM, put it. In the past, the Association organized legislative dinners in conjunction with its Annual Meeting to forge a closer relationship with lawmakers in Albany. According to Reilly the dinners died off in the mid-1970s, and NYSBA's influence in Albany started to wane: "They wanted to have more of a presence. They clearly needed to have more influence in Albany and in Washington. We really didn't have a lot in those days."

A search committee lead by Phil Beuth, one of the first employees at CapCities and vice president and general manager of WKBW-TV at the time, was established. Joe Reilly, who headed stations in neighboring New Jersey where he launched the careers of television impresario Roger King and many others, quickly emerged as the leading candidate. Of course, he was no stranger to the Association. He had served as its treasurer in 1973 while vice president and general manager of WWOM-FM in the Capital District. In 1979, he had just signed a two-year noncompete when he sold his station in Albany. As part of the agreement, he couldn't work in radio within 85 miles of Albany for two years. However, he was attracted by NYSBA's opportunity to serve his peers, and the political aspect of the job also really caught his attention. He enjoyed the idea of shifting back and forth between the two worlds of broadcasting and politics, easily moving between the two.

Among all the impressive archives of William O'Shaughnessy's recollections, one of his favorites involves the hiring of Joe Reilly as NYSBA's executive director. O'Shaughnessy, president of Whitney Radio in Westchester, had been conducting some business in Albany on the same day the NYSBA Board of Directors was meeting at the historic Fort Orange Club to discuss whether to establish a true presence in Albany by hiring a full-time executive director. After his appointments, he decided to "swing by" the Fort Orange Club around 4 p.m. to see what the board had decided. A former NYSBA President from 1973–1974, he claimed he wanted to "test" a recently passed resolution, permitting past presidents the "privilege of the floor." When O'Shaughnessy arrived, he was surprised to find that the board was still in session as the sun began to set over the capital city, and there was still no definitive resolution on the issue of hiring an executive director after an exhausting day of contentious debate.

After making his presence briefly known at the meeting, he decided to head home. As he walked to his car, Bob Peebles, vice president and general manager of WROW in Albany, rushed out to catch up with him. O'Shaughnessy remembers Peebles saying: "Look, O'Shaughnessy, you and I have disagreed about darn near everything. But I'm trying to get them to open an office and set up a real presence in Albany. We may not need it now, but we will need it down the road. The board is not quite sure they want to make the investment! Frankly, I haven't got the votes." The two quickly devised a plan to have the chief steward of the Fort Orange Club send waiters into the boardroom with silver trays full of cocktails, sure to be a welcome sight after a long day of debate. After a few relaxing drinks, the board was "inspired" by their new found wisdom, as O'Shaughnessy recalls, and decided to hire Reilly as executive director.

Reilly, it seems, was sent by central casting and took to the job immediately. In July of 1980, he began serving as the Association's first full-time executive director. Marty Beck, NYSBA's president at the time, said the hiring of Joe Reilly was one of the highlights of his career: "NYSBA had more legitimacy when Joe came in. He gave it more dignity. He gave it a little more excitement, too. Joe's enthusiasm is very catchy."

Reilly's work was certainly cut out for him. During the summer of 1980, the Association literally had no money in the bank. In fact, he would forgo his salary during his first nine months, an early, but certainly not the last, indication of his total dedication to the interests of New York's broadcasters. NYSBA members quickly discovered a new resolve to start paying their dues, according to Walter Maxwell: "In those days our dues were not very high, and I think it was in '81 when we all had to chip in to pay Joe because there was literally no money in the pot. We all made a commitment to pay our dues or pay something extra, because we didn't want Joe to leave because we didn't have any money." Maxwell got his start in broadcasting when he joined his family's station WGHQ in 1973. His stepfather was the famous, rip-roaring Hudson Valley broadcaster, Harry Thayer, who had once been general manager of the Philadelphia Eagles and publisher of a weekly newspaper in the Catskills. Thayer was known for his provocative and hard-hitting editorials.

Reilly spent his first year crisscrossing the state armed only with his charm, wit, and personality, or "CWP" as he jokingly calls it, attempting to meet every broadcaster in New York. He got his start at WERA as an announcer in Plainfield, New Jersey. Reilly then went on to build stations of his own in New Jersey, New York, and Virginia. His roots in broadcast sales suited him perfectly for his new role at NYSBA, notes Bob Ausfeld: "Joe is a real, authentic broadcaster. He went out to each of the markets throughout the state and talked to GMs to determine their needs. He kept that going for years." Ausfeld is currently regional vice president for Regent Communications in Albany and has spent over 30 years in the market, managing almost every single radio station in the Capital District.

When Reilly wasn't on the road, he kept in regular touch with broadcasters via the Association's revamped newsletter, "Newsbreak." Neil Derrough, general manager of WCBS, was NYSBA president from 1980–1981 and offered the services of one of his graphic designers, Gary Cummings, to create a "new look" for the Association's newsletter. He designed a new logo for NYSBA, retiring the familiar radio microphone image. Ellen Cody referred to the new look of the newsletter as "that gray thing" because of the gray paper it was printed on. Reilly's goal was to put something on broadcasters' desks at least once a week, either a current edition of the newsletter or an update on a developing issue. The new "Newsbreak" publication would be chock full of pictures of broadcasters Reilly snapped on his travels around the state. He would gather all the latest information from stations, including new hires, promotions, and recently launched programs and publish them in "Newsbreak." His goal was to "promote the heck out" of what people were doing on behalf of their communities and the Association. In his first article, "From the Executive Office," Reilly outlined his primary initiatives for NYSBA: "My major goal will be to increase participation throughout the Association. We need to open the ranks to greater numbers. . . . We must broaden and expand our present membership to include some fresh, new-thinking members. . . . NYSBA is a strong, solid, viable 'sleeping giant' about to be awakened!"

Reilly would deliver on those promises, offering an explosion of services within a few years, as well as dramatically boosting membership and overall participation in the organization. Based on the feedback he gathered from broadcasters around the state, the changes he would introduce were nothing short of a revolution. John Kelly, like many broadcasters from small and medium-sized markets, felt like an "outsider" crashing an "exclusive club" when he first attended NYSBA's annual Executive Conference at the venerable Otesaga Hotel in Cooperstown. Changing the tone of the conference was a symbol of the new outlook Reilly envisioned for the organization, explains Kelly: "He told the board from the beginning that his goal was to include all broadcasters, make it more democratic, and I think he's done that." John Kelly retired in 2001, after almost 40 years of service in the Albany market; he was president of Albany Broadcasting. He now serves as an advisor to the president of Siena College and oversees the activities of the campus radio station.

Over and over, Reilly would hear complaints from many of the smaller rural markets about the Association's focus on larger broadcasters. In response to this feedback, he recommended some fundamental changes to the leadership of the organization: "I suggested we reconfigure the board to show more parity between upstate and downstate, small market and big market, TV and radio." He understood that to bring about real change, the leadership of the organization had to broaden and be more reflective of the members it was intending to serve.

From time to time, Reilly would conduct surveys to get a better sense of the different kinds of services NYSBA members expected from their Association. While lobbying was the number-one concern among the majority of broadcasters, he knew he had to add additional services to give smaller broadcasters more bang for their buck. Jim Champlin knew that Reilly recognized the need to forge a bond between the upstate and downstate broadcasters to get more clout in Albany and Washington. "Downstate was always very critical to our major lobbying efforts, but upstate was just as important because we needed the numbers and their unique, intimate relationships with their hometown legislators. Joe recognized that additional services had to be provided to attract smaller broadcasters from upstate." Prior to 1980, only about half of the broadcasters in New York were dues-paying members. Smaller broadcasters felt they were essentially second-class citizens, excluded from the overall efforts of the Association because there weren't any services that addressed their needs as small business owners. They also had a difficult time justifying the contribution of money from their tight budgets and felt that their time would be better spent running their stations. When Reilly started off in 1980, he admits there was very little to offer the "little guy," but soon that would all change as well.

Long-time legal counsel to NYSBA, John Tabner observed Reilly's insights into the changing needs of broadcasters early on: "He started an insurance program and organized sales workshops. In those early years, the broadcasters needed an advocate. By the time Reilly arrived they also needed services to show them how to be more efficient and how to improve their revenues. He really gave them something for their money." Reilly would deliver in a number of ways. To get a sense of the vast amount of additional services the Association would come to offer over the last 25 years, its budget would expand by 20 times.

Listening to the concerns of broadcasters was just half the formula necessary to turn NYSBA into a powerful force in Albany and Washington. Reilly also worked tirelessly to gain the trust, respect, even admiration from leaders like Governor Mario Cuomo, Governor George Pataki, State Senate Majority Leader Joe Bruno, Senator Daniel Patrick Moynihan, Senator Hillary Clinton, and

Senator Charles Schumer. Former Senator Alfonse D'Amato was an early friend and admirer. "Joe Reilly has an extraordinary ability to galvanize the group. When and if he did take a position, it was one that was sound. We were very effective in warding off the tentacles of the bureaucracy," said Senator D'Amato, now himself a potent lobbyist. Reilly would raise the voice and profile of broadcasters, not only in New York but also of broadcasters all across America. " Joe Reilly is not only a highly respected leader in the Empire State, but he has also become a national leader. I've seen Reilly operate at many different levels, and when they have high councils in Washington at our National Association, he's like the pied piper. The other state presidents follow him everywhere," affirms Bill O'Shaughnessy.

Seminars in the Art of Sales

"I pushed NYSBA pretty hard to get a lot of sales trainers. I thought it was something stations needed that could be provided by our organization. Rather than a station going it alone, it would be nice to have NYSBA help with the sales effort," opines Eric Straus, a former Hudson Valley broadcaster and son of R. Peter Straus, an NYSBA president and former head of the Voice of America during the Carter administration. His sentiments were held by many other broadcasters and provided Reilly with an opportunity to provide a truly valuable service to smaller broadcasters. Drawing upon his extensive sales background, Reilly understood the day-to-day struggle of most broadcasters in the marketplace and out on the streets.

Broadcasters were united in their belief that serving their communities was priority number one. However, there was no denying that sales was the essential life blood in sustaining that mission. "Our biggest challenge is our sales department. NYSBA has been great about giving us essential tools to work with, like seminars on CD and workshops on how to sell against newspapers. We actually pulled in a couple of buyers as a result of those resources," notes Adrienne Gaines, general manager of WWRL in New York.

One of the first sales seminars Reilly organized was led by Maurie Webster, "Selling Against Newspapers." Webster was probably the best-known "sales guru" in radio. Over his 60-year career in radio, he was an announcer for KNX in Los Angeles, a station manager at KCBS, and spent 17 years as a vice president at CBS. In 1977 he started a company with his son, Scott, and daughter, Susan, called the Center for Radio Information. A frequent speaker at NYSBA meetings and seminars, Webster was constantly thinking of new sales tactics to make broadcasters more competitive. At one meeting he reminded NYSBA members:

"Radio stations must be willing to invest more dollars than ever in research if they are to put radio measurements on a standard equaling that of TV and magazines." As radio became more segmented he advised radio sales reps to think in terms of demographics and not just a broad-based audience: "If media buyers or advertisers don't have a demographic customer profile in mind, they're probably researching it and looking for one. Nobody has a budget large enough to reach everybody anymore. Advertisers are looking for their best, core customers. . . . That's why ratings alone aren't enough."

At the time of Webster's first NYSBA Seminar in 1982, newspapers were the primary competitor of local broadcasters. Over 150 people attended to learn why newspaper circulation was in decline while their rates increased. Webster also taught them about the concept of "positioning," an emerging buzzword in the retail world in the early 1980s. The one-day seminar was just $39 for members, a fraction of the cost for an individual station to bring in a sales trainer on its own. This was exactly the type of service Reilly wanted to deliver to members. Twenty years later, NYSBA designed a similar seminar to offer strategies on how to sell against cable, a sign of the evolving landscape in broadcasting.

Reilly would go on to organize many more sales workshops, one of the most popular NYSBA services to this day. At times, he organized a five-city tour, setting up shop in places like Buffalo, Rochester, Syracuse, Albany, and Long Island, attracting more than 800 people statewide. However, he would always pay particular attention to smaller markets: "I would especially reach out to the Boonvilles and towns a hundred miles away from Buffalo or Rochester because they had little access to training."

Reilly never really regarded pros like Maurie Webster as just "trainers"; he thought of them more as "motivators." Some of the motivational speakers Reilly signed on included Jason Jennings, Chris Lytle, Lindsay Wood Davis, Jim Doyle, Roy Williams, and John Mitton, an expert in selling broadcast classified advertising. There would be sessions for "newbie's," as well as seminars geared for sales "veterans." The goal of each seminar was to provide sales reps with educational tools they could bring into their daily work and to measure the ongoing results of their new techniques.

Workshops to Expand Broadcast Knowledge

Most small broadcasters in the early 1980s were still "mom and pop" operations, for the most part. They didn't have access to training programs or were unable to justify the cost of regular access to expert advice or legal counsel. Recognizing their disadvantage, Joe Reilly developed the "Great Idea Exchange." He organized one-day seminars for smaller markets by first contacting all the stations within a 50-mile radius of the meeting. Initially, some broadcasters were skeptical about possible cooperation with competitors, but Reilly soothed their fears: "There was a little bit of concern about being too close between towns, but this really wasn't a problem. Of course, this wouldn't have worked in some of the larger markets like Albany or Rochester, where there is a fierce competition for sales talent."

At these seminars, the day was spent discussing legal issues of concern to smaller broadcasters with a lawyer Reilly brought up from Washington, D.C. He would also invite a representative from the National Association of Broadcasters to update them on federal legislation, and he also provided a status report on affairs at the state level. Broadcasters would spend the rest of the day opening up and tapping into each other's expertise: "Once they got going they would share sales ideas, news ideas, and promotional strategies."

The first Great Idea Exchange was held in the fall of 1982. Dave and Nancy Atwood from Boonville, Bill Brown Jr. from Batavia, and Chuck Stewart from Newburgh would play host to over 70 broadcasters. Dick Zaragoza—a D.C. lawyer from Fisher, Wayland, Cooper, and Leader—was available for legal concerns, and Barry Umansky from NAB addressed questions pertaining to the FCC and Washington regulatory matters.

During the 17th Annual Meeting in 1971, the first-ever NYSBA workshop was held at the suggestion of Phil Spencer, vice president and general manager of WCSS in Amsterdam. For broadcasters who traveled a long distance to the meeting, there were a few hours of free time between the sessions during the day and the dinner at night. With license renewal legislation always on their minds, Spencer organized a discussion about the nuts and bolts of license renewals. Over 70 members attended the workshop. It became an annual tradition, covering topics like training for employees, government relations, and public relations. It also helped spark interest for more special seminars throughout the year.

Not all NYSBA seminars and workshops dealt exclusively with business topics. One of the most well-received seminars was the "Fred Friendly Roundtable." The 26th Executive Conference in 1987 presented a special two-day seminar tackling ethical issues facing broadcast journalists. CBS News legend Fred Friendly, a professor at the Columbia University School of Journalism, and Arthur Miller, the brilliant Harvard law professor, led broadcasters, lawmakers, and businessmen in a Socratic dialogue. Both Friendly and Miller presented the group with real-life scenarios they may one day encounter on the job. Then the participants delved into their own experiences and perspectives to determine how they would handle the ethical situation confronting them. It was a rare, spellbinding opportunity for broadcasters to peal away the layers of complicated issues like the criminal justice system, the Fairness Doctrine, the First Amendment, license renewal, and AIDS prevention advertising outside of their day-to-day decision-making process.

Many other targeted seminars and workshops would be organized by NYSBA, reflecting the changing needs and opportunities of New York broadcasters through the years. In the early1970s, Paul Dunn, president of WTLB in Utica, helped bring together a seminar focused on small and medium-sized radio markets. As FM broadcasting grew stronger vis-à-vis its AM counterpart, an "AM Radio Day" was organized in Syracuse in 1987 to help AM operators seek new opportunities. Panel discussions included "The Secrets of Successful AM Radio Stations," "Programming: Recapturing and Keeping AM Listeners," and "Best Money-Making Ideas." Following the success of the "AM Radio Day," a "Country-Western Radio Day" was created to maximize opportunities within the growing popularity of the country-western format.

Affordable Insurance for Broadcasters

Of the many new services Joe Reilly would introduce to NYSBA members, health insurance would be one of the first. He saw the opportunity to offer small broadcasters affordable health coverage, giving them more value for their NYSBA membership. On April 27, 1981, the NYSBA board of directors voted to designate five trustees to manage and administer all group insurance plans. Walter Maxwell, owner of WGHQ and WBPM in Kingston, would serve as chairman of the Insurance Committee for approximately 15 years. While most larger broadcasters had enough clout to negotiate insurance rates for themselves, smaller broadcasters didn't have that luxury, explains Maxwell: "Lots of small broadcasters couldn't get health insurance, dental insurance, or workers comp because the rates were too high. You were pretty much at the mercy of whoever was around your base because you didn't have an "experience" rating. When we started the Insurance Program, it was a real big help for local broadcasters."

A. W. Lawrence & Company in Albany would serve as the NYSBA group manager, while the Insurance Committee would set benefit and premium levels. Initially, two insurance plans were offered, a dental plan and New York State disability coverage. To take advantage of the program, broadcasters only had to be a member of NYSBA. Just a couple of months after its introduction, six stations had already expressed an interest in taking part in the new Insurance Program. A year later, roughly 10% of NYSBA members were in the Disability Program, and the Dental Program had over 200 participants.

To make the Insurance Program more attractive, the board of directors approved the addition of a new Group Medical Insurance Program in the fall of 1982. It offered comprehensive medical coverage one would expect from a large corporation, but at a cost most small broadcasters could afford. Four years later a 401(k) Plan would be added. This retirement investment service had previously been limited to larger corporations because of the high administrative cost. Now smaller broadcasters were able to participate by uniting together under the NYSBA banner. At that time, individuals could set aside up to $7,000 tax-free.

In 1997, NYSBA changed to Rose & Kiernan as administrator of its insurance programs. This new partnership introduced a service from AFLAC New York to help broadcasters with all aspects of installing their 125 Program at no extra cost and allowed AFLAC New York to offer its Supplemental Health Insurance Program to employees on a voluntary basis. As with the other insurance programs offered by NYSBA, this program was designed to help further reduce broadcasters' administrative costs.

Investing in the Future: Internship and Recruitment Services

Over the last two decades NYSBA has been very active in helping students launch their careers in broadcasting, as well as helping stations meet FCC EEO requirements through the creation of internships, a job bank, and career fairs. In 1971, the Association created a Placement Service to collect résumés from people interested in entering the business and then matched them up with vacancies at stations across New York. Ernie Anastos, an anchor for more than 20 years in New York City, believes that helping young people is a distinguishing characteristic of NYSBA: "It's important for us to give them our time and help them participate in some way, so they can become good broadcasters. When we're gone, we will have perpetuated something that will be of real value in the future."

In 1976, the NYSBA Scholarship was introduced. Campbell Thompson of WGNY in Newburgh served as chairperson of the Scholarship Committee. Other committee members included James O'Grady Jr. of WALL AM-FM in Middletown, Marion Stephenson of NBC Radio in New York City, and Oscar Wein of WDLC AM-FM in Port Jervis. A $500 scholarship was to be awarded each year to a deserving undergraduate majoring in broadcasting at a New York State institution of higher education. Elliot Klein, a junior enrolled in the Ithaca College Broadcast Management Program, was the first recipient. Two scholarships were awarded the following year at the Annual Meeting in 1977. After just a few years the scholarship evolved into a new Minority-Training Program.

"My internship . . . proved to be a valuable and memorable experience. I will never forget this special summer," wrote Cheryl Carter to NYSBA about her internship in the summer of 1979 at WUTR-TV in Utica. Carter was one of 11 lucky students to be chosen to participate in what was believed to be the first internship program of its kind in broadcasting. She learned to write, produce, and report, all under the guidance of news director Gary Kennerknecht.

There were just five internships available that first summer, but thanks to a grant from the New York State Division for Youth, an additional six were able to participate. At the suggestion of Martin Beck and Bill O'Shaughnessy, the program came to be known as the "Nelson A. Rockefeller Minority Intern Program," honoring the work of the late governor of New York and vice president of the United States. It was a unique opportunity for young minority adults to gain first-hand knowledge about the various aspects of broadcasting. The 11-week internships were open to both college and high school students. They were paid $2.90 an hour, minimum wage at a time when most students were toiling for just academic credits, and most of them, not in the NYSBA program, still are today.

Arthur Harrison, vice president of sales at WWRL in Woodside, served initially as chairman of the program. Soon after, Dick Novik would guide its growth and development for well over a decade. Novik owned stations in Brewster and Poughkeepsie after working for 20 years with his father Harry Novik at WLIB-AM in New York City. In 1984, Dick Novik secured additional funding to expand the training to make it a year-round program. In the early 1990s, interest in the program had begun to wane. With Joe Reilly's unwavering support and Novik's persistence, the program was restructured. Funding from the New York State Division for Youth enabled a minimum of 10 students to participate and helped reimburse stations for up to $1,000. By the turn of the century, participation was at an all time high, with 50 students securing internships each year.

In addition to creating internship opportunities, NYSBA created a Minority Job Bank in 1995 called "NYSBA EEO Job Bank." Two years later its name was changed to "NYSBA Job Bank." It would serve as a central clearinghouse by member stations to match up available positions across the state with qualified minority candidates. By the fall of 1995, the Job Bank was already a qualified success, hosting over 300 résumés and responding to over 200 job requests.

To help stations comply with new FCC outreach requirements, NYSBA co-produced several career fairs with radio and television stations across New York in 2003. Fairs were held in Buffalo, Albany, Syracuse, Rochester, and New York City. Upstate attendance was between 450 and 700, and an overflow crowd of approximately 10,000 candidates showed up at the Javits Center in New York

City. Many NYSBA board members hired candidates from the career fairs. Always having a tough time finding new sales talent, Adrienne Gaines recalls discovering one of her most interesting hires at a NYSBA Career Fair: "I pulled a fella from the casket business. He sold caskets to funeral homes all over New York State. He came to the NYSBA Career Fair. Thousands of people came. I remember his résumé and I was quite intrigued by it. I called him back for an interview, and guess what? He has become one of my highest billers. He opened up two new categories for me—funeral homes and assisted-living. You just never know. . . ." NYSBA's Dick Novik is credited with much of the success of organizing these career fairs.

NCSA: Funding for the Expansion of NYSBA Member Services

In 1992 the creation of the Non-Commercial Sustaining Announcement (NCSA) program greatly influenced the dramatic expansion of services the Association would be able to offer. The idea was first presented to Governor Mario M. Cuomo in 1989 by Joe Reilly. Due to state budget constraints, it would take a few years to get the program up and running. At that time, 35 other state broadcast associations already had an NCSA program, and some were fully funded by the revenue generated from the program. The initial goal was to raise $150,000 annually for educational services like speakers, management conferences, scholarships, and convention booths.

Reilly worked with Randy Bongarten, currently the president of Emmis Television, to get the first NCSA program launched in the fall of 1992. A campaign for the Urban Development Corporation started airing in six markets: New York, Long Island, Syracuse, Buffalo, Albany, and Rochester. Approximately $180,000 in time was donated by member stations, yielding $40,000 for NYSBA. Other clients would eventually include the New York State Bar Association, the Army National Guard, and the U.S. Coast Guard. The Governor's Traffic Safety Committee and Department of Motor Vehicles became regular clients, airing campaigns against drinking while driving. On the radio they ran a campaign called "Snooze and Booze," and on television, "Driver Ed" offered New Yorkers driving safety tips.

Broadcasters like Steve Baboulis, vice president and general manager at WNYT-TV in Albany, view these public service announcements (PSAs) as a way of giving back to their community: "I think the traffic safety spots we air throughout the state, the Coast Guard spots, and the DWI spots do a great public service through a not-so-formal channel. It's not your standard advertising buy, but it allows those PSAs to be aired across the state."

In 2002, Dick Novik was hired to oversee the NCSA Program and Member Services as senior vice president of NYSBA. To help with the continued expansion of the program, Sandy Messineo was promoted to NCSA administrator that same year. Through the years the program proved to be a resounding financial success for the Association, but there was some concern that the Association could become too dependent on NCSA funds. Reilly argued that the program enabled NYBSA to hold down dues increases and offered a wide array of services like sales seminars, lottery and gambling primers, the Job Bank, the FCC Inspection Checklist, and a "5-Minute License Protection Plan" video, services that would not have otherwise been possible. Jim Morrell, CEO of Pamal Broadcasting in Albany, appreciates the value of the services funded by the NCSA Program: "NYSBA takes the money generated as a result of stations like ours airing these PSAs, and they bring trainers into the community who will help our salespeople or our engineers. We rely on the Association to provide some of those benefits, and they've done a good job at that."

A few years ago, WNBC was honored by the Ad Council for running the highest percentage of public service announcements in the country. Dennis Swanson, general manager of WNBC at the time, also points out that "doing good" through the airing of PSAs is actually good for the bottom line: "At the same time we were the number-one station in the U.S. in terms of revenue. When I received the award, I thought to myself, 'Well, for people who say you can't generate significant revenue if you run too many PSAs, I guess we proved otherwise.'"

Annual Gatherings to Exchange Ideas and Share Stories

Through the years, many members looked to NYSBA for opportunities to interact with and as a source of camaraderie with their fellow broadcasters. The Association would fulfill this need through the organization of meetings and conferences. Eddie Fritts, president of the National Association of Broadcasters, candidly admits that he often organizes his busy travel schedule around NYSBA's meetings because of the special weight they carry in the industry: "You have the New York City universe as a starting point. Then not only do they represent that city but they also represent markets like Albany, Syracuse, Buffalo, and Long Island to smaller markets like Poughkeepsie or Plattsburgh. As you bring all those people together, you have a microcosm of what broadcasting is all about in America."

The Annual Meeting was held each year to elect new officers and was generally administrative in nature. Year by year, it became more elaborate as high-profile speakers were invited to address the Association. The event would eventually be combined with the annual Legislative Dinner, an opportunity for broadcasters to get to know their Albany lawmakers better.

Responding to the desires of its members for a yearly get-together centered around a program of seminars analyzing the latest industry trends, the first Executive Conference was held at the Gideon Putnam Hotel in 1962. Herb Mendelsohn of WKBW and Hal Neal of WABC Radio served as co-chairmen of the first conference. Early in his career, Neal had been the announcer on the fabled "Lone Ranger" radio program. He retired as president of ABC Radio after a long career. Legendary newsman Lowell Thomas was invited to be the keynote speaker. Sam Slate of WCBS Radio led the very first session, "Revitalize-Editorialize," discussing the role of editorializing in broadcasting. The 100 attendees to the first Executive Conference paid a registration fee of just $55, and $35 for a room. One of highlights of the conference was the running of the First NYSBA Pace at Saratoga Raceway; Highley's Sadie placed first in the race.

Many broadcasters fondly remember the Executive Conference as a place where they met lifelong friends. It also served as an opportunity to talk shop with your peers outside the office, recalls Al Primo: "Everybody's involved in the same business, with a lot of the same problems, so you get to share things with your counterparts. It's 'our tribe,' as Bill O'Shaughnessy might say." Primo served as news director for WABC-TV during the 1970s, developing the famous "Eyewitness News" format, revolutionizing local news programming.

During the second Executive Conference, broadcasters participated in panel discussions on ratings, trade press relations, FCC relations, and the image of advertising. This annual event is one of the few times where both big and small broadcasters meet under the same tent, observes Gordon Hastings: "It brings together the media capital of the world, New York City, with owners and operators of some of the smallest radio and television stations in America. It brings them together under one constituency. The discourse that can go back and forth in that kind of environment is amazing, when you have such a cross section of broadcasters within that community." Hastings was an insightful executive at Katz Media during the 1970s and 1980s. Understanding the potential of FM, he made Katz a leader in FM representation. He was also responsible for the build out of Katz Television. Later on, he owned stations in the Glens Falls and Saratoga region. Currently, he is the president of the Broadcasters' Foundation, a highly regarded national charity that helps broadcasters in need.

Both the Annual Meeting and the Executive Conference quickly became places to see big names and to be seen, as well as to spend valuable time with your own peers. The list of invited speakers over the last five decades reads like a "who's who" of legendary broadcasters and policymakers, including Arthur

Godfrey, Henny Youngman, Senator Jacob K. Javits, Charles Osgood, Dan Rather, Jane Pauley, Chris Matthews, Bill O'Reilly, Lou Dobbs, Maureen O'Boyle, Maury Povich, Larry King, Joy Behar, Geraldo Rivera, Frank Stanton, Senator Hillary Clinton, Rush Limbaugh, Edwin Meese III, Phil Donohue, Senator Charles Schumer, Lowry Mays, Gloria Steinem, Howard Samuels, Ossie Davis, WilliamB.Williams, Regis Philbin, Cardinal John O'Connor, Tim Russert, Governor Malcolm Wilson, Billy Bush, Ruby Dee, et al. "We would have meetings that were the envy of other state associations because of the turnout we would get and the VIPs who would show up. We always used to have the governor visit with us, and many different radio and TV stars came to our meetings all the time," recalls Leavitt Pope, long-time president of WPIX-TV.

Representing the "fourth branch of government," NYSBA events also held considerable weight in the realm of state and national politics. Governor Nelson Rockefeller was a frequent and valued presence at NYSBA functions. The image of Rockefeller swooping down from the sky in a state police helicopter, landing on the 18th green at the Otesaga Hotel, and being whisked away in a golf cart by an NYSBA officer is etched into the minds of many New York broadcasters. Rocky's first words to broadcasters upon his arrival were, "Hiya fellas . . . this is fabulous!"

With the clouds of Watergate hanging over the nation in 1973, Congressman Ogden Rogers Reid, the former publisher of the *Herald-Tribune* and a First Amendment champion, would use the Past President's Dinner at the Executive Conference in 1973 as an opportunity to advocate his support for Newsman's Privilege: "The FCC must not be allowed to make moral judgments; we must not permit censorship of broadcasting under any guise. A vigorous free press helped save us in the worst Constitutional crisis in our history. We need clear Newsman's Privilege, an absolute shield for broadcasting as well as print media." In 1982, the Executive Conference would even play host to important and timely gubernatorial debates between Democratic candidates Ed Koch and Mario Cuomo, as well as among Republican candidates Paul Curran, James Emery, and Lew Lehrman.

Governor Hugh L. Carey was honored at the Annual Meeting for his efforts to improve the state's business climate in 1981. He had just been married to real estate mogul Evangeline Gouletas and arrived at the meeting right from his honeymoon. In his address, the governor promised New York State's broadcasters investment tax credits. To demonstrate its appreciation for his work on behalf of the state and its broadcasters, NYSBA presented the governor with a special gift. It was a pricy Steuben glass beaver, a likeness of the official state animal of New York. It also happened to be Joe Reilly's first Annual Meeting as executive director, and it was his idea to give the beautiful glass beaver to the governor. "It was all glass, with garnet stones for eyes, truly a work of art. It came with a pedestal, but wasn't attached to it," recounts Reilly. As much as he thought it was a clever gift to reflect the spirit of New York's broadcasters, Neil Derrough, then NYSBA president, was slightly less keen on the idea, but went along with it anyway. Derrough was the vice president and general manager of WCBS-TV at the time. At the appointed hour during the banquet, he presented the glass beaver, delicately perched on its pedestal, to a delighted Carey. Holding onto the pedestal, the governor quickly maneuvered himself for an obligatory photograph at the podium. The momentum, however, sent the glass beaver flying to the ground in front of the dais, scattering into a million pieces! Reilly was certain his tenure with NYSBA would be cut short, but fortunately his charm and wit guided him through that day and far greater challenges over the next 25 years. Incidentally, Governor Carey howled with delight when Reilly rushed to the podium microphone promising to replace the beaver . . . "as soon as we can find the garnet eyes!"

"I remember there was a serious discussion each year as to where the Executive Conference was going to take place. Part of the issue was the convenience for the various members who were coming from all over the state and partly for where they thought the food was best," remarks R. Peter Straus about the "weighty" decisions over choosing the site of the annual Executive Conference. Straus was owner of the celebrated station WMCA in New York City and a previous candidate for governor himself, who also owned stations in Middletown, Geneva, and Utica. The conference was held at the Gideon Putnam in Saratoga Springs for the first couple of years, before moving to the lovely Otesaga Hotel in Cooperstown. While it was a hike to get to from New York City, Bill Brown III always thought the Executive Conference was more of a vacation for the big shots than a business trip: "The people from the city viewed it as a real getaway . . . even the people who were very influential and had the big jobs. It was great to go up there and spend part of a week far removed from the hustle and bustle of metro New York. I think those people looked forward to it, perhaps even more than we did, as a vacation." Brown helped his father, Bill Brown Jr., operate and manage WBTA in Batavia.

Bill O'Shaughnessy would recall many "rollicking late night sessions" in the Leatherstocking Lounge, located in the basement of the Otesaga Hotel. "They would go late into the night, long after the formal sessions." Jim Champlin was one of those "young" broadcasters sharing a few laughs during those late night hours with peers like Tony Malara, Larry Levite, Bob Peebles, Dick Novik, and their wives. No one had more fun at these late-night soirees, it would seem, than the execs from ABC Radio. Dick Beesemyer, Bob Mahlman, George Williams, Dick Foreman, and Wally Schwartz were members in good standing of a swashbuckling group presided over by Ed McLaughlin and occasionally by Hal Neal. "The other networks had some 'colorful' representatives at these confabs, but ABC ruled when the sun went down," remembers O'Shaughnessy.

On at least two occasions, the elders of the Association opted for a change of scene away from the upstate resorts. Twice the Executive Conference was moved to suburban Westchester County. Although the "Golden Apple's" proximity to the "Big Apple" made it easier to snag big-name guests, the execs from the New York City stations didn't bring their families. Still they dutifully attended the business sessions. On another occasion, the Association set up its tent at the Lake Placid Club, an aging resort in the Adirondacks, and for a time, in the Catskills too. Another vivid and memorable location was Mrs. Cornelius Vanderbilt Whitney's home, Cady Hill. Marylou Whitney is the indomitable "First Lady of Saratoga." During NYSBA's summers at the Gideon Putnam, Mrs. Whitney always insisted on entertaining the entire conference at her home.

When Reilly attended his first Executive Conference at the Otesaga, he quickly realized it would not keep pace with his new vision for the Association. Purely from a physical point of view, it was too small to accommodate the additional members he hoped to attract. Walter Maxwell always remembered the associate members and suppliers complaining about having to stay at a motel down the road with no phones because the Otesaga was booked solid by NYSBA members.

Beyond capacity issues, Reilly quickly got the vibe that it was time to change the traditions embodied by the annual jaunts to the Otesaga: "If you ran a station in a small market and you sauntered into one of these meetings at the Otesaga, you'd sit there for three days with your wife and nobody would talk to you." The Executive Conferences confirmed many of the sentiments he had heard from small-market broadcasters that the Association was too much of a "big-boys club." Tony Malara was one of those small town broadcasters: "My wife, Mary, and I were sent to a meeting as a kind of reward. Here we were from Watertown, and we went to the summer conference in 1962. Man, we were sitting there like wallflowers, watching these big-time executives. All I could say to Mary was, 'This is the big time, honey.' I was just like a little kid enjoying that."

Malara's natural charm and jovial nature would not only get him accepted into "the big-boys club" but would also eventually land him one of the top jobs at CBS, as president of the television network. He would also become a beloved institution at the Executive Conference, serving as M.C. to this day, making everyone feel like they are part of the gang.

Reilly reported to the board that if they wanted real change, things could no longer stay the same. He eventually moved the Executive Conference to the Sagamore Resort Hotel in Bolton Landing on Lake George and perked up the Annual Meeting to make it more worthwhile for smaller broadcasters to attend.

The Executive Conference was also a family affair for many broadcasters. When Wally Schwartz was offered the chairmanship of the event in the 1960s, he told the board he would accept the honor on one condition—there would be no afternoon meetings. Schwartz was general manager of WABC Radio at the time, rising to become president of ABC Television. He believed the best way to get more broadcasters involved was to position it as a family affair. Schwartz had lots of ideas about how to get more broadcasters to attend. Most importantly he wanted to organize activities for the whole family instead of meetings in the afternoon. "If the wives and kids wanted to come, there was no way that the old man wasn't going to go to the Executive Conference. The first year we had meetings right up till noon and then everybody could do whatever they wanted to do in the afternoon." There would be movies, cartoons, a teen swim party, and special games with prizes for the younger folks, and bridge, a golf tournament, tennis matches, and softball for their parents.

"When you say the Otesaga or Gideon Putnam, it puts smiles on people's faces. You have to remember our kids grew up with us through this process. Those kids are now married with kids. All of us have such great memories of those meetings being a great family reunion," reflects Dick Novik. The conference even sparked teenage romance, remembers Phil Beuth: "My daughter and Tony Malara's son used to sneak off together to hold hands by the lake. They used to be an 'item' year after year. It was the only time they'd see each other, and everybody said they looked perfect for each other."

To recognize the achievements of their peers, a Special Awards Committee was established in 1965. Herb Mendelsohn served as chairman, with Bill Sullivan of WOTT in Watertown, Dick Landsman of WOKR-TV in Rochester, and Bill McKibben of WGR in Buffalo also served on the committee. The first Special Awards plaques were given out at the 1966 Executive Conference for best commercial announcements, news reports, documentaries, and special programs. In later years, silver bowls were awarded. There were separate categories for radio and television, as well as for New York City and the upstate markets. During the first Awards ceremony, Richard Beesemyer accepted an award for best public affairs programming in New York City on behalf of WABC-TV in recognition of its documentary "Who Will Tie My Shoe?" Other winners included WKBW-TV, WHCU, and WROW. In 1979, Phil Beuth revamped the entire "Awards for Excellence in Broadcasting," as the awards become known, to get even more broadcasters involved in the process. More categories were added, including best local news and best feature report. He also established a new framework for competition by market size, dividing up the state into red, green, and blue categories. That same year, he was awarded the Delaney-Cuneen Award for his efforts.

Individual Dedication to NYSBA

Joe Reilly would be the first to admit that his efforts alone have not made NYSBA the powerful and influential force it is today in broadcasting. During the Association's first 50 years, there were countless other broadcasters who took time out from serving their communities to help their colleagues make broadcasting even better.

Since the founding of NYSBA, 48 broadcasters have served as president or chairman. The position was renamed "chairman" in 1986 when Reilly was given the title of president to give both his office and NYSBA more clout. "It takes a lot of time. The chairman of NYSBA sounds like an honorary position, but you are very busy. It is a lot of responsibility," explains Shell Storrier. While never having served as president himself, Storrier is all too familiar with making commitments to his fellow broadcasters, serving in a variety of capacities within the Association. A consummate volunteer, Storrier was one of the first inductees in the Association's Hall of Fame.

The achievements and contributions of each NYSBA member are invaluable, and their service will always be remembered in their own unique way by other New York broadcasters: John Kelly for his tireless efforts to maintain the Emergency Broadcasting System (the predecessor to EAS); Mary Anne Jacon, NYSBA's vice president of operations, for her 11 years of dedicated service to the Association; Phil Spencer for vocalizing the rights of broadcasters in a clear, direct, vigorous style; Bob King for limiting the number of consecutive terms any one person could sit on the board, to encourage fresh thinking in NYSBA; Bob Klose for becoming the first chairman of the National Legislative Committee; Maire Mason for becoming the first woman to serve two terms as NYSBA chairman; William O'Shaughnessy for being an unrelenting champion of free speech and the First Amendment; Ed Levine for establishing the NYSBA Hall of Fame; Bill McKibben for a decade of service as NYSBA secretary; Barbara Munderville for working tirelessly on the frontlines as NYSBA's current administrative assistant; and Neal Moylan's government service at the New York State Department of Commerce. Moylan also served for many years as counselor to NYSBA.

The late Robert Peebles, vice president and general manager of WROW in Albany, a CapCities veteran, is fondly described by his fellow broadcasters as "endearing," "passionate," and "dedicated." He served as president of the Association in 1978. In his 30 years of service to NYSBA, it is believed that he never missed the Annual Meeting or Executive Conference. He was never afraid to pepper speakers and presenters with questions about their take on a wide array of broadcast issues. "Bob Peebles was one of the nicest people. He always had a smile, and he was just a huge hulk of a guy, but he ran a tight ship and was fair, always outspoken, not negative, but he always told you what he thought about an issue and how we should either go after it or forget about it. He would always volunteer to do something if we needed something done in Albany," remembers Jim Champlin.

C. Glover Delaney, an enormously respected elder of the Association, served NYSBA with distinction as only the second president to serve two terms. As president and general manager of WHEC in Rochester, he held a seat on the NYSBA board for a decade and was named the first president emeritus of the Association. In 1976 his dedication to New York broadcasters was recognized through the creation of the Delaney-Cuneen Award. Each year, members of NYSBA's board recognize an individual who has made the most significant contribution to the Association during the past year. Some of those who have been presented with this award include Robert Peebles, Richard Hughes, Martin Beck, Vincent DeLuca, and Lawrence Sweeney, a popular and much-loved BMI executive, who was a fixture at NYSBA functions. The spirit of Delaney's service was also memorialized by naming after him the trophy presented to the winner of the annual tennis tournament at the Executive Conference.

The Delaney-Cuneen Award itself also honors the service of Michael Cuneen, general manager of WDLA in Walton. His vigorous service was not limited to that remote mountain town in Delaware County; it extended to the broadcasting fraternity throughout New York and America. He contributed to NYSBA and served on the board of the National Association of Broadcasters, as did Joe Bilotta, Marty Beck, Les Arries, Dick Novik, Bill O'Shaughnessy, Bill Stakelin, Carol Reilly, and Al Vicente, but Cuneen had the distinction of being from the smallest station to ever hold a seat on the board of the NAB, an achievement he was very proud of. According to Amos Finch, he took the time to get in touch with broadcasters from all over New York State: "Very often he would take a day just to go and visit with two or three other broadcasters just to stay on top of what was happening in the business." Finch had the privilege of working with Cuneen before he became an owner of a few stations himself in the mountains of western New York. Tragically, Cuneen's life was cut short in a car accident in 1974.

There were many broadcasters serving the Association in quieter but important ways, as head of a committee or simply to help organize the Executive Conference. Elliott Stewart, one of the founders of NYSBA, dutifully served as its first secretary, a position he would hold for almost a dozen years until his death in 1966. In 1939 Stewart joined WIBX in Utica, rising to become executive vice president and general manager of the station. He was a "broadcasters' broadcaster," serving on many boards and service organizations, including president of the Utica Chamber of Commerce, the Utica Kiwanis Club, and the American Cancer Society. To recognize his contributions to broadcasting, UPI established the prestigious Elliott Stewart Award, awarded annually to an individual who is recognized for "outstanding news coverage and excellence in reporting" in broadcast media. In the early 1970s, NYSBA added the Elliot Stewart Award to its Annual Editorial Awards to recognize the best public affairs program or series produced outside New York City.

John Lynch holds the distinction of serving as NYSBA's longest serving treasurer, from 1962 to 1970. He founded Normandy Broadcasting, parent of WWSC AM-FM in Glens Falls, in 1959. Prior to becoming a broadcaster, he was a career diplomat serving in American embassies in Stockholm, Oslo, and Helsinki. As one of many father-and-son teams in New York broadcasting, his son, Chris Lynch, would follow in his footsteps, serving the community of Glens Falls and becoming treasurer of NYSBA.

As more and more doors began to open for women in broadcasting in the 1970s and 1980s, it was due in part to trailblazers like Marion Stephenson. She was the first woman vice president at NBC and would also be the first female president of NBC Radio. The New York State Broadcasters Association welcomed her as their first distaff member in the 1970s. Her position gave women in the industry a template from which they could articulate their stand on a wide variety of issues in the industry. At the 13th Executive Conference, Dr. Stephenson, who was also chair of the board of trustees of Hamilton College, shared her views as to why it was difficult for women to enter the management ranks: "Childhood attitudes prevent women from aggressive pursuit of management jobs. Without access to lunches, the locker room, or the bar, women don't have the opportunity to learn of available jobs. Both women and the bosses need sociological training." In any season, Marion Stephenson was considered a class act by her colleagues.

During the 1980s, Pat Tocatlian, president and general manager of WSLB and WPAC in Ogdensburg, took up the cause for women within the Association. After attending one of her first NYSBA meetings, she knew things had to change for women: "They opened every conference with a joke about women. It was really bad. I said to my husband, Chris, 'You know, maybe this is a group we should join, but I really don't want to.' Well, he wrote a letter about it because he was kind of irritated too. I think because I protested what they were doing, Joe Reilly thought eventually it would be cool if I became president." In the early years of his tenure, Reilly knew that the Association needed a lot of change, and he agreed with Tocatlian. She became president in 1989, undaunted by the task that lay before her. Frank Boyle, the noted station broker, remembers how well she rose to the challenge: "At the time, people wondered how this woman from a small town was going to tell the ABC, CBS, and NBC guys what the hell to do. Well they were very pleased to have her because she was talented and a take-charge lady with lots of skills."

It wasn't all a bed of roses, but Tocatlian stayed the course. She handled her battles one at a time. She recalls being caught slightly off guard at a luncheon during one of the Association's Calls on Congress: "I sat down, and this guy across from me says, 'How does it feel to be the only woman here?' I said to him, 'You know, I never thought of it, I just thought of myself as a broadcaster.' When I came home and told a friend of mine about the incident, she told me, 'You should have told him you weren't really a female, you were in drag!'"

Some women, perhaps, regarded themselves as "trialblazers," but Carol Reilly did not. Despite the obvious positive example she set for women in broadcasting during her service at Albany area stations, "she was possessed of a smile that lit up the room," "an enormous presence," and "a role model," are just some of the ways New York broadcasters remember Carol Reilly. As the wife of Joe Reilly, she held the unofficial title of "First Lady of NYSBA." More importantly, she was a broadcaster in her own right. When Merv Griffin bought WTRY and WPYX in Albany, he hired Carol to run the stations. According to her husband Joe, Merv loved Carol and invited them often to his home in Hollywood.

Although she did not seek to be a trailblazer for women, her actions undoubtedly set an example for many young women. "Wherever she would go, women would surround her. She was strong, tough, and smart. She was a role model for women. She wasn't Gloria Steinem, but was happy, I guess, just to be Mrs. Reilly," explains Joe. At one point she was asked to run for the "woman's seat" on the NAB board and won. In today's world, it's hard to believe there was ever a separate, designated seat for "women," but Carol took it in stride.

Like Pat Tocatlian, Carol Reilly had her share of run-in's with less enlightened men, Joe Reilly recalls: "The president of Albany's biggest bank bought advertising on Carol's station. She met with him one time, and as she was leaving, he called his secretary to 'get that girl back here.' She saw a lot of that." She never lost her sense of self as she helped to change the broadcast industry in her own quiet, dignified way. After she lost her battle with cancer in 2000, the Association created the Carol M. Reilly Award to recognize women in New York who reflect "general excellence, leadership, and professionalism," exemplifying the many attributes of Carol's character. Past winners include Maire Mason, Olympic ice skater Sarah Hughes, Lieutenant Governor Mary Donohue, and socialite Marylou Whitney.

The services NYSBA provide and the assistance members extend to one another highlight only part of the Association's work in support of New York broadcasters. Balancing the needs of smaller upstate broadcasters with the clout of the networks in New York City has made the Association a powerful force in defending the rights of broadcasters in Albany, as well as giving it unparalleled influence in matters involving broadcast regulations and policies at the federal level.

2

Defending the Rights of Broadcasters

"Broadcasters are responsible, concerned citizens, while always remaining competitive in business."

—John Tabner, former NYSBA legal counsel

From NYSBA's nascent beginnings, lobbying would be the top priority among New York's broadcasters. As early as 1957, the Association hosted its first Legislative Dinner, so broadcasters could build stronger relationships with their state lawmakers. The event was used also to help lawmakers better understand how various legislative actions in the state assembly would affect television and radio in the Empire State. In time, the Legislative Dinner was held in conjunction with the Annual Dinner to draw big-name broadcast talent, as well as governors, senators, and FCC commissioners. At its height, the event drew as many as 400 broadcasters and state lawmakers. Interest in the event, however, waned by the mid-1970s, possibly due to fewer state legislative issues directly affecting New York's broadcasters. As a result, more and more state senators and members of the assembly dispatched their legislative aides and staffers in their place. This forum was eventually abandoned in favor of more effective and meaningful one-on-one sessions with key lawmakers and annual breakfast meetings hosted by the sitting governor for NYSBA's board.

These candid, off-the-record sessions were often complemented by similar confabs with legislative leaders of both houses of state government. Over the years, Joe Reilly and NYSBA directors would meet privately with many key Albany solons, including Warren Anderson, Joe Carlino, Perry Duryea, Stanley Steingut, Jim Emery, Stanley Fink, Joe Bruno, and Sheldon Silver.

As the Association matured, broadcasters regarded their collective energies as an important avenue to protect their rights and to raise their image in the eyes of the public.

The drive to ban cigarette advertising on radio and television in the 1960s forced broadcasters to circle their wagons in a way they never had to do before. As responsible citizens and parents, they understood the potential harmful effects of cigarette smoking, particularly among children, but they never believed that government intrusion into broadcast content of any kind was the best possible solution to combat this or any other health problem. They also felt they were being treated unfairly, in light of the fact that their print counterparts were not asked to pull cigarette ads from their newspapers and magazines. Fighting for freedom of speech and equal treatment for all media were to be reoccurring themes as New York broadcasters defended their rights over the last 50 years.

"I think the most important thing we do is look out for broadcasters' rights on the state and federal level. A lot of that is 'defense' work. It's not proactive legislation in most cases," comments Dick Novik, senior vice president of NYSBA, on the lobbying initiatives of the Association. After Joe Reilly's initial tour around New York State in 1980 as the Association's new executive director, broadcasters confirmed their resolve that lobbying would continue to be the principle area in which the Association should focus its efforts. That determination remains to this day.

Tracking Legislative Matters

At the conclusion of the very first Legislative Dinner, the Association established an ongoing Legislative Committee under the direction of Mike Hanna. He would guide the new committee for over a decade and a half before Bob Peebles took over the reins as chairman in the 1970s. The mission of the committee was to monitor legislation in both Albany and Washington. They would report the latest developments back to the Association's board of directors so NYSBA leaders could formulate positions on legislative matters of direct consequence to the state's broadcasters.

To monitor national legislation more effectively, NYSBA established a separate National Legislative Committee in 1970. The new body would also be responsible for aligning the Association's efforts more closely with NAB's national initiatives and strategies. Robert Klose, general manager of WNBF-AM in Binghamton, served as its first chairman. Bill O'Shaughnessy of WVOX-AM in New Rochelle, Robert Peebles of WROW-AM-FM in Albany, Shell Storrier of WKTV-TV in Utica, John McArdle of WNYS-TV in Syracuse, Hal Fisher of WNYR AM-FM in Rochester, and Bill McKibben of WBEN AM-FM in Buffalo also served on the committee. Its first call to action was to encourage all NYSBA member stations to contact their congressmen and senators, urging them to vote in support of a presidential veto of a bill that would limit the amount spent by political candidates on broadcast media during a campaign.

The Legislative Committee would also serve as liaison between the board and the legal counsels serving NYSBA. John Titus, from the law firm Whalen, McNamee, Creble and Nichols in Albany, was the Association's first lawyer. He helped establish the basic framework for NYSBA's activities before being replaced by John Tabner in 1960. Tabner is currently a partner at Tabner, Ryan & Keniry in Albany. He was already well acquainted with the inner workings of the state legislature, having served as a state assemblyman representing the Third District of Albany County. During his 30-year tenure as NYSBA's legal counsel, Tabner studied and dissected thousands of assembly and senate bills. He then submitted memoranda to the Legislative Committee and various subcommittees in support of, or in opposition to, proposed legislation. Tabner also advised the board on possible effects of new legislation, helping them craft their positions on a plethora of issues.

Alternatively, Tabner would also find it necessary to share his insights into the broadcast world with local and national lawmakers from time to time. He once advised Senator Daniel Patrick Moynihan on how best to accommodate the senator's own view that there was too much "right-wing" coverage on the airwaves in New York State. Initially, the senator decided to distribute a letter to all broadcasters demanding, "in no uncertain terms," that they change their coverage. Tabner got wind of Moynihan's letter. The NYSBA counsel clearly understood the acute sensitivity that existed among broadcasters in regard to *any* government prodding in relation to news coverage. Tabner decided to talk to the senator as "one lawyer to another" to avert a potentially explosive confrontation with this towering intellect of the United States Senate. He recalls asking Moynihan if he had any relationships with broadcasters. The senator responded, "No." Tabner then told him: "The fastest way to get this issue on television and radio (something neither wanted) is to actually tell broadcasters how they should cover the news." The savvy lobbyist refrained from specifically telling the senator what to do, but he wanted to give him fair warning as to how the broadcasters would react. Moynihan wouldn't relent. However, Tabner's advice wasn't completely lost on the senator, because while a letter was ultimately sent to the state's broadcasters, it was a much more "toned-down version" from his original inflammatory draft. Tabner was held in such high regard by the broadcasters that he was awarded the Delaney-Cuneen Award in 1989.

Essentially, NYSBA represents a unique, dual relationship between lawmakers and broadcasters. Not only is it an association representing broadcast journalists and their craft, it is also a potent lobby working with lawmakers to protect the economic and political interests of its members. As previously indicated, most politicians have a long-established "love-hate" relationship with broadcasters. They often accuse broadcasters of reporting only "bad" news, seeking, of course, to keep negative reports about themselves and their colleagues to a minimum. To be fair, lawmakers are a bit more tolerant of coverage they view as "unfavorable," just as long as broadcasters balance their coverage with some more positive news about the achievements public officials have worked so hard to secure on behalf of their constituents. They are also keenly aware that broadcasting is still the number-one source of news for the average New Yorker, thus remaining a powerful and often irresistible platform for lawmakers.

New York broadcasters had no greater friend in the Albany firmament than Governor Nelson A. Rockefeller. He rarely turned down an invitation to meet with broadcasters at NYSBA's Annual Meeting or at its Executive Conference. Shell Storrier remembers the warm rapport Rockefeller had with broadcasters: "Anytime we had an event, he was there. In fact, one day at the Otesaga in Cooperstown we were having a meeting, and he came to speak at length on a wide range of issues. When Rockefeller concluded his formal presentation he said, 'Why don't we go down and have a couple of glasses of wine with lunch.' We told him we couldn't do it. He asked, 'Why not?' We told him because it was Primary Day and we were busy with our stations' coverage, so we couldn't have a drink before 9 o'clock that night!" The governor could hardly contain his laughter and dismay.

A relentless and consistent defender of the First Amendment, Governor Mario M. Cuomo would be another kindred spirit for New York broadcasters. A broadcaster himself, from time to time, the articulate Cuomo often participated in a popular talk show on WAMC Northeast Public Radio with Albany political commentator Dr. Alan Chartock. "I miss it. I did a show in Albany for 18 years . . . I guess every week . . . without missing a show," reminisces Governor Cuomo, now a partner in the prestigious Manhattan law firm Willkie, Farr and Gallagher. It is widely believed that part of the political success of Governor Cuomo was attributed to his use of radio to help build his political network, launching him into the governor's seat in Albany. He once famously remarked, "I have a *face* for radio." Born in the golden age of radio, it was the medium Mario Cuomo felt most comfortable using to communicate with his constituents: "I never lost my fascination with radio. If you gave me the opportunity to write an important national column or do a radio talk show, I would choose radio. Why? There's something about the medium that makes it easier to be candid. Perhaps because you aren't seen. It provides a more intimate relationship than television or the Internet."

In 1985 John Tabner passed the baton to Matthew Mataraso, now an attorney at Pryor Cashman Sherman & Flynn in Albany. Mataraso serves the Association to this day. He has guided it through some of its toughest legislative battles, fighting to keep New York's courtrooms open to cameras, as well as passage of the sales tax exemption on capital expenditures.

Affairs of State

The Legislative Committee reviewed a wide range of bills that cascade year in and year out from the state legislature, which directly or indirectly affected broadcasters, from taxes to labor concerns to journalistic privilege. In the early days of NYSBA, bills were frequently drafted to censor broadcasters at the state level. For example, legislation was actually introduced in the Assembly in 1961 to give the director of the Television Bureau in the State Education Department the power to review all television scripts and films for censoring! The bill would require the issuance of a license for each television script, with fees of $50 for each half hour and what amounted to the "policing" of all advertising by broadcasters themselves. In cooperation with Madison Avenue and the advertising community, the Association successfully prevented its passage.

Often NYSBA worked with lawmakers to modify bills with good intentions, so they would not adversely affect broadcasters, and thus their listeners and viewers. The New York State Senate once proposed allowing the state attorney general to bring civil action against false advertising claims, holding both advertisers and broadcasters accountable. John Tabner moved right in and worked with lawmakers to exempt broadcasters from penalties arising from false and misleading statements made by their advertisers.

As yet another indication of how broadcasters sought to achieve "equality" with newspapers in the eyes of the state assembly, an exemption from jury duty was sought for radio and television news personnel as was afforded to their print counterparts. After much debate throughout the late 1960s and early 1970s, a bill was finally passed granting the privilege of jury duty exemption to all broadcast professionals involved with the direct gathering and distribution of news.

To enhance the Association's lobbying efforts in Albany, the board of directors created a Political Action Committee called "COMPAC" in 1984. With Joe Reilly's support, Arthur Angstreich, an NYSBA director with an accounting background, set up and administered the new committee. It was believed to be the first PAC of its kind in the broadcast industry on the state level. Its intended purpose was to enable NYSBA members and corporations alike to support the legislative efforts of the Association. Individuals were permitted to deduct contributions of up to $50, or $100 per couple (for a joint filing from their federal tax return), each year. Companies were able to donate up to $5,000 each calendar year. All activities of the NYSBA PAC would be confined to New York State and could support only state candidates, not those standing for federal offices. At its inception, $5,500 was raised with an initial annual goal of $50,000. NBC, ABC, Metromedia, and RKO were some of the first corporations to support COMPAC. Over time the success of various legislative victories was attributed to this new political entity that existed outside the formal structure of NYSBA. It helped open many more doors in Albany, giving broadcasters a stronger hand in shaping legislation that affected their profession and its business dealings.

State Tax Relief

Throughout much of its history, NYSBA of course took a more defensive posture on issues involving discriminatory state taxes, generally focusing on preventing new taxes from being levied unfairly on broadcasters. In the mid-1970s Stuart Subotnick, then assistant controller and director of taxation at Metromedia, remembers banding together with his peers from CBS, NBC, and ABC to help lawmakers in Albany better understand how their tax policies affected the broadcast industry: "We would trek up to Albany, week in and week out, pleading our case on a variety of issues like taxes on advertising. We told them there can't be a tax on advertising. It would be unconstitutional. It's essentially a tax on speech. Ultimately, we were pretty successful in those battles."

Through the 1970s, the Association would further ratchet up the activities of its Tax Committee. Arty Angstreich, then vice president for tax matters at NBC, became chairman of the committee in 1979. Walter Maxwell, former owner of WGHQ in Kingston, like most broadcasters, deeply appreciated the impact of his work: "Arty Angstreich, who was our tax expert, is probably the most unsung guy of them all. He really saved the New York broadcasters millions of dollars in taxes."

Angstreich's stated long-range goal at the time was to achieve "parity" with other industries in terms of how broadcasters were taxed: "Every couple of years there were industry issues that if we couldn't legislate them out, we were able to get some kind of exemption, or at least a pronouncement from the state supporting our position." Members of the Tax Committee also provided an additional service to general managers and station owners by making themselves available for questions on tax issues and providing tips on how to save some additional revenue by leveraging tax benefits.

Subotnick and Angstreich led a 10-year fight with the State Tax Commission over granting franchise tax relief for stations whose signals went into neighboring states. This issue was the Tax Committee's first victory, recalls Angstreich: "The issue dealt with the ability to allocate income within and without New York State. Particularly for stations located near the borders, like Albany or New York City where a station's signal goes within and beyond New York." The state had always held the position that all the broadcasters' income was taxable to New York because their broadcast signal *originates* from New York. Subotnick and Angstreich argued that the state couldn't tax broadcasters' *total* incomes because they had audiences in places like New Jersey, Connecticut, and Massachusetts, as well as a national audience via the networks. The State Tax Commissioner would eventually concede the point, issuing regulations enabling broadcasters to allocate their receipts for franchise tax purposes based on the location of their respective audiences. In the October 1980 edition of "Newsbreak," Angstreich reported to NYSBA members that the Tax Committee saved broadcasters an estimated $1 million in the first three years of its existence.

The Tax Committee scored another victory for broadcast tax relief in 1983, when the New York State Tax Commission issued new guidelines for valuing film and tapes. The new valuation technique enabled broadcasters to produce original television programs without any adverse tax affects. When preparing their New York State Franchise Tax Return, broadcasters would now value their own produced property based on the percentage of audience within New York State, thus reducing their taxable value for state taxes.

A couple of years later, broadcasters received an investment tax credit for the first time with respect to the equipment and facilities used in producing radio and television programs. Roderick Chu, commissioner of the New York State Tax Commission under Governor Mario Cuomo, announced the new policy at the NYSBA Annual Meeting in 1985: "By the time you get back to your stations, your tax people will have heard that we are extending investment tax credits to put you on an equitable basis and to encourage you to invest in New York and its future."

Over the past 40 years, at one time or another, the New York State Assembly would try to tax broadcast advertising. "Whenever the state got into financial trouble, which was a good share of the time, they'd look for new revenues and try to tax advertising," remembers Phil Spencer, former owner of WCSS in Amsterdam, New York. During the 1980s and early 1990s, the reality of a tax on advertising became very real, says Arty Angstreich: "Sales tax on advertising reared its ugly head when many states were having trouble balancing their budgets. It became a national issue as many states saw this great 'giveaway' called advertising." In 1986, the Florida state legislature passed a "tax on advertising" bill, the first of its kind in the country. The State of Florida anticipated raising $1 billion in new revenue annually from the new tax.

In the early 1990s, with New York in the throes of a recession along with the rest of the country, and facing a budget shortfall as well, the fight to prevent a sales tax on advertising was brought dangerously close to home for NYSBA. Legislative leaders and the governor proposed an expansion of the sales tax to include public relations, which would have resulted in the imposition of a 4% sales tax on advertising services. Broadcasters dodged their first bullet in this 1990 battle remembers Angstreich: "We, the Association, along with the advertising agencies and publishers, worked together to kill the ad tax in 1990."

But the battle was far from over when the issue was raised again just a year later. New York was again looking for solutions to alleviate its budget deficit and still regarded advertising services as an untapped resource. After the longest, drawn-out budget process in the state's history up until that time, a new $51.9 billion state fiscal budget was approved without an ad tax. A gross receipts tax, in which all companies with annual receipts of at least $1 million would have faced up to $75,000 in additional annual taxes, also failed to find its way into the budget. Fortunately for broadcasters, the economy rebounded a year later, quelling future attempts at an ad tax for years to come.

The tax relief provided for broadcasters during the 1980s and 1990s was indeed sizable, but Joe Reilly's proudest achievement for New York's broadcasters was the sales tax exemption on broadcast equipment in 2000. "It was probably the single most important thing we did for the industry, getting that sales tax eliminated," comments Reilly. Signed into law by Governor George E. Pataki, broadcasters would no longer have to pay a sales tax on any of their capital expenditures, including their transmitters, tape machines, studio furniture, and new digital equipment.

The newspaper industry had never been taxed on its capital expenditures. Angstreich always insisted that the real issue behind the sales tax exemption was achieving parity with print media: "We do the same thing the print industry does, but we do it in an electronic format. There was a huge disparity, however, because of this quirk in the law. Broadcasters were paying sales tax on all of their equipment and were being forced to compete with their hands tied behind their backs."

Although Governor Cuomo was a great admirer of Joe Reilly, and remains so to this day, Reilly's arguments fell on deaf ears during the Cuomo years. The governor didn't want to hear about cutting taxes for broadcasters at a time when the state was desperately struggling with its finances.

Undaunted, Reilly revisited the issue when Governor Pataki was elected, along with Bob Vonick, vice president of taxation at The Walt Disney Company, and Matt Mataraso, NYSBA's legal counsel. They pointed out to the newly elected governor that not only did the newspaper industry get this tax break, but the broadcasters in all the surrounding states did as well. Pataki gave as good as he got, suggesting that he knew New York's broadcasters wouldn't move their towers out of state. However, around this time, NBC did just that, when they decided to build their new 24-hour cable network, MSNBC, across the river in New Jersey.

NYSBA decided to apply additional pressure to their cause by hiring Bill Powers, a well-connected lobbyist and former state Republican Party chairman. The charming Powers was a tough-talking ex-Marine known for making things happen. Powers opened doors for New York's broadcasters, and Reilly presented his arguments once again to lawmakers. He went so far as to demonstrate how the exemption would actually help save the state money. He also indicated that the exemption would help broadcasters upgrade to digital even faster: "It was a huge issue because it came on the heels of having television go digital." Reilly estimated the typical cost of a station to upgrade to digital was between $3 and $5 million: "When you lop off the 8% sales tax, you are talking a minimum savings of around $250,000 per station. No small potatoes for a small broadcaster . . . ," and then Reilly couldn't resist the observation, "All of a sudden those NYSBA dues looked more like an investment than a cost."

NYSBA, no shrinking violet when it comes to defending the economic interests of broadcasters, has never let its members' business prerogatives take precedence over the welfare and interests of the general public. New York's broadcasters have traditionally viewed their efforts as a "profession," guiding mass audiences in a democratic dialogue, rather than as an "industry," merely mass-producing widgets. Thus, one would be hard pressed to find any example where the Association devoted its considerable clout and lobbying muscle to anything inimical to the public trust.

Protecting New York's Public Broadcasters

Fighting for the economic life of broadcasters was not limited to commercial television and radio stations, but extended to New York's PBS stations as well. A representative of public broadcasting has held a seat on the board of NYSBA through much of its history. Currently, Norman Silverstein, president and chief executive officer of WXXI Public Broadcasting in Rochester, serves in that capacity. He voices the concerns of all nine public television stations in New York. According to Silverstein, NYSBA membership has given public stations access to lawmakers they would not otherwise have had: "Our stations have always been included each time NYSBA has meetings with key officials. Every time the state legislature or Congress threatened to cut our funding, Joe Reilly was quick to draft a letter of support on our behalf."

A decade ago, former House Speaker Newt Gingrich (R-GA) led a high-profile campaign to eliminate federal funding for the Corporation for Public Broadcasting (CPB), which passes on that funding to thousands of PBS and NPR stations across the country. Those funds represent about 15% of the total revenue for the public broadcast industry. Ultimately Gingrich's efforts ended in failure. Public broadcasters dodged another bullet recently, when a House sub-committee voted to phase out all federal subsidizes for CPB over the next two years amid criticism by conservative groups of the perceived "liberal bias" in the programming of public broadcasting. After vigorous lobbying by supporters of public broadcasting, $100 million in proposed cuts for CPB's budget next year were restored by a vote in the House of Representatives.

Aside from the lobbying influence of NYSBA, services like sales training to improve underwriting efforts and career fairs to help with recruitment have been very useful to PBS stations as well. While funded differently, Silverstein says publicly supported stations have always felt right at home with their commercial brethren in NYSBA: "It has been a very supportive relationship, and the result has produced a strong commitment to public service. We have always found ways to work with our commercial counterparts to better serve our communities."

Shield Law

It was a historic occasion when New York State lawmakers gave reporters complete protection from being found in contempt by any court for failing to disclose confidential sources obtained in the course of newsgathering with the enactment of the Shield Law (also referred to as the Betros Bill) in 1970. The law was initially interpreted as guarding from disclosure only those news materials that were received under a cloak of confidentiality. As a result, journalistic privilege would not be attached in the event the materials weren't received in confidence.

The Shield Law would be used in the controversial case of *Beach v. Shanley*. In 1983 Dick Beach, a reporter at WRGB-TV in Schenectady, was subpoenaed to testify before the Rensselaer County grand jury regarding one of the sources he used for a story broadcast on WRGB-TV, about the contents of a sealed grand jury report in connection with alleged misfeasance and malfeasance in the Rensselaer County sheriff's office.

After the broadcast, special prosecutor Donald Shanley was assigned to direct an investigation regarding the disclosure. He argued that whoever leaked the information may be guilty of a crime, and therefore Beach was "witness to a crime." As a result, the reporter was a possible "accomplice" and thus not covered by the state's Shield Law. WRGB-TV maintained that he was in fact covered by the law.

Beach was subpoenaed to testify and ordered to provide his documents to the special grand jury, but he refused, citing protection under the Shield Law. Justice Paul Yesawich Jr. would say of Beach's refusal: "It seems to us inarguable that the Shield Law was never intended to serve as a shield for, or to conceal the commission of, a crime." The judge argued that, at the time of its passage, the Shield Law was not intended to bar reporters from testifying relative to crimes they actually witnessed. The purpose of the law was to protect a news source, so that members of the news media would not be subject to disclosure of those communicating information to them. Justice Yesawich ruled that the disclosure in and of itself constituted a crime, therefore the Shield Law did not apply in this case.

Another precedent-setting case would then clarify the parameters of the Shield Law. In 1986 Knight-Ridder Broadcasting sought to quash a subpoena by the Albany County district attorney's office. The case would become known as *Knight-Ridder Broadcasting v. Sol Greenberg*. Greenberg was the Albany County district attorney attempting to secure the outtakes of an interview by WTEN-TV with a man later accused of his wife's murder.

At issue was whether or not the Albany County district attorney could compel WTEN-TV in Albany to produce nonbroadcast materials obtained and prepared in the course of newsgathering under subpoena for a grand jury investigation. The supreme court in Albany would side with Knight-Ridder, quashing the subpoena on grounds that the materials sought were privileged and protected from disclosure by the Shield Law. Shortly thereafter, the appellate division would reverse the decision. The court of appeals would uphold this final decision on grounds that the materials have to be received in a confidential capacity.

In September 1987 an amendment was introduced into the legislature at the urging of NYSBA to amend the Shield Law to eliminate the confidentiality requirement, but it failed to gain necessary support. However, since then, attorneys have been reluctant to pursue information gathered by journalists protected under the Shield Law because of the strength and clarity of the law.

A recent string of high profile cases involving *The New York Times*, *Time Magazine*, and WJAR-TV, the NBC affiliate in Providence, Rhode Island, have found reporters threatened with subpoenas, contempt, and even jailed for not revealing their sources. Senator Christopher Dodd (D-CT) has led the charge for a federal Shield Law, in response to the mounting legal maneuvers being unleashed against journalists and their ability to do their job, primarily to maintain a free and fair press.

Daylight Savings Time

After year-round daylight savings time, also known as "war time," was abandoned in 1945 by the federal government, state and local governments were left to determine whether or not they would continue to observe daylight savings time. In 1963 Senator Edward Speno introduced a bill in the New York State Senate to place New York on daylight savings time year-round once again. The intention of the legislation was to reduce traffic accidents by having more daylight during the late-afternoon commute. While there would be more daylight later in the day, the early morning drive would be left in the dark. New York's daytime radio station owners fought vigorously against the legislation because they would be unable to broadcast during that critical time of the day. Paul Godofsky, president of WHLI-AM, Hempstead, Long Island, was one of the NYSBA members who led the fight against year-round daylight savings in New York. He was quoted in NYSBA's newsletter: "The case for the broadcasters was pointed up as a serious deprivation of public service so necessary to the communities in these early hours." It would also mean a loss of revenue for the daytimers. By the time the bill was introduced in 1964, NYSBA, led by John Tabner, made sure it never saw the "light of day."

Daylight savings time was not only causing trouble in New York but also across the country. Rather than leave the daylight savings time issue to the discretion of local laws and customs any longer, Congress decided to end the confusion with the passage of the Uniform Time Act of 1966. The original law created a uniform pattern across the country, with daylight savings time beginning on the last Sunday of April and ending on the last Sunday of October. Any state that wanted to be exempt from daylight savings time could do so by passing a state law. Over the next decade, there would be repeated attempts by New York's legislature to amend daylight savings time.

Cameras in the Courtroom

As early as 1961, John Tabner had been working to amend section 52 of New York State's Civil Rights Law to open up the state's legislative and committee proceedings to the public by permitting coverage by broadcasters. Initially, legislation called the Mitchell-Savarese Bill to grant this privilege was passed by both the assembly and the senate, only to be vetoed by Governor Rockefeller. But a decade later the state's legislative and committee sessions would finally be opened to broadcast coverage.

The Association would push for further reform of section 52 in the 1980s to allow for coverage of all courtroom proceedings in the State of New York. In 1982 Reilly got a call from Ben Chevat, who was then working on the staff of Assemblyman Saul Weprin (D-24th District), the powerful chairman of the New York State's Assembly Judiciary Committee, to set up a meeting. Weprin was a lawyer and a big advocate for getting cameras into the state's courtrooms. He was seeking to have the courts of New York "reformed." He believed that the public was ignorant of the inner workings of the judicial system and sought broadcast coverage of courtroom proceedings as a way to educate them.

Chairman Weprin explained to Reilly that he was having difficulty getting the legislation passed and sought the support of NYSBA. Neighboring states like Connecticut, Massachusetts, and New Jersey all permitted cameras in their courtrooms. Reilly also knew that larger markets like New York City and Albany would be excited about it, especially his television constituents. He presented the idea to the board, and they voted to support the repeal of section 52. They regarded the closed judicial system as injurious to the legal system and believed that the public had a right to know what went on behind closed doors.

Around the same time, Chief Judge Lawrence Cook of the Court of Appeals had recently opened the state's powerful appellate courts to television cameras. For the most part, the coverage of the proceedings had been well received. Justice Cook was invited to speak at NYSBA's Annual Meeting in 1982 and indicated his strong support for an amendment to section 52 to assure the public that justice was being carried out by opening New York State's courtrooms.

That same year, Assemblyman Weprin and Senator Douglas Barclay introduced bills in the state legislature that would provide for an "experimental" 18-month program. The bill would provide for broadcast access to both criminal and civil courts. On June 7, 1982, by a narrow vote of 76 to 61, the bill passed the assembly. The victory would be short-lived when the bill failed in the senate by a vote of 36 to 19. The fight, however, was far from over.

A modified bill was introduced in both the assembly and the senate a year later. It would include rules for courtroom media procedures and increase the power of the presiding judge in a case covered by the media. It also provided a limited experiment of a sampling of urban, suburban, and rural jurisdictions. John Tabner recalls that many minority groups were opposed to the legislation because they felt that having cameras in courtroom proceedings would cast a negative light on African Americans, Hispanics, and other ethnic groups. The NYSBA counsel, however, saw the issue as a matter of principle to open up the courts and believed that the bill had plenty of constraints to protect witnesses.

Court of Appeals Judge Sol Wachtler would address a joint session of the New York State Legislature in support of the measure. He recognized concerns about the potential effect on witnesses, but believed the benefits to the judicial system outweighed the shortcomings: "It seems ironic that this state, which spawned the principals of the First Amendment, should be one of the very few that has shown reluctance to even experiment with allowing cameras in our trial courts."

The debate would continue for another few years, until the bill was defeated once again in the senate by just two votes in 1986. There was a proposal on the table to amend the bill to require the consent of all parties involved in courtroom proceedings. However, supporters of cameras in the courtroom argued that the measure would be rendered completely ineffective. Some of the reasons why detractors in the senate said they wouldn't support the bill included a general mistrust of the media's intentions and the fear that clips of trial coverage aired during the 11 o'clock news would hardly educate the public on the judicial process, and some believed witnesses would be intimidated by the exposure and publicity.

Governor Cuomo, always a tireless defender of the First Amendment, wholly supported the concept. The senate was the only hold-out. NYSBA worked vigorously with its members to reach out to their representatives to support this legislation.

Finally, in 1987, after a five-year struggle, the senate approved a bill, by a vote of 35 to 25, to allow an 18-month experiment of cameras in New York State's courtrooms. The bill was drawn up with a sunset provision. If the critics were right, the bill could die or be altered when it was set to expire on May 31, 1989. Eager not to give any ammunition to critics of the hard-fought legislation, the Association quickly distributed 400 "how to" action kits to its members. The kits included the rules governing audio/visual coverage of judicial proceedings, official forms requesting trial coverage, a copy of the statutes, a list of the most frequently asked questions with answers, and a list of local contacts for broadcasters with specific questions about coverage of trials. NYSBA's Reilly was also appointed to the Advisory Committee on Cameras and Microphones by Albert Rosenblatt, chief administrative judge of the courts of New York.

Feedback from judges in early 1989 showed that two-thirds of the state's jurists were favorable to the presence of cameras in their courtrooms. This indication of support would help the passage of a modified bill on May 31, 1989, the day the initial bill was set to expire. Cameras would be allowed in New York's courtrooms for another two years.

Unlike the first bill, when the second bill expired in June 1991, cameras were temporarily banned from New York's courtrooms due to an impasse in the state legislature. Both the assembly and senate had passed their own versions of the bill, the senate's version being somewhat more restrictive.

Governor Cuomo led negotiations between Weprin, who was then speaker of the assembly, and State Senator Christopher Mega, sponsor of the bill in the senate, to work toward a compromise to extend the experiment. The issue at hand was the question of consent by nonparty witnesses to allow broadcast coverage in the courtroom. Mega believed that witnesses shouldn't be recorded without their consent. Weprin argued that such a provision would render the bill useless.

A compromise was eventually reached, and broadcast coverage of trials was reinstated on July 1, 1992, through January 1995. Much of the teeth had been taken out of the bill, laments Reilly: "What they ended up with was a watered-down version that produced only a two-year experiment. Defense lawyers hated the bill and tried to insert provisions, like victim's consent. They wanted to enable either side to give the OK to coverage. Of course, most cases would never end up being covered if you have to get consent from both parties."

The new bill would prohibit the coverage of a victim of a sex crime unless the victim requested coverage. It would also allow nonparty witnesses, except an expert witness, the right to deny coverage, as well as family members, except when testifying. News organizations that violated provisions of the bill would be fined up to $5,000 a day, and news personnel faced imprisonment for up to 30 days.

Saul Weprin, often referred to as the "Father of Cameras in the Courtroom" in New York, died in 1994. His son, Mark, was elected to his seat in the state assembly that same year, taking up his father's cause. He vowed to introduce legislation to make cameras in the courtroom permanent, but once again supporters of the concept would have to settle for an extension. On January 30, 1995, the state senate voted to continue coverage of courtrooms until January 30, 1997, by a razor-thin margin of just four votes.

According to Reilly, it would be the "trial of the 20th century" that would finally end New York's decade-long experiment with cameras in the courtroom: "We all saw this coming, and I said this is gonna kill it, it's gonna kill it. I was right." It would be Judge Ito's famous lack of control of his courtroom during the O. J. Simpson trial that would play right into the hands of the detractors of cameras in the courtroom here in the Empire State. Unable to reach a compromise, on June 30, 1997, the state legislature allowed the statute to "sunset." Interestingly, no one called Reilly when the bill died. Not one broadcaster. "I didn't get the feeling of passion from broadcasters that they wanted this bill that badly anymore," said Reilly. Tabner thinks that since most of the cases that appeared on dockets for litigation were just dull, routine, mundane "lawsuits," cameras in the courtroom simply didn't make for very good theater.

In 2000, Judge Joseph Teresi of the state supreme court opened the courtroom to cameras for the Amadou Diallo trial in Albany. There have been some other courts opened up across the state since the experiment ended. Without the force of law, courtroom access for broadcasters was now left up to judges. Looking toward the future, Steve Baboulis, general manager of WNYT-TV in Albany and chairman of NYSBA for 2005, believes it's time to pick up the issue again: "I would love to do more to reinstitute cameras in the courtroom and have effective, resilient legislation passed. I think that would be a wonderful achievement."

Opening New York's courts to cameras again may still be a long-time coming. New York's highest court, the Court of Appeals in Albany, recently ruled against Court TV to allow television coverage of courtroom proceedings. The cable network, dedicated to the coverage of legal affairs, sued the State of New York, claiming the policy unfairly prevents television reporters from executing their full newsgathering responsibilities. The court said television reporters had every right to attend trials and to report on their proceedings, as long as they didn't bring their cameras. State lawyers argued that the presence of television cameras in court would unduly influence the judicial process. The court also found that broadcasters did not have an inherent constitutional right to cover trials with cameras and microphones.

Alerting New Yorkers

The full potential and effectiveness of the Emergency Broadcast System (EBS) in New York through much of its existence was held back by a chronic lack of funds. The first statewide test of the Emergency Broadcast System was held on October 7, 1986. Through the persistent efforts and dedication of Albany Broadcasting President John Kelly and other volunteers, the system was maintained with what little resources they had available to them. Broadcasters were all too familiar with its shortcomings and hoped it would never have to be used. According to Kelly, priorities in the state assembly drastically changed after the attacks of 9/11: "It was difficult to build this system, but 9/11 changed all that. They were tripping over dollars to create a viable emergency broadcast system because no one wants to be unprepared again."

The existing Emergency Alert System (EAS) was designed to enable the president of the United States to reach every broadcast station in the country. September 11th demonstrated some of the faults with the system. Neither Governor George Pataki nor Mayor Rudolph Giuliani was able to access the system to communicate with frightened New Yorkers. Shortly thereafter, NYSBA teamed up with State Emergency Management Office (SEMO) to build a statewide EAS system.

Dick Novik headed up the project to build the new system, enabling the governor to reach all radio and television stations simultaneously. In the event of a future crisis, an EAS message would first be sent from SEMO headquarters to SEMO facilities across the state via satellite. These messages would then be sent to the radio and television stations' EAS receivers. The receivers and satellite equipment installed at each station were completely funded by the state. Not only does the new system reach out to the entire state of New York but localized messages can also be sent directly to county executives in the event of a local disaster to communicate with local constituents.

During the summer of 2002, NYSBA worked with the New York State Police, the Division of Criminal Justice Services, the State Emergency Management Office, and the National Center for Missing and Exploited Children to establish a different kind of alert system to locate recently abducted children, called the "Amber Alert Program." John Kelly brought the program to the attention of NYSBA. It was started in Texas and named after Amber Hagerman, a little girl who was kidnapped and murdered there. Once a missing child has been reported, local or state police trigger the alerts, which are then received in broadcasters' control rooms. The stations then make an announcement, passing along information to listeners and viewers to help find the missing child. The program will be eventually integrated into the New York EAS system.

Calls on Congress

Joe Reilly not only made broadcasters' issues heard in the capital district but in the nation's capital as well: "Frankly, the Washington scene became more important to us than the Albany scene because we are regulated by the federal government." In the fall of 1981, with the help of Bill Williamson from WIBX/WIBQ in Utica, Reilly organized the first ever "Call on Congress." A party of 23 broadcasters had the opportunity to visit with 25 members of the New York congressional delegation, including both Senator Daniel Patrick Moniyhan and Senator Alfonse D'Amato. They discussed a wide range of issues, including deregulation, longer license terms for broadcasters, Senator Bill Bradley's proposal to move a New York television station to New Jersey, cable television, copyrights, and direct-broadcast satellites.

During their visit, broadcasters were able to convince two New York congressmen, who also happened to be co-sponsors of the bill, to withdraw their support from the Performers Royalty Bill. The legislation would have forced broadcasters to bear additional financial burdens. They were already paying fees to ASCAP, BMI, and SESAC for the right to air music from recording artists, not to mention the enormous promotion and on-air exposure broadcasters gave to the record companies and the artists they represented. The potential cost of the bill was $1 million-plus each year for the entire broadcast industry in New York, but fortunately for broadcasters, the measure was eventually defeated.

The Call on Congress in 1990 also helped bring about the demise of the so-called "spectrum fee." The federal government was facing a $50 billion deficit, so a tax of 5% on the gross revenues of broadcasters was proposed. It would have potentially raised $10 billion over a five-year period, but broadcasters argued that it was unconstitutional. Over dinner the night before officially visiting with New York's delegation, broadcasters expressed their concerns to Senator Robert Dole's chief of staff, Jim Wholley. He relayed those concerns to Senator Dole the next day. The senator arranged a meeting with the director of the Office of Management and Budget, Richard Darman, to request that the concept of the spectrum fee be dropped from the proposed budget. Congress eventually abandoned the idea. This adroit piece of lobbying was just one of many examples of NYSBA's influence on the national scene.

The Washington meetings, with both senators and congressmen, were regarded as a huge success and became an annual tradition for over a dozen years. Senator D'Amato remembers those meetings as an opportunity to better understand the needs of broadcasters: "I always wanted to let them know I was available and open to them. Those meetings gave us an opportunity to listen to their various concerns, so we could try to respond favorably to their needs and be on the lookout for overregulation."

In late 1988, a committee of 18 NYSBA officers and directors met to develop a "near term" strategy for the Association. There was a strong consensus to increase the Association's lobbying efforts in Albany. The committee felt more emphasis needed to be placed on the state legislature because of the continued deregulation activities by the FCC in Washington, leaving the states increasingly responsible for issues that may adversely affect broadcasting. Some of those issues included a tax on broadcast advertising, restrictions on tower construction, libel and slander laws, and restrictions placed on certain types of advertising. As a result, they recommended creating a "Call-on-Albany" Day based on the success of the Calls on Congress. Thus, in the spring of 1989, the NYSBA board began a new annual tradition in Albany, meeting with state legislative leaders, including Senate President Ralph Marino, Assembly Speaker Mel Miller, Senate Majority Leader Manfred "Fred" Ohrenstein, and Assembly Minority Leader Clarence "Rapp" Rappleyea. Vital lines of communication were established between state legislature and broadcasters at that meeting, helping lawmakers better understand the importance of the broadcasting industry as one of the largest employers in the state, in addition to their standing and stature as custodians of New York's local airwaves.

Federal Affairs

Many state issues obviously directly affect how broadcasters conduct their affairs, but ultimately New York's broadcasters were regulated from Washington via the Congress and the FCC. Those regulatory bodies could dictate such policies as Equal Employment Opportunity (EEO) programs, ownership rules, and indecency guidelines. For example, in 1981 the FCC relieved broadcast stations from having to file EEO programs relating to the employment of minorities, but only if the members of minority groups constituted less than 5% of the local labor force.

In an effort to diversify broadcast ownership, the FCC introduced two new methods of transferring licenses in 1978. The FCC's intent was to get more broadcast stations into the hands of minority groups to be more reflective of their actual proportion of the population. One method made sellers of a station eligible for a tax credit to reduce or delay their capital gains tax on the sale of the station, but only if the station was transferred to a minority licensee. Alternatively, a station could be sold to a minority group in a "distress sale" for no more than 75% of the fair market value of the station. Stations transferred via a "distress sale" were those currently under investigation by the commission or in violation of FCC rules. By 1989 it was estimated that 160 stations had passed into minority hands via the tax credit method alone.

In 1970, the FCC introduced the Prime Time Access Rule in an attempt to encourage the production of local public affairs programming. The rule limited network programming to three hours during prime time. However, an unintended side effect was the creation of a new market for "off-network" shows, as well as a tidal wave of inexpensive syndicated entertainment programming.

That same year, the commission introduced the Financial Interest and Syndication Rules (Fin-Syn Rules) to further promote program diversity and to limit the market share held by the networks. The rules prohibited the networks from owning a financial interest in programs beyond their first run or owning the means of syndication for those programs. The introduction of this ruled forced CBS to spin off its in-house syndication arm into what became Viacom. During the 1990s, the networks argued vigorously for the repeal of the Fin-Syn Rules, citing increased competition from cable. The share of the network's audience had dropped to around 60% from around 85% in the early 1980s. In an ironic twist of fate, Viacom would acquire its former parent, CBS, in 1999.

Fairness Doctrine

Most broadcasters would argue that the most ambiguous guideline crafted by the FCC was by far the so-called "Fairness Doctrine," also known as Section 317. In 1949, the FCC overturned its "Mayflower Doctrine," prohibiting broadcasters from editorializing. It now enabled broadcasters the opportunity to be advocates, but only if they permitted opposing views, as well as the right of the public to respond to a controversial issue.

Many broadcast journalists regarded the guidelines as an infringement on their rights afforded by the First Amendment. Reporters believed they should make their own decisions about what is fair and balanced in their stories. Addressing the NYSBA Executive Conference in 1964, FCC Commissioner Lee Loevinger called the Fairness Doctrine a good rule with a bad name: "Many people are misled to thinking that the Fairness Doctrine guarantees that everything you put on your air is 'fair.' The only thing that the Fairness Doctrine requires of you is that you permit the right of reply. The Doctrine gives broadcasters a wide latitude and is really a means of helping reporters develop a professional 'conscience.'"

Governor Mario Cuomo's view on this issue could not be more clearly defined. He used his Albany bully pulpit to summon up arguments against the dreaded Fairness Doctrine. Cuomo's opposition to this misnamed FCC rule sent a signal to liberals and academics that broadcasters' First Amendment rights ought to be protected and preserved.

To sidestep the pitfalls of this requirement, some journalists went so far as to avoid coverage of controversial issues altogether, the exact opposite of the FCC's intentions. To address this importance, the commission required each station to report on its efforts to seek out issues of concern to its community each time its license renewal came up. This process became known as the "Ascertainment of Community Needs."

The proliferation of news outlets in the 1980s and the drive toward deregulation by the Reagan Administration made the Fairness Doctrine increasingly irrelevant. President Reagan appointed Mark Fowler chairman of the FCC in 1981. The new FCC chairman vowed to kill the Fairness Doctrine. In August 1987, Fowler made good on his promise, when he unilaterally decided to stop enforcing the doctrine. Congress then attempted to turn the Fairness Doctrine into law, thus requiring the FCC to enforce it.

NYSBA rallied its members in response to the congressional momentum, calling for "a stronger stand against content regulation." The legislation was eventually vetoed by President Reagan, who was greatly influenced in the matter by the legendary Ward Quaal, an iconic broadcaster who once ran the mighty WGN in Chicago. Quaal was a fierce opponent of the Fairness Doctrine. Congress had also failed to muster the necessary votes to override the president's veto. The Fairness Doctrine was no more.

Michael Collins muses that the death of the Fairness Doctrine ushered in a new era in radio: "In 1987 the Fairness Doctrine ended. That ruling led to the start of the Rush Limbaugh show and other controversial radio talk shows. That's how talk radio became the very partisan platform it is today." Collins is a former broadcaster who worked at stations in Connecticut and New York. Most recently he served as an adjunct professor at Quinnipiac University in Hamden, Connecticut, teaching broadcast history and serving as general manager of WQUN, Quinnipiac's student radio station.

Equal Time

Another FCC regulation affecting coverage of political campaigns would prove to be equally as vague and troublesome in its interpretation and application as the Fairness Doctrine at times. Section 315, more commonly referred to as the "Equal Time Amendment," sought to treat political candidates equally when selling or giving away airtime, as well as preventing broadcasters from unduly influencing the outcome of an election.

A controversial amendment to section 315 was made by the FCC in 1959. Broadcasters interpreted the ruling as now requiring equal time for any candidate anytime his or her opponent appeared on air, even outside of purchased commercial airtime. To clarify the ruling, Congress eventually outlined four exemptions. Broadcasters would not have to provide equal time to candidates appearing on regularly scheduled newscasts, news interviews shows, documentaries, or on-the-spot news events. These new guidelines, however, would obviously give incumbent candidates the upper hand by virtue of the fact that they would be making news as the current office holder.

Broadcasters' interests would be further threatened by amendments made to the equal-time clause in 1971. Congress now required broadcasters to offer candidates a similar rate they would offer to their most favored advertiser. If an advertiser was given a special discount, then political candidates would have to be offered that lower rate as well. Phil Spencer of WCSS in Amsterdam expressed the view held by many broadcasters in New York at the time: "I'll tell you how bad it was. Let's just take my little radio station. My biggest advertiser was a men's store that spent about $6,000 a year with me, which was a lot of money back then for a little station. In those days, I used to get, like, $3 a spot. For them to get a $3 rate, my lowest rate, they had to buy 2,000 spots. A politician coming in off the street says, 'I want to buy one announcement for $3.' My rate card was $6 for one announcement, but now radio and TV were forced to sell at what they called the 'lowest unit rate.' It was crazy. . . . "

Around the same time there was growing support for "counter-advertising," a close cousin of equal time. Proponents for counter-advertising sought to balance the views of commercial sponsors. They believed it would enhance free speech and break the perceived monopoly sponsors had over the public's airwaves. The Federal Trade Commission, in its drive to provide greater protection for consumers, recommended that the FCC mandate counter-advertising. Broadcasters were outraged by the FTC proposal, saying it would "ruin" the industry if enacted. In an editorial aired April 11, 1972, and reproduced in "Newsbreak," Gene Bohi, vice president and general manager of WAST-TV, Channel 13 in Albany, made a direct appeal to his audience about the dire consequences of counter-advertising: "We as broadcasters, would be required to give away the only commodity we have to sell—airtime. And since time is limited, and criticism of our commercials wouldn't be so constrained, pretty soon there wouldn't be enough time left to sell. Many stations might have to fold . . . . not only broadcasting but also all kinds of industries would be affected. The economic impact could cause job losses at a time when we are concerned about unemployment." He would go on to say that advertisers would most likely abandon broadcast in favor of print out of shear frustration. In the end, counter-advertising was never given the force of law, and only a few limited test spots were aired throughout the country.

Advertising Regulations

The surgeon general's release of its report on the dangers of smoking to Americans in 1964 would ultimately take a chunk out of broadcast revenues. Cigarette ads accounted for about 10% of broadcast revenues in the 1960s. Two years after the release of the surgeon general's report, a New York lawyer, John Banzhaf, requested time for antismoking spots on WCBS-TV, but the station refused. The FCC eventually ruled in favor of Banzhaf under the provisions of the Fairness Doctrine.

Both the FCC and Federal Trade Commission soon began to push for the total ban of cigarette advertising in broadcasting. There were questions as to whether the government could ban advertisements of a legal product. Another approach was to air anti-smoking spot announcements using the Fairness Doctrine, as in the case of WCBS-TV. Many broadcasters, like Phil Spencer, felt it unfair to prevent cigarette advertising in one medium and not another: "If they'd knocked out cigarette advertising for everybody, I wouldn't have said a thing. I used to get a little money—not much because we were in a small market—from cigarette advertising every year. All of a sudden, I drive down the highway and I see billboards advertising cigarettes, or I pick up the newspaper and they've got cigarette ads, too. Magazines did, too, but radio and television were shut out."

Other broadcasters believed the industry should self-regulate itself before the government did it for them. R. Peter Straus, former owner of WMCA in New York, was one of the first broadcasters to make adjustments to cigarette advertising over his airwaves by banning it during hours when kids would be listening. He ended giving up about a third of his revenue, hoping his colleagues in the industry would follow suit, but they didn't. As he feared, Congress banned cigarette advertising in broadcasting after January 1, 1971, so no one ended up with any revenue from tobacco companies.

As with cigarette advertising in the 1960s, there was movement in the 1980s toward banning beer and wine broadcast advertising. In 1985 a bill was introduced in Congress by Representative John Sterling (D-OH) calling for mandatory counter-advertising to balance the perceived large amount of beer and wine broadcast advertising. The lobbying efforts of groups like Project SMART (Stop Marketing Alcohol on Radio and Television) to reduce drunk-driving fatalities were certainly admirable, but broadcasters felt their own voluntary educational campaigns were sufficient. During the NYSBA Call on Congress in 1985, Senator D'Amato expressed support for the broadcaster's approach to the issue: "Our state's citizens are now, more than ever, aware of the tragic consequences of drunk driving, notably because of your efforts." He understood that a simple ban on beer and wine advertising alone would not curb the abuse of alcohol.

That same year, NYSBA organized a panel discussion at the Executive Conference that focused on the bill introduced by Representative Sterling, moderated by Joe Reilly. Terry Mahoney from NBC, Don Shea from the U.S. Brewers Association, Paula Roth from the National Council on Alcoholism, and George Hacker from Project SMART served as panelists. Hacker and Roth argued that they merely wanted to help reduce the deaths attributed to drinking and driving. Broadcasters demanded evidence of a direct correlation between broadcast advertising and drunk-driving fatalities. The view among broadcasters for the proposed counter-advertising measure was regarded as intrusive, as expressed by the feisty Oscar Wein, owner of WDLC-AM/WTSX-FM in Port

Jervis: "I resent SMART taking away my First Amendment rights."

NYSBA supported a number of initiatives to educate the public on the dangers of drinking and driving, providing an alternative to government intrusion. The New York State Bar Association aired three different PSAs in 1985, using the theme "When in Doubt, Don't Start Out." A year later NYSBA teamed up with the State Department of Education, the Governor's Traffic Safety Committee, the Department of Motor Vehicles, and the County STOP-DWI coordinators to sponsor an Alcohol and Highway Safety PSA contest for high schools across the state to create awareness about the dangers of drinking and driving, as well as how broadcasting impacts lifestyle choices. The winning PSAs were aired during the 1986–1987 school year.

State and federal legislation didn't necessarily always have a negative impact on broadcast advertising as was the case with the establishment of the New York State Lottery in 1967. The New York State Constitution was amended to allow for a state-run lottery, with all proceeds earmarked for educational purposes. New York became the second state after New Hampshire to establish a lottery.

It would be several years, however, before New York broadcasters would see revenue derived from the broadcast advertisement of the lottery because FCC regulations at the time forbade it. Governor Rockefeller worked closely with NYSBA to overturn the statute, insisting that the New York State Lottery was being used for educational purposes. It would not be until 1975 when a new federal law was passed allowing state lotteries to be advertised on radio and television.

As soon as the new legislation was passed, Commissioner Ronald Maiorana of the New York State Wagering and Racing System met with NYSBA to discuss the results of its study to maximize its advertising budget to reach 100% of the state through broadcast outlets. The commissioner told the NYSBA board he "was of the opinion the Lottery will start to boom." In time, not only would it "boom" for the state, but for broadcasters as well. The New York State Lottery, under the leadership of Director Nancy Palumbo and her predecessor Margaret DeFrancisco, is one of the largest broadcast advertisers in New York today, spending almost $20 million annually.

Congress eventually expanded the right to advertise lotteries on radio and television with the passage of the Charity Games Advertising Act of 1988. When it went into effect two years later, not-for-profit organizations, governmental organizations, and commercial organizations were now permitted, under certain conditions, to use broadcast advertising to market their games of chance, only if the state in question allows it. In the State of New York, however, the law is more restrictive. Only the New York State Lottery can be advertised, since state law supersedes the federal law in this particular case.

NYSBA also played a very important leadership role in the "issue" advertising battles on Capital Hill. When Congress tried to prohibit corporations from deducting issues or advocacy advertising as a legitimate expense, the Association teamed up with NAB and Herb Schmertz, the dynamic public affairs chief of the Mobil Oil Corporation, to mount a national effort to maintain the right of free expression, even for giant multinational corporations. Issue advertising had significant impact at the local level as many advertisers (especially the electric, gas, telephone, and water utility companies) threatened to curtail expenditures for public affairs. Advocacy and even some marketing budgets were struck as a result of the proposed new policy. Bill O'Shaughnessy, who was chairman of NAB's Public Affairs Committee at the time, organized a road show with Mobil's Schmertz and other advertisers to lobby Congress and the New York legislature as the idea was gaining momentum. This fight would continue all through the 1970s.

Federal Deregulation

Rumblings to replace or reform the Communications Act of 1934 grew louder and louder throughout the 1970s. More competition from the rise of cable and other new technologies on the horizon made many broadcast regulations increasingly obsolete. Broadcasters like Al Anscombe applauded efforts to get rid of the regulatory underbrush: "There were too many rules, until Ronald Reagan got in and cleaned out some of them that weren't being used anymore. There was just no market for them." Anscombe was a visionary broadcaster and a "triple" pioneer, having been active in radio, broadcast television, and cable. One of his most notable accomplishments in broadcasting was his transformation of the venerable WKBW-AM into one of the leading rock stations in America.

One of the biggest proponents for reforming broadcast regulation was Congressman Lionel Van Deerlin of California. Coming from a broadcasting background, he would assume the chairmanship of the House Communications Subcommittee in the late 1970s. His ill-fated Communications Act of 1978 would seek to replace the FCC, revise the Fairness Doctrine, and completely deregulate radio. Over time there would be a shift toward providing broadcasters a structure in which they could operate more freely. While the FCC would maintain control over ownership limits and employment guidelines, they would have less involvement in developing policies for advertising and programming. However, there would be an emerging feeling in Congress that if broadcasters were not held to their obligations as "trustees" of the public's airwaves and were to be treated just as any other business, then they should pay a special fee to the government for the use of those public airwaves, a scarce resource.

President Reagan's appointment of Mark Fowler as chairman of the FCC would usher in an era of aggressive deregulation. Fowler moved quickly by first extending television licenses to five years and radio to seven. Two years later, the three-year ownership requirement was dropped. The original intention of the guideline was to encourage a new owner's commitment to the community they were now obligated to serve and to demonstrate why they deserved to have their license renewed after three years. Former CapCities executive Phil Beuth cites this ruling as the reason for the "commoditization" of broadcast licenses: "The worst thing that happened was when the FCC dropped the three-year rule. Television stations became pieces of real estate and merchandise. They were just traded like commodities or chattel, and as a result, public service suffered." No doubt this would begin the buying and selling frenzy of television and radio stations, dramatically increasing their value over the next two decades.

In the mid-1980s, ownership rules would be relaxed for the first time in 30 years. The number of television stations any one entity could own would expand from 7 television stations to 12. However, no more than 25% of the nation's population could be served by a given licensee. The radio ownership cap would also be expanded to 12 stations. Amos Finch, a small radio broadcaster in Deposit, New York, remembers making his opposition known to the FCC's new policy: "I remember writing some letters to the FCC, when they started allowing owners to acquire many more stations than they could in the old days. That policy has had a lot to do with the change we've seen in broadcasting. Radio has just become a jukebox, and community information has just about been cut out. It's just not the same."

FCC guidance as to how broadcasters were to serve their local community were also relaxed when the "ascertainment" requirement was dropped. Previously, when broadcasters went to renew their license they had to provide detailed program logs, as well as documentation to demonstrate how they "ascertained" what their community needed or wanted in the way of programming. Phil Beuth believes that this new policy has left broadcasters out of touch with their local communities: "All they are required to do now is answer eight questions and send in a postcard. It's ridiculous. We used to have to go and visit charitable organizations, civic groups, and business leaders to get a feel for the community. We had to address that in our news and in our public affairs programs. Nobody does that anymore." The FCC would eventually bring back "form 395" (as the ascertainment requirement was also known) after Janet Jackson's "wardrobe malfunction" during the 2004 Super Bowl on CBS. The commission took a dangerous turn toward content regulation in general in 2004 when, under pressure from Congress and the public, the FCC began to

Fig. 1. Former NYSBA legal counsel, John Tabner, served the Association for over 30 years, helping New York's broadcasters develop their position on a wide range of legislative matters.

Fig. 2. NYSBA's current legal counsel, Matthew Mataraso, with the late Carol Reilly, who once managed Merv Griffin's radio stations in Albany and, as the wife of Joe Reilly, was affectionately known as the "first lady" of NYSBA. Her husband, Joe, says, "She had a smile that would light up the room." Carol was also a role model for women broadcasters.

Fig. 3. NYSBA's "mother hen," Ellen Cody, waves goodbye to New York's broadcasters in the early 1980s, after more than 25 years of dedicated service to the Association.

Fig. 4. NCSA administrator Sandy Messineo (left) and Mary Anne Jacon (right), NYSBA's vice president of operations, with NYSBA's 2004 Broadcaster of the Year Dan Rather.

Fig. 5. Former chairman of the New York State's Assembly Judiciary Committee, Saul Weprin (D-24th District), known to New York's broadcasters as the "Father of Cameras in the Courtroom," addresses NYSBA members after a 10-year struggle to keep New York's courtrooms open to cameras.

Fig. 6. Congressman Ben Gilman records an anti-drunk-driving PSA in the U.S. House of Representative's recording studio as (left to right) Maurie Webster of NYMRAD; Dick Novik, former owner of WPUT in Brewster and WRVH in Patterson; and Jerry Gillman, former owner of WDST in Woodstock look on.

Fig. 7. A young Joe Reilly signs on WERA-AM in Plainsfield, New Jersey, for the very first time on September 16, 1961. Pasquali Tominaro, known for 20 years on WCBS Newsradio 88 as Pat Parson, is seen in the background.

Fig. 8. Left to right: Paul Dunn, former owner of WTLB-AM in Utica; Walter Maxwell, former owner of WGHQ and WBPM in Kingston; NYSBA president Joe Reilly; and Don Snyder look over the books, taking care of NYSBA business.

Fig. 9. King World chief Roger King built the number-one syndication company in all of broadcasting, distributing programs that have become cultural icons, like "Oprah," "Jeopardy!" and "Wheel of Fortune." The media mogul owes his very first break in broadcasting to Joe Reilly, who landed him a job selling time for WERA-AM in Plainfield, New Jersey.

Fig. 10. A young Bill O'Shaughnessy, president of Whitney Radio in Westchester, makes one of countless First Admendment pleas to Association members as a former NYSBA president, conference chairman, NAB Radio representative, and a local, hometown broadcaster. The greatly admired and legendary former president of WPIX-TV in New York City, Leavitt Pope, looks on.

Fig. 11. Governor Nelson Rockefeller engages Dr. Frank Stanton (center) just before Merl Galusha (right) is about to introduce him to NYSBA members for the first time since the CBS president was called before Congress to testify about the CBS documentary "The Selling of the Pentagon."

Fig. 12. "Colonel" Larry Sweeney, a popular executive at BMI, was a regular at NYSBA events, with his wife, Lauretta.

Fig. 13. Now pitching for NYSBA . . . Phil Beuth, one of CapCities's first employees and Tom Murphy's right-hand man, generously contributed his time and effort to NYSBA, even organizing the annual softball tournament at the Executive Conference and winning the Delaney-Cuneen Award for revamping NYSBA's awards for broadcast excellence.

Fig. 14. NYSBA icon Tony Malara has everyone in stitches as the perennial M.C. of the Executive Conference, a role he performs to this day. Malara's jovial nature, and a reputation for getting things done, sent him from relative obscurity in tiny Watertown to the upper echelons of broadcast management at the CBS Television Network in the 1970s and 1980s.

Fig. 15. ABC Television president Wally Schwartz congratulates CBS executive Bob Hosking on winning the annual NYSBA golf tournament at the Executive Conference in 1966.

Fig. 16. Two-term NYSBA chairperson Maire Mason accepts the "Carol Reilly Award" from John Kelly (left), former president of Albany Broadcasting, and Dennis Swanson (right), head of Viacom's television station group, for her distinguished leadership in broadcasting. Mason is currently the vice president and general manager of WNEW.

Fig. 17. Sports broadcaster Greg Gumbel just about manages to juggle his haul of NYSBA Awards for Broadcast Excellence. The awards were created in 1965 to recognize the achievements of broadcasters throughout New York State, in markets both large and small.

Fig. 18. Legendary Long Island broadcaster Marty Beck is the guest of honor at a luncheon at the 21 Club in the early 1980s for his years of service to NYSBA, including serving as president in 1979–1980. left to right: Bill O'Shaughnessy, president of Whitney Radio, who hosted the event; NYSBA president Joe Reilly; Jim Greenwald, former Katz Media CEO; Tony Malara, former CBS Television president; Marty Beck, former owner of Beck-Ross Communications; Carl McCall, then comptroller of New York State; Jim Champlin, former president of Beck-Ross Communications; and Dick Novik, senior vice president for NYSBA.

Fig. 19. Long-time NYSBA secretary Bill McKibben of Buffalo (left) and beloved former two-time NYSBA president C. Glover Delaney of Rochester (right) recognize Glens Falls broadcaster John Lynch for his achievements in broadcasting. Lynch was treasurer of the Association for many years. His son, Chris Lynch, eventually served NYSBA in the same capacity.

Fig. 20. Many theatre luminaries and literary giants stars would drop in at NYSBA events over the years. (Left to right) The famed writer Peter Maas; author and columnist James Brady; the first woman member of the New York Stock Exchange Muriel Siebert; Ruby Dee and Ossie Davis. Dee and Davis were more than frequent guests of the NYSBA; the First Amendment advocates were old friends of the Association.

Fig. 21. Zany comedian Foster Brooks has former WABC executive Dick Beesmyer (center) and powerful former state senate majority leader Warren Anderson (right), gasping for air as he entertains a packed hall of New York broadcasters.

Fig. 22. Only at a NYSBA dinner would one find local politicians and television stars locked in engaging conversation with each other, as we see TV talker Sally Jesse Raphael listening intently to former New York City Mayor David Dinkins. His honor was wearing the special shades following a tennis accident.

Fig. 23. The press circles around an impromptu meeting between television talk show host Jerry Springer with New York's junior senator, Hilary Rodham Clinton, at a NYSBA event.

Fig. 24. Broadcasting's most famous interviewer Larry King dances with Marylou Whitney, generous supporter of the Association, who entertained New York's broadcasters in grand style at her estate in Cady Hill during several ExecutiveConferences at the Gideon Putnam Hotel in Saratoga.

Fig. 25. Entertainment legend Arthur Godfrey checks in a the 1963 Annual Dinner. Godfrey's straightforward, infor mal radio style landed him a morning show on CBS Radi in 1945, called "Arthur Godfrey Time." The show ran for years, until it was canceled in 1972.

Fig. 26. Governor Nelson A. Rockefeller was unarguably one of NYSBA's best friends. He rarely turned down an invitation to speak with NYSBA members. Seen here in a golf cart with NYSBA's very first president, Mike Hanna, after touching town on the 18th green at the Otesaga Resort in Cooperstown.

Fig. 27. Former NYSBA president Neil Derrough is seen here presenting Governor Hugh L. Carey with the now infamous Steuben glass beaver. Moments after this picture was taken, the beaver met its demise when it flew off its pedestal, shattering into a million pieces in front of the dais, to whooping laugher!

Fig. 28. In 1982, NYSBA hosted a debate between the Democratic contenders for governor, former New York City Mayor Ed Koch and the then Lieutenant Governor Mario Cuomo. The two are seen here continuing their informal debate as WCBS Newsradio 88 anchor Lou Adler looks on.

Fig. 29. New York's 53rd governor, George Pataki, holds court with a delegation of New York broadcasters including (left to right) Maire Mason, WNEW general manager; Betty Ellen Berlamino, WPIX-TV executive; Tim Busch, WROC-TV general manager; and Steve Baboulis, WNYT-TV general manager.

Fig. 30. One of many NYSBA's Calls on Congress, Buffalo broadcasters are seen here meeting with former Congressman Jack Kemp, including (left to right) Larry Levite of WBEN, Al Fetch of WYRK, Frank Lorenz of WBLK, Jack Kemp, Les Arries of WIVB-TV, Bill Brown Jr. of WBTA in Batavia, and Lyn Stoyer of WGRZ-TV.

Fig. 31. Left to right: Congressman LaFalce's chief of staff, Gary Luczak, meets with Rochester broadcasters Arnold Klinsky, Vince DeLuca, and Andy Langston.

Fig. 32. Frank Smith, one of CapCities' co-founders, and his wife are shown here turning on the transmitter for WROW-TV (later WTEN) for the first time in 1954.

Fig. 33. Tom Murphy, the first general manager of WTEN-TV in Albany, sits atop a bulldozer for the groundbreaking of WTEN's current studios in the early 1960s. WTEN was the cornerstone of the CapCities empire Murphy would build over a 40-year span.

Fig. 34. From its earliest days, broadcasting has proved to be an enormously influential tool in helping connect local citizens to those in need. Under the leadership of Phil Beuth, WKBW-TV hosted many successful telethons, raising millions of dollars for local charities. Beuth is pictured here second from the right.

levy draconian fines for indecency.

Requirements to promise a specified minimum amount of public service programming or to limit the maximum amount of advertising to be aired would also be dropped during the 1980s. The FCC would, however, maintain control over political programming and obscenity.

In the fall of 1995, the FCC waived its rules to allow for the unattended operation of broadcast stations. An FCC press release at the time of the announcement stated: "In many areas of broadcast operation, automation is seen as affording more accurate and controlled operation than that performed by humans." It would go on to say that the waiver would provide broadcast stations with "the more effective use of financial resources to enhance other station operations and services." Critics charge that the ruling has led to a dramatic increase in automated and "homogenized" programming, and has left news coverage of many local communities in a vulnerable state. Many stations are no longer staffed on the weekends or overnight, as is the case of the radio station previously owned by Jim and Keela Rodgers in Lake Placid: "They leave the station at 5 o'clock on Friday night and don't return until 5 o'clock on Monday morning."

Coverage of the "Great Northeast Blackout" on August 14, 2003, by WSYR-AM in Syracuse has been held up as an example of the industry's shortcomings as a result of deregulation by Dr. David Rubin, dean of the Newhouse School of Public Communications at Syracuse University. Listening to almost four hours of the station's coverage on that desperate day, Rubin called it "extremely disappointing" because of the station's reliance on CNN feeds and calls from local citizens, rather than on local reporters. Clear Channel, which owns WSYR, has defended its coverage, stating it did in fact use three of its own reporters, as well as coverage it simulcast from Channel 9 in Syracuse, a television station Clear Channel also owns. The horrific attacks of September 11, 2001, however, would demonstrate broadcasting's continued ability to serve as a platform and sounding board in a time of crisis. Many stations in New York and across America won kudos and praise for their "heroic" and dedicated service in the dark days following 9/11.

Docket 80/90

During the 1980s, the FCC allowed the creation of a few thousand new FM stations under docket 80/90, so called because it was the 90th proceeding initiated in 1980. The intention of the FCC was to promote diversity in medium- to smaller-size markets, recalls *Radio & Records* publisher Erica Farber: "If you look at where the additional licenses were added, it's not like they were added in

New York City or Los Angeles. They were in markets where one could say they were 'under-radioed.' What's under-radioed mean? It's so subjective. There's so much diversity today in broadcasting, yet you'll still find dissatisfaction out there among a segment of the audience that says they are not being served."

An unintended side affect of docket 80/90 was oversupply and not enough demand in many of these smaller markets. Just prior to the FM expansion, radio broker Frank Boyle knew that markets like Utica or Rome couldn't support these new stations: "There were about 8 different owners in each market and 3 of the 10 or 12 stations were already broke at the time. With the 80/90 rule we went from 10 radio stations in each market to about 20. It couldn't even support 10, and now there were 20!" Boyle is an articulate heavyweight in the radio station brokerage business, rising through the ranks of Eastman Radio, the rep firm, over 30 years. In the early 1970s, he became president and chairman of the board, serving at Eastman until 1985. He now operates out of Stamford, Connecticut.

Not only did many new stations struggle to gain a foothold, but also many existing outlets were forced to reduce their staffs just to survive. In the mid-1980s, Walter Maxwell employed roughly 35 full- and part-time employees. By the time he sold his station in 1999 he was down to seven employees. Increased competition forced him to air more and more satellite programming and less local news: "We had four full-time people in news at WGHQ in 1986. We had live announcers on both AM and FM from 6 a.m. to midnight. We did a lot of local stuff because there was no competition. Between myself and the other AM in town we did well. Then 80/90 came along and took away all the money. The pie stayed the same, but everybody got a smaller slice."

By the early 1990s, the glut of radio stations in the red would become a powerful argument for consolidation. Many believe that the shortcomings of the 80/90 rule were one of the reasons for the drive toward consolidation. Central New York broadcaster Ed Levine, a benefactor of the policy, has mixed feelings: "I got into ownership because of 80/90, so I can't say anything bad about it, but at the same time it begat hundreds of stations that were on the verge of going, or were going, bankrupt. Hence consolidation was probably an overreaction to all these new stations coming on board."

1996 Telecommunications Act

"The rewrite of the Communication Act of 1934 changed the radio business overnight. The consolidation of the industry saw the radio business go from being primarily an industry of mom and pop companies to multibillion-dollar corporations literally within a 12-month period," comments Erica Farber on the sweeping affects of the Telecommunications Act of 1996. The primary goals of the act were to increase competition among new communications services and to discard antiquated regulations. It was also used to frame the new communications policy of Congress for the next century, to replace governmental regulatory guidelines with marketplace competition. After almost a decade, Senator Alfonse D'Amato reflects on the landmark legislation: "On balance it was not bad legislation, but the world of telecommunications is changing continuously." At the time, FCC Chairman Reed Hundt was quick to remind the industry that while the world of telecommunications had indeed changed forever, the Telecommunications Act of 1996 "amends" but does not replace the Communications Act of 1934.

The Act brought down many of the cross-market barriers that prohibited companies from one communications industry from providing services in other industry sectors. The elimination of these barriers would open the floodgates of mergers, acquisitions, and the integration of services previously barred under FCC rules. By the turn of the century, cable providers would be offering both telephone service and access to the Internet in addition to their core business of television distribution, competing in what was once regarded as two distinct fields of media and telecommunications.

Broadcasters would see great relief in the area of ownership requirements. Ownership limits on television stations were lifted. Group owners were now able to purchase television stations with a maximum service area cap of 35% of the U.S. population. The previous limit was 25%, established in 1985. The FCC would come to rule that one owner could control two TV stations in the same market if there were a minimum of eight stations in a particular market.

Limits on the number of radio stations were completely lifted, although the bill does provide regulatory guidelines on the number of licenses that may be owned within specific markets. In cities with 45 or more stations, one owner could have up to eight stations. No owner could control more than half the stations in any market, and the Justice Department eventually ruled that no owner could control more than half the advertising in one market.

Broadcast license renewals would now be every eight years instead of five. Previous rules allowing competing applications for license renewals were dramatically altered in favor of existing licensees. Stations could also choose to be affiliated with more than one network. Broadcasters would also be allowed to own cable television systems, but television licensees would still be prohibited from owning newspapers in the same market.

The biggest concession to the broadcast industry limited eligibility for advanced television licenses (ATV) to existing television licensees, assuring broadcasters a future in providing digital and enhanced television services. While broadcasters vehemently oppose the notion of paying for the digital spectrum, the Act does include provisions that would allow the commission to impose spectrum fees for any nonbroadcast services that broadcasters may provide with these new allocations.

Beyond ownership rules and the establishment of new communications services, the Act also mandated that the industry develop a ratings system to identify indecent or objectionable programming. In conjunction with the establishment of a ratings system, television set manufacturers were also required to install a V-chip, a blocking device, in television receivers larger than 13 inches.

Under the banner of NYSBA, broadcasters have come together through all these years to overcome daunting challenges, generating widespread goodwill, influence, standing, and stature within the State of New York and beyond. They have made the Empire State safer through the creation of Amber Alert and the EAS system. NYSBA-generated public service announcements to stop drunk driving and to improve traffic safety have undoubtedly saved countless lives. By making legal proceedings transparent through cameras in the courtroom, New York's broadcasters have made citizens more aware of how judicial decisions may affect their daily lives. While these achievements are indeed remarkable, it is the dedication each broadcaster expresses to the community they served day in and day out that forms the inherent bond between the individual members of the New York State Broadcasters Association. It is these shared values that have sustained the Association through an ever-changing regulatory environment and mounting pressure from broadcasting's competitors.

3

Public Interest, Convenience, and Necessity

"It is the nonspectacular events of daily life that give greatness to broadcasting. Its availability day in and day out, provides the average citizen with the opportunity to learn about the world, but more importantly, about his or her local community."

—Senator Alfonse D'Amato (D-NY)

Members of the New York State Broadcasters Association have always understood that the heart and soul of broadcasting is not about ratings, profits, or star power. It is about delving into the problems and aspirations of local citizens, and then illuminating and responding to their needs. Broadcasting is informed by a confluence of ideas. It is an instrument of communication guiding a community toward the greater good, as well as helping individuals realize their full potential.

Many of NYSBA's founding members grew up in a culture of community service, recognizing the duty to give back to one's community. Some of those broadcasters lived through the hardships of the Depression, others risked their lives in World War II, and still others channeled their innovative energies to help build the United States into the mighty nation it is today. The idea of community service was second nature to the broadcast pioneers who built radio and television in New York at this time. It did not need to be dictated or learned, it was understood.

It is true that the broadcast licenses awarded to them by the federal government mandated that they operate in the "public interest, convenience, and necessity" of their communities in return for the commercial use of the public's airwaves. Ironically, this mandate was probably not as necessary as it might be today in American society. At their core, broadcasters are in the business of entertaining and informing the public. Yet they also perform a quasi-governmental function of directing people to safety and security in times of crisis. As the "fourth branch" of government, they serve as the eyes and ears of their communities as well. Broadcasters possess the awesome responsibility of guiding democratic discourse, in addition to playing their role in maintaining the balance of power at the federal, state, and local levels of government by resembling a forum for the expression of many different viewpoints.

Those New Yorkers who dedicated their lives to the broadcast profession did so for a variety of reasons in addition to the opportunity to serve. Whether they saw it as a vocation, a reason to carry on a family tradition, or a "fun" way to satisfy their insatiable curiosity, they did so with a deep sense of purpose and pride. The very word *broadcasting* sounds almost too impersonal to reflect the deep connection the medium had with New York's local communities. The true essence of the medium can perhaps only be drawn from the individual reflections of those who chose to serve and made it the most "human," personal, and accessable of all the mass media ever created.

Broadcasting, a Life Passion

For many broadcasters, the love of broadcasting was coursing through their veins at a very early age. It was almost part of their DNA. For as long as they can remember, broadcasters like James Duffy knew there was nothing else they wanted to do in life: "I had always envisioned myself, even as a kid, being a broadcaster. I used to 'pretend' to broadcast ball games. I would play with cutout figures and baseball cards, doing the play by play." Duffy's passion would fuel his determination to succeed in this electrifying profession, eventually becoming president of the ABC Television Network. Before Duffy assumed the top spot at ABC, it was frequently described as the "fourth network in a three-network race." During his tenure as president in the 1970s, however, Duffy would guide ABC from worst to first.

As a child, Jim Delmonico, a broadcast icon in central New York, quickly became infected with a lifelong passion for broadcasting while he was quarantined in his home recovering from scarlet fever. As an antidote to pass the time, he remembers playing with a shortwave radio his father gave him: "I could get stations from all over the world, and it made that three months go by really quickly because I would write down everything I heard." Delmonico was general manager of WRGB-TV during the 1970s and 1980s. His enthusiasm and commitment reinvigorated the pioneering spirit of America's first television station and gained him the admiration of his peers as a quintessential broadcaster.

Like Delmonico, Buffalo broadcaster John Zach's interest in radio was also sparked by his father, who, as a radio enthusiast, built one of the first crystal sets back in the 1920s. Zach got into listening to long-distance stations via DX, using old radios. Temporarily distracted by dreams of becoming a rock star, Zach eventually found his calling by sharing the triumphs and tragedies of Buffalo with three generations of listeners, and counting. Currently, he is the co-anchor of "Buffalo's Early News" with Susan Rose on WBEN-AM.

In the mid-1950s, as rock and roll was sweeping the nation, no one could just walk into a radio station, remembers Zach. The doors were *always locked*, and an appointment was required to gain admittance. However, Zach managed to befriend Dan Neaverth, who would become the most listened-to disc jockey in Buffalo. After helping establish WBNY as Buffalo's first rock station in the late 1950s, Neaverth went on to become one of WKBW's most popular personalities. Zach hung out at WKBW's studios, watching Neaverth's show. One day he built up the courage to tell Neaverth he had a band. Zach remembers him asking: "How would you like to play at my dances?" Before he knew it, he was playing at Neaverth's "record hops." Neaverth would nurture Zach's interest in radio, helping him practice announcing A&P and Sears-Roebuck commercials. He would also advise him how to give the copy more flair. "I owe a great deal to him," Zach recalls fondly.

First-generation broadcasters are described by long-time WBEN-TV (now WIVB-TV) news executive, William McKibben, as "guys who were down in the basement tinkering with radios when they should have been working for a living." He admires their devotion to broadcasting even before it really proved itself as a business. One can hardly escape the comparison to today's devotees of the Internet. McKibben describes himself as a second-generation broadcaster who played witness to the genius or "wackiness" of the first-generation's achievements. Rock and roll would be the defining characteristic of his generation of broadcasters. Starting out at rock stations in the Midwest, McKibben drew upon his rock-and-roll sensibilities to develop a new, fast-paced, cutting-edge style of news programming for WGR Radio in Buffalo and then for WBEN-TV. Despite his "hip" programming style, the importance of belonging to local civic organizations to better understand the needs of the citizens of Buffalo was not lost on him. During McKibben's most active phase at WBEN-TV, he estimates he served on as many as 10 different boards, including service as secretary for NYSBA.

The founder of Galaxy Communications in Syracuse, Ed Levine's love for broadcasting was also fueled by rock and roll. In high school he dreamt of landing a gig as a disc jockey at WNEW-FM in New York. He remembers the excitement of being on the radio for the very first time: "I was 15 years old when tickets for the Concert for Bangladesh went on sale in 1971. A buddy of mine and I slept outside Madison Square Garden all night long to get tickets. I remember calling up Alex Bennett, who was probably my first radio hero, the following morning to talk about being on line for tickets and hearing myself on the radio." His passion only grew. By the time he went off to Syracuse University, Levine knew what he wanted to do with the rest of his life: "I'm such a simpleton. I pursued one career path at 18, and I've never thought about doing anything else for one moment in the succeeding 30 years." Like so many others, he was hooked.

Too young to be a first-generation broadcaster, popular New York City anchor Ernie Anastos did, however, share their zeal for building radios. He even built his very own "station" in his parent's basement at the age of 13: "I ran wires into the kitchen and put up speakers there, so my parents and sister could hear me while I was 'on the air.' I would sit down there and be a DJ, as well as reading the news."

Content with the prospect of just being able to sweep the floors of his home-town radio station, Anastos walked in the door of WOTW in Nashua, New Hampshire, looking for a job at the age of 16. Exceeding his expectations, the program director gave him a chance to do a reading: "He put me in the studio and I started to read. I felt like I was back down in the basement just practicing. You know, I got pretty good at it because I was practicing so much." Impressed with the teenager's abilities, the program director gave him his first radio pro-gram, a teenage talk show called "Saturday Morning Discussion." Soon after, Anastos became the weekend announcer for the station: "You know what the real love story is? I bought that radio station, WOTW in Nashua, about three years ago. I even have the original WOTW microphone in my office at home." Anastos now also owns four other stations in the Albany-Saratoga region. In fact, Joe Reilly was part owner of the first station Anastos bought in Albany, WQAR.

Anastos wasn't the only one to build his own radio station at a young age. Dick Foreman, former president of programming for ABC Radio, did as well. Foreman's uncle, who owned a radio shop, gave him a book on "electronic the-ory" at the age of 11. Undaunted by the weighty material, Foreman decided to build a radio station to serve his entire neighborhood! He also published a newspaper, even selling ads in it. When he went off to prep school, he founded a radio station there. It continued to operate long after he was gone, until the school closed its doors in 1988. Foreman would continue his "hobby" of build-ing radio outlets, revamping the ABC Radio Network in the 1970s, and building a satellite distribution system that would come to be used by all three major broadcast radio networks.

The allure of radio and television quickly seduced many broadcasters into lifelong careers dedicated to the profession, but for some it would take some time before they found a niche in which they could thrive. "I always wanted to be in the business because I wanted to be an announcer. I wanted to be a writer," remembers Phil Beuth, former president of early morning and late night programming at ABC. He attended Union College in Schenectady to pursue his ambition of becoming a broadcaster. He majored in English so he could learn how to improve his writing and verbal skills.

Beuth also had a passion for baseball. In 1948 he entered a contest organized by WPIX-AM, in New York, to predict the final standings for both the National and American Baseball Leagues at the end of the season. He got every one of them right, winning a $500 gift certificate to Howard Clothes in New Jersey. When he went to pick up his prize at WPIX, Jackie Robinson and his wife, Rachel, were in the studio, along with the famed sportscaster Red Barber, one of Beuth's heroes. As both of his life passions intersected at that moment, Beuth didn't pass up the opportunity to strike up a conversation with Barber. He got up the nerve to tell Barber he wanted to become a broadcaster. Beuth recalls being told: "First you've got to get rid of that New York accent." He admits to having an unforgiving "dees, dems, and doze" accent at the time. Barber told him to get someone to coach him as he read a newspaper aloud into a tape recorder. Beuth acted on Barber's sage career advice for the next three years.

In 1952 Beuth landed a gig as a page at WRGB in Schenectady, then part of General Electric. One of his duties was to give tours of the entire GE plant, including the radio and television studios. One day the hosts of GE's program "True," a drama on Sunday nights sponsored by True Cigarettes, paid a visit. Beuth was assigned to show Ronald Reagan and Red Barber around the studios. Hardly able to contain himself as he escorted them back to their limo, he said to Barber: "Well, gentlemen, it's been great being with you all day, and Mr. Barber, you may not recall, but I met you before with Jackie Robinson and his wife at the Jimmy Powers studio in New York. I predicted all the baseball standings correctly." He responded, "Oh yeah, I remember that." Beuth went on to remind him of the advice he gave on how to get rid of his New York accent. Full of pride about how much he had already accomplished since he left New York City, he awaited Barber's response. He told Beuth: "You still need to get rid of that New York accent." Temporarily dejected, Beuth would go onto a long and successful career at Capital Cities as chairman Tom Murphy's first hire and right-hand man.

"Accidental" Broadcasters

Many broadcasters admit to having "fallen into the business" almost by accident. Fortunately for the industry their career stumbled or lurched forward in the right direction. After graduating from college in 1951, Shell Storrier moved to Pennsylvania to sell cement, never imagining he would spend most of his career in broadcasting. The construction industry paid well, but he was laid off during the winter when there was little building activity. He was bored, so when a friend asked him if he wanted to start selling ads for television, Storrier jumped at the chance. He moved to Utica in 1953 and started selling ads for WKTV-TV. Spending more than 40 years at the same station, he retired in 1992 as general manager.

Not surprisingly, there were some other broadcasters who "fell" into broadcasting completely by accident. Stephanie McNamara, general manager of WADO in New York, shares her tale of how she made a career switch from working in a department store to selling airtime: "There was a little index card in the job placement office for a job at Time Buying Services, and it was 25 cents more an hour than I was making at the department store." The job involved buying airtime, something she knew absolutely nothing about. "I went on the interview and got the job." She told the gentleman who interviewed her that she decided to apply for the job only because it paid more than what she was currently making. "The guy thought it was such an honest answer that he gave me 50 cents more an hour instead of 25 cents, just for being honest."

McNamara wasn't the only one going in blind when she applied for her first job in broadcasting. Looking to move on from his job in textile sales early in his career, Jim Greenwald, a former chief executive of Katz Media, starting pounding the pavement in search of a higher-paying job. He saw an ad in *The New York Times* one day: "Rep Salesman Wanted." He went to the employment agency to apply for the position. The man interviewing him asked him why he wanted to be a rep salesman. Greenwald responded: "I work for a firm that prints ties on gray goods, and I assume this is a job selling rep *ties*." The interviewer told him to get out of his office. Confused, Greenwald asked him, "What are you talking about?" The gentleman informed him that a rep salesman sells *broadcast* time! Greenwald begged to be allowed to interview for the position. He said he wouldn't embarrass the headhunter, and he probably wouldn't get the job anyway. Several rounds of interviews later, he found himself as one of the final two candidates. The other person was offered the job, but flunked the company's mandatory *mental* exam, Greenwald was hired. Thus began his 40-year career at Katz Media.

Walking into the lobby of the wrong company would become one of the happiest mistakes of former WABC-TV news director Al Primo's life. Looking for a job to save up money for college, he tossed his résumé out to companies all over Pittsburgh. Visiting the last building in Pittsburgh's economic hub, the Golden Triangle, he took the elevator up to the 10th floor to a company he had heard of before. He walked into the office and requested an application. He was surprised by the frenetic activity of the place. He was then called into the human resources office to fill out an application. At the top of the application it read "Dumont Television Network," but it wasn't the name of the company he thought he was visiting. "I kept my mouth shut out of pure embarrassment and submitted the application." Primo's family was too poor to even afford a television at the time. He was called the next day to work in the mailroom of WDTV. Immediately he caught the bug for broadcasting: "I just fell in love. I mean I really fell in love with television."

Not sure of their exact path in life, some broadcasters were given a gentle nudge into the business. "My best friend in high school worked at WDLA as an announcer. He told me when we graduated in 1954 that he was leaving WDLA to go work for another radio station in Binghamton," recounts Amos Finch. His friend told him he should apply for his old job at WDLA. He did just that and got the job. "Being low man on the totem pole at a 1,000-watt rural AM station, I also got the duties of mowing the lawn and putting the garbage out." The dues he would have to pay would be well worth the mentoring he received in return from WDLA owner Mike Cuneen, a fixture in upstate broadcasting.

Before Nick Verbitsky was building radio empires like United Stations, encouragement from one of his college professors helped him get a foot in the door at J. Walter Thompson, the renowned advertising agency in New York. He was working in retail at the time, while a student at St. John's University. After an interview, Verbitsky was offered a position as a night watchman in 1964: "It entailed accepting packages at night in the lobby of the ad agency's building on Madison Avenue. In those days people who worked past 7 o'clock got $2.50 in supper money. We were responsible for having people sign for it. I made a lot of friends that way." When he returned from a tour of duty in the Marine Corps he was offered a position as a buyer in the media department at J. Walter Thompson.

The Family Business

Prior to the 1980s, broadcasting was still very much a "mom and pop" business. Husband and wife teams ran the local radio station in many of the towns across New York State. Sons and daughters followed in their parents' footsteps. This should come as no surprise. Broadcasting after all was tightly knit into the fabric of New York's villages and hamlets. The local radio station was a beacon of ideas, as well as a familiar communal hearth that broadcasting families proudly tended and watched over.

New York's quintessential "broadcasting family" is without a doubt the Gamblings. Collectively, John B., John A., and John R. Gambling have graced New York City's airwaves for well over 75 years. What made them so special was their ability to widen the bond of their own family with millions of listeners. "What they established with the audience was a connection and an emotional link that made them in every sense 'part of the family' of the listener. They were just the nicest people, and they were respectful of being in people's homes. They never crossed the line into poor taste. That was their hallmark, just being very nice people you could relate to," explains Bob Bruno, vice president and general manager of WOR-AM in New York City and a NYSBA board member for over a dozen years. WOR was the long-time home of "Rambling with Gambling" before the program was canceled in 2000. Responding to changing demographics, WOR decided it was time to take its morning programming in a new direction. John R. Gambling, the third-generation member of the Gambling tribe, quickly found a new home at WABC-AM.

There are also examples of entire families filling the ranks of local radio stations throughout New York. Such is the case with "Ramblin" Lou Shriver's station, WXYR-AM in Buffalo. "It's a family-run business. My son is the sales manager and my daughters work at the station part time," says Shriver. His wife also helps operate the station. Ramblin' Lou's "family business" is more than just a radio station. It actually resembles something of a local multimedia entertainment empire. The entire family is part of a band, the "Ramblin' Lou Family Band." The radio station is integral to helping promote the family's overall musical activities. They perform regularly in Buffalo and also take the show on the road, making annual pilgrimages to the country-western mecca in Branson, Missouri. During their performances, the family shares a joke about how much they are paid by their father. They tell the audience he doesn't pay them much. He quips: "Don't make your dad look bad in public. I pay you weekly!" They respond tongue-in-cheek, "Yeah *weakly*, Dad!"

Bill Brown Jr. said he never paid his children an allowance, he just put them right on the payroll. He, his wife, and four children all worked at his station, WBTA-AM, serving the Batavia community. One of his sons (also named Bill) eventually became sales manager of the station. As one might imagine, there was some confusion from time to time for those who called the station looking to speak with "Bill." To clarify their respective roles, Bill Brown Jr. would joke with callers, telling them: "I'm in management and he's in sales. Are you calling to bitch . . . or buy?" Bill Brown Jr. also lent his voice to the Batavia Downs harness race track as its announcer. Young Bill is now a communications executive at AARP in Georgia.

Husband and wife teams were also not uncommon. Jim and Keela Rodgers ran WNBZ in Lake Placid, Chris Coffin and Pat Tocatlian ran WSLB and WPAC in Ogdensburg, and Jerry and Sasha Gillman ran WDST in Woodstock. Interestingly, the husbands gravitated toward programming responsibilities, while the women handled all the finances. Jerry Gillman explains the division of labor at WDST: "Sasha had literally everything to do with money, including buying the equipment, buying the building, attending conventions, etc. My end was personnel and programming." Jerry would broadcast editorials and commentaries, as well as cutting-edge programs and talk shows that appealed to the "hippie" intelligentsia in that fabled mountain town in the Catskills. Long before "books on tape" became popular, he would literally read books on the air!

Keela Rodgers admits she got into radio because she married a "radioman." Jim Champlin would also marry into the broadcasting business. After working in the marketing research and sales department of *Time/Life*, he was asked by his father-in-law, Marty Beck, to come work for him. "I decided why not? It was a family business he had just started, and I was thrilled to join him," recalls Champlin. He started in national sales, eventually becoming the company's president.

The Beck family laid its roots in media long before broadcasting even existed. According to former Katz chief Jim Greenwald, Marty Beck's father joined Katz Media, the nation's first media representation firm in 1903. He stayed with the company for an astonishing 65 years. Beck also worked at Katz for many years before going out on his own, building radio stations on Long Island. Imbued by the family tradition in broadcasting, Stuart Beck followed in his grandfather's and father's footsteps, rising to become president and chief operating officer of Granite Broadcasting, owner of nine television stations. Last year, Stuart Beck left broadcasting to become the ambassador and permanent representative of the Republic of Palau to the United Nations, the first person to ever hold the post. Beck has a long history with the country. He was retained as chief counsel in 1977 to assist the island nation in securing its independence from the United States, as well as establishing its own constitution. His wife, Ebiltulik, is also from Palau.

Ellen Sulzberger Straus, a member of the fabled Sulzberger clan, owners of *The New York Times*, also found herself in the broadcasting business when she married R. Peter Straus. Through their 45 years of marriage, Ellen was deeply involved in the running of WMCA. She loved to discuss the issues of the day and even had her own program, "Call for Action," focused on consumer awareness. Listeners could call in to get answers to questions about housing, consumer fraud, and other social problems. The program proved so successful it was copied across the country. Ellen Straus died in 1995 of cancer.

The broadcasting gene would be passed on in their family, as was the case in many New York broadcasting families. The Straus's son, Eric, helped his father run WMCA before it was sold in 1986. After being out of the business for a few years, he went on to build a radio station group of his own in the Hudson Valley before selling the company in 1999. Today R. Peter Straus owns a chain of newspapers in the Hudson Valley and northern New Jersey.

In Westchester, 16-year-old Matthew O'Shaughnessy once persuaded his father, Bill O'Shaughnessy, to let him experiment with the midnight-to-dawn "wee, small hours." Young Matthew came up with a slam-bang, heavy-metal format called "Midnight Metal" that attracted suburban teenagers from all over the New York metro area in the early 1980s. His brother, David, took a different route into the family business. David, who had joined Miramax after college, left the movie business to pick up two masters degrees. He's now ensconced at Whitney Radio as executive vice president for administration.

Over the last decade many broadcasters have been given "offers they couldn't refuse" to sell their stations. Andrew Langston, owner of WDKX in Rochester, has been approached to sell his station many times over. However, he wanted to offer his son the opportunity to continue what he started: "I have a son who grew up in the business, and I wouldn't sell it. I know he could do a better job by owning the station and pursuing some of his own ideas than if I sold it to someone else."

The idea of "family" in broadcasting goes beyond blood ties and marriages. Adrienne Gaines, general manager of WWRL in New York, considers one of the biggest accomplishments of her career is building a staff that has worked with her for over 20 years. They are now like family to her: "At the end of the day, there isn't as much focus on Arbitron ratings here as there is on my ability to lead these people and for them to believe in me. We've all been able to put visions and goals on the table, and we accomplished them together." She is also proud of being able to pass on the spirit of broadcasting to future generations of WWRL employees: "I have even employed several children of members on my staff, or I have been able to get them employment elsewhere in the business."

License to Serve

"Your license required you to operate in the public's interest, convenience, and necessity. Broadcasters were supposed to serve the public with local news, information about community events, and, of course, entertainment. The license was regarded as an obligation to serve," explains Joe Reilly, conveying the original intention of broadcast licenses as laid down by the Communications Act of 1934. Since there was a finite number of signals that could be used in the analog spectrum, Congress developed the concept of issuing licenses that would be granted to the private sector for commercial use. Every three years those licenses would come up for renewal, and broadcasters had to demonstrate how they were serving their community. Tom Murphy, co-founder of Capital Cities, took those renewals very seriously: "We thought about what we promised, and we made sure we lived up to the promises we made to the FCC."

Unlike a utility company (like power or water), broadcasting has the potential to influence public opinion, positively or negatively. It has the power to shape the public mindset for better or for worse. It is omnipresent, and the government has granted licenses with the understanding that this "power" will be used in the best interests of society. Through the last 50 years, the concept of "public interest" has been interpreted both narrowly and broadly. Don Angelo, currently local sales manager at WGRZ in Buffalo, has taken the broader definition as his mantra: "All this was put in place for one specific purpose. The government said, 'we will give you a license only if you operate in the public interest.' This has always been kind of my motto living in this industry through my entire adult life. You can transpose that concept as a philosophy of how you should serve the community in terms of community outreach, news coverage, and all the way through, even into the advertising end of it, too."

Other broadcasters have also interpreted "public interest" as going beyond the stated or intended needs and wants of the public. Paul Dunn, former owner of WTLB-AM in Utica, views the concept from an even more enlightened perspective: "To me it's a necessity, and the public interest does not always mean what the public is interested in." Most broadcasters are vehemently against directing public opinion, preferring to regard themselves as moderators in democratic discourse. Some have championed the opportunity to offer editorials but have always provided airtime for opposing views. Since the abandonment of the Fairness Doctrine in 1987, many established broadcasters are bewildered by the partisan talk shows that now dominate the airwaves.

Licenses were also viewed as an invitation into the homes of communities where broadcasters were privileged to serve. The bond between individual members of the community and broadcasters is a special one, says Tom Murphy, now a director of The Walt Disney Company: "Being a broadcaster you have the chance to be intimately involved in the community where you operate." Announcers were guests at the breakfast table, someone to keep you company in the car or a companion to take you to the local Fourth of July parade when you couldn't go yourself. Many people still use radio in their homes, just for the "background noise" of human companionship. Jim Greenwald thus describes station operators as "part of the community, not some distant person."

An invitation into someone's home is always treated with the highest degree of respect by broadcasters, whether in person or via a broadcast signal. Even as the proliferation of media outlets has relaxed attitudes towards dress, sex, and violence, the majority of the public is still intolerant of indecent programming coming into their homes, especially over the airwaves *they* own. While New York broadcasters were always steadfast in defense of the First Amendment, they were also mindful of operating within the perceived boundaries of good taste within their communities.

In the 1950s there were fewer broadcast licenses, as well as much less competition from the total sum of available media outlets. As a scarce resource with limited competition, many broadcasters found it fairly easy to generate revenue from their stations. Television in particular would become flush with cash. One broadcaster remarked: "It wasn't a question if you would make money in television, it was how much." Nonetheless, most broadcasters tried to strike a balance between reasonable profits and acting in the interest of the public.

"Old-time" broadcasters argue that the passage of the Telecommunications Act of 1996 has encouraged today's broadcasters to become too concerned with profit rather than the public good. They believe their peers should still be operating under a higher standard than just the bottom line. Dennis Swanson, currently President of Station Operations for Fox Television Stations, doesn't see the issue as mutually exclusive, but rather one and the same: "Normally if a television station has the most credible or best news in a local market, and serves its community as well, it will have the success it needs on the bottom line. As a result, you are actually accomplishing a couple of things at the same time." Swanson's extensive service to broadcasting includes syndicating "The Oprah Winfrey Show," "Jeopardy!," and "Wheel of Fortune." Before he went to Viacom, he served as general manager of WNBC-TV in New York, the number-one television station in the market. He also presided as chairman of NYSBA for two terms, in 2000 and 2001.

Stewards of Localism in New York

A common thread among the most admired broadcasters in New York is not how much money they made or how many stations they owned or how famous they became, but rather their deep commitment to the community their broadcast license entitled them to serve. "Marty Beck is emblematic of the type of broadcaster that everyone would like to be associated with. He is a broadcaster who understood localism and who had incredible loyalty to the communities in which he operated his radio stations," proclaims Gordon Hastings, president of the Broadcasters' Foundation. One would be hard pressed to find a broadcaster in New York who does not hold Beck in admiration for his loyalty to his employees, for being forthright in his business dealings or for serving in the best interests of the public. He has been described as a "steward," an "exemplar" in broadcasting, and a "mentor." He truly exemplifies all the virtues of what one would think a holder of a broadcast license should possess.

"The purpose of local broadcasting should be local. Radio achieves its highest calling when it is a platform and a forum for the expression of many different viewpoints," articulates Bill O'Shaughnessy. Some would refer to O'Shaughnessy as the "last of his kind." He religiously observes his duty as the "Johnny Apple-seed" of ideas in Westchester, promoting and exchanging ideas in the influential "Golden Apple" of New York. Many of its residents commute into New York City each day, living just outside the grasp of big-city life. At a time when everyone else is thinking globally, he is acting locally. He happily turns over the airwaves to their rightful owners, the residents of the influential community he serves. He is known for his persistent prodding of on-air talent: "I tell our talk show hosts to use their genius to encourage feedback." David Hinckley, critic-at-large for the *New York Daily News*, once had this to say about O'Shaughnessy's station: "WVOX is a glorious hodgepodge, much of which even O'Shaughnessy can't get excited about." Make no mistake, Bill O' Shaughnessy does not practice a dying craft, but one that will carry broadcasting into the future. He embodies the essence of what it means to be a broadcaster. The *Wall Street Journal* has de-scribed WVOX as "the quintessential community station in America."

Serving local communities courses through the veins of someone like Richard Novik, growing up under the direction of his father, Harry Novik, former owner of WLIB-AM in New York. From his father, Richard Novik learned the basic principals of what it meant to be a broadcaster. He would eventually take his "big market" experience and buy stations of his own upstate in Brewster and Pough-keepsie. In his estimation, once you've decided to become a broadcaster, you have no choice but to become involved in the community you are to serve: "I think it is delightful that we are obligated to serve the community as broadcasters based on our licenses, but then from there on it is just a lot of fun. I think all of us in management have come to that understanding, and you find very few managers who don't want to get involved. You have to get involved." As an owner in smaller markets, he often found it easier to get involved with the community: "I think or-ganizations felt they could obtain more exposure or airtime if they got the man-agers of stations involved. Although that may not always be the case, I think it is the reason broadcasters have an easier time making their way in a community." Like other small market broadcasters, Novik covered all different types of local events from fairs to parades to charity events. Not every event exactly "worked" for radio, he recalls: "The funniest thing we ever did was to broadcast from a local pub on St. Patrick's Day. We were broadcasting Irish tap dancing one year, and I suddenly said to myself, 'What are we doing? This is radio!'"

Broadcasting in the mountains along the southern tier of New York, Amos Finch and Myra Youmans were worlds away from the influence of New York City. Their stations— WDLA-AM/FM, WIYN, and WDHI— were the primary sources of local information for the Catskill Mountains. "When it comes to serving an audience, we tried to give them everything they wanted to know. We attended all types of meetings and dinners to keep abreast of what was going on in the county, and passed on the information and local color to listeners," says Finch. There was nothing too local about anything they covered. If it was important to a group in the community, they were there. "We had one of the finest county fairs in New York State. We would set up a studio at the fair each year and broadcast there for the solid week. We also did live broadcasts of local election debates, new business openings, and various high school sports in the county, including football, basketball, baseball, and soccer games. We used to broadcast the 'Big King of the Hill' bowling tournament live, and there were a lot of other events. The point is that people knew we were part of the community and interested in the community." While Finch took great pleasure in sharing a slice of life as he traveled around his rural county, it was his morning show that had the greatest impact. "From 5 o'clock to 9 in the morning, I just felt there were so many things I could tell people that they needed to know. It really provided a service to people. I just loved working that early-morning shift."

In 1955, Si Goldman built WJTN, a radio station in Jamestown, a sleepy little community tucked away in the farthest reaches of western New York near the Pennsylvania border. He understood that the people of Jamestown cherished an easygoing lifestyle and a commitment to familiar institutions. Just as New York City thrives on change, a place like Jamestown strives for stability. According to Dennis Webster, the long-time morning announcer for WJTN, Goldman's deep sense of the community was reflected in how he ran his station: "He had a very keen sense of the people, so he would allow good people to sort of create their own comfort zone. He wouldn't get in the way very much. If you wanted to show some initiative, he would be helpful in allowing you to develop your project. He allowed you to make your own way, so that even though people used to say he never paid very much, nobody left. They just got into the rhythm of the station and the community. It became important to them in ways that didn't have anything to do with money."

At the age of 20, Merrill Rosen was hired by Goldman. He would rise through the ranks to become manager of the station, and he is still at it today. "We're pretty laid back here. If you can make it in Jamestown, New York, a small, little community, you can make it anywhere else in the world. I mean, you don't get on the wrong side of somebody in the community, because it will take a long time for them to forget you did something that was not proper," comments Rosen on the audience he has served for almost 45 years. Without a doubt, Jamestown is the kind of place where everyone knows everyone else. In fact the station still runs obituaries twice a day: "The reason we still run obituaries is because if you're 55 years or older in Jamestown, you probably were born here and you're probably going to die here. Half of the people also do not get the newspaper. When someone dies, people really want to know. I mean, hundreds of people turn out for a funeral, *whoever* it may be. It's absolutely incredible."

Jim Delmonico, former general manager of WRGB-TV, achieved success at an Albany area station that would have easily landed him a job elsewhere in the upper echelons of broadcasting. However, the management of General Electric once referred to him as a "pimple on the path to progress." His commitment to his family and community outweighed monetary pursuits. "My kids grew up going to school in the same neighborhood. Their mother was home every day when they got out of school. That's the way we wanted to bring them up and we didn't want to move. It worked out okay," explains Delmonico.

He never saw staying in the same market as an impediment to his career but rather a benefit. If he needed a favor or to come up with some money for a charity, he knew immediately which sponsor would be willing to help out: "I've watched other operations, some of them here locally, where it's just a revolving door. You never know who's going to be there. I think the nature of the business is to get somebody who's not necessarily going to stay forever, but somebody who's rooted in the community, while they're here. Somebody who 'gets it.' Somebody whose family lives there. It's a public trust."

When Walter Maxwell sold his station in 2000, he wasn't ready to stop serving his community, so he formed a public corporation called "Kingston Community Radio," which leases airtime from WGHQ-AM from 7 a.m. to 9 a.m. each morning: "People send us 10 bucks a month and we broadcast from 7 to 9 in the morning. As far as I know it's the only station of its kind in the country." For the past year, the program has been one of the highest-rated programs in Ulster County according to Arbitron. It's a wonderful testament to Maxwell's dedication to localism. He learned from the best; his late stepfather, Harry Thayer, was a legend in the Hudson Valley. While they named a park after Thayer for his contributions as a broadcaster in Kingston, Maxwell hopes for a more poignant remembrance from the community he has served for over 30 years: "I would just like it if somebody would say he made the town a nicer place to live, I'd be happy with that. . . ."

Up in the "north country," Lake Placid conjures up images of picturesque snow-covered mountain landscapes, a winter wonderland stopped in time. Like Jamestown, life plods along at a gentle pace with few interruptions, except of course when the entire world comes to pay a visit. Lake Placid has had the distinction of being one of only two towns to host the Winter Olympic Games, not once but twice. "We covered the 1980 Olympics, too, and that was a real highlight," reflects Jim Rodgers, former owner of WNBZ. He hired additional staff just for the Olympics, with a person at every venue providing five to six hours of live coverage each day. Of course there was play-by-play coverage of the U.S. hockey team's "Miracle on Ice" victory.

Rodgers fondly remembers the preferential treatment his station received as the local broadcaster from the Olympic organizers: "We couldn't afford to hook up for the remote from the press center. It was $500 for a phone, and a fee had to be paid to the organizing committee. Because we were local, we 'bypassed' the fee and the local high school principal gave us his office to use as a workplace. The school served as the press center." Tiny WNBZ would serve as a major source of "local flavor" for all the major American networks, as well as those from abroad. Their sports director would be hired by NBC for the summer games in Moscow in 1980. Unfortunately he would never go because the United States chose to boycott the games that year to protest the Soviet invasion of Afghanistan.

In the world of public broadcasting, listeners and viewers quite literally vote with their dollars to demonstrate their support of a station. If dollars are indeed the barometer of success, Alan Chartock seems to be doing his job very well: "When 6,000 people give you $600,000 in four days, it just really goes to show that they have come to think well of this radio station." WAMC is affiliated with NPR, but Chartock is so committed to the local communities he serves that he prefers to develop much of his own local programming rather than using a lot of syndicated programming from NPR. It is a strategy that has been working for him. Allowing individuals to air their grievances has also been a critical component in connecting with the community: "We read every single comment on the air, so if somebody writes us and says, 'I hate that darn Chartock!' . . . we'll read it because it's both entertaining and it gives people a chance to hear themselves in a way they wouldn't have gotten otherwise. Now if somebody does say they hate me, there'll be 10 right afterwards saying: 'What are you talking about? He's wonderful!' But that doesn't matter, because I think they sense there's a commitment to making this a community."

Bob Ausfeld, regional vice president at Regent Communications, has served the Albany market for his entire career, working for almost every broadcaster in the area at one point or another: "What's nice about being a broadcaster in Albany is it's so close to New York and Boston, so we get overlapped by major markets. It's an advantage because we can be up with the latest trends just as quickly as they can. We do some really good radio here. This market's always produced good radio. We've had some terrific broadcasters." Although Ausfeld has never been an owner, preferring the role of "hired ranch hand," as he likes to think of himself, he is completely committed to localism. Eric Straus describes him as the "face" of the stations he now manages for Regent: "I don't think he is thought of any differently in their market than I was thought of in mine. Yes, I was an owner and he is a manager, but he is still the face of the station. He still 'super serves' his local audience, so I think people still go up to him in restaurants and ask for help for upcoming public service events. It is still very much a local, townie business."

Eric Straus sold his stations in the Hudson Valley in 1999. It is exactly that type of interaction with the local audience he misses most about the business: "I really do miss making a difference in my local community. Right now I'm just a guy with some money going to eat in a restaurant. It used to be I was a guy sitting in a restaurant and people would come up and ask me to get something on the air about their event this weekend for their church or some other public service organization. I really felt like I mattered in the community. I matter less now . . . and that's tough. I think every ex-broadcaster feels that way."

Two years after Oscar Wein helped get WDLC on the air in 1953, he bought the station, immersing himself in the concerns and needs of his fellow citizens, quickly becoming the voice of Port Jervis. He was a member of the Port Jervis Elks Lodge, the Tri-State Chamber of Commerce, the Port Jervis school board, and the Taxpayers Association. Wein gained notoriety for his editorials, as well as his morning program, "Reveille Ranch," announcing birthdays and community events.

There's no doubt, Martin Stone will be forever remembered in the annals of television history for his role in the development of "Howdy Doody," one of the most popular and enduring children's programs of all time. As Buffalo Bob Smith's agent, Stone suggested putting his WEAF radio program, "Triple B Ranch," on the new medium of television. They brought the idea to NBC and launched a new show, "Puppet Playhouse" in 1947. A week later, the show was renamed, "Howdy Doody."

Stone was a true broadcast pioneer for that alone. In addition to producing "Howdy Doody," he developed other programs, including, "Author Meets the Critic" and "Americana." To the citizens of Mount Kisco, New York, in the rolling hills of northern Westchester, however, he will always be remembered as the conscience of their community. In 1957 he established a new radio station there with the appropriately named call letters WVIP. To launch the new station, he held a benefit for Northern Westchester Hospital, demonstrating the positive impact broadcasting could have on the community. M.C.s for the event were Howard Cosell and Merv Griffin, who had gotten their start thanks to Stone.

The station became part of the Herald Tribune Radio Network in 1959, a network of suburban radio stations. The charismatic Stone oversaw the building of those radio stations in the wealthy, upscale suburbs of Long Island, the Hudson Valley, Westchester, and New Jersey to help prop up the fortunes of the *Herald Tribune* newspaper. For a number of different reasons, the concept struggled and the network broke up in 1975. Harry Thayer and Bill O'Shaughnessy, who were part of the original group, took over ownership of their respective stations, WGHQ and WVOX, and Stone retained WVIP.

Stone hosted a daily interview show on WVIP called "Meet the VIPs" through the 1990s. In a sad twist of fate, broadcasting would lose two great legends in New York broadcasting in 1998; both Stone and Buffalo Bob Smith passed away. The WVIP building, which had been designed by famed architect Edward Larrabee Barnes to resemble a seashell (for better acoustics), burned to the ground in 1997. No longer a broad-based community station, WVIP today primarily programs religious music.

Although famous as a television pioneer, one must also give Martin Stone his due as the "spiritual father" of suburban radio. Prior to the establishment of WVIP, stations located outside the "big city" played a bland mixture of Mantovani and Jackie Gleason type background music because their owners thought that was the extent of the musical palate of their listeners. Many formats in suburbia were merely carbon copies of the more successful New York City outlets. Stone changed all that with a dynamic mixture of community-based programming.

Several able and highly talented broadcasters were attracted to WVIP during its 30-year run. Jean Ensign was one of the first women to run a radio station in the suburbs of New York City. She often called WVIP a "pristine jewel" of a radio station. Nicholas Orzio, General Douglas MacArthur's chief photographer, served as the station's first manager. Before Morton Dean's distinguished career as a correspondent for ABC News, he cut his teeth as a newsman at WVIP. Kenneth Harris, now at Clear Channel in Florida, and Bob Bruno of WOR in New York City, also got their start with Martin Stone's WVIP. At just 18 years old, a young Bill O'Shaughnessy worked as one of the station's first account executives, using his charm to haul in a sizable portion of WVIP's revenues during its first year on the air in 1957.

Stirring Goodwill in the Community

The role of broadcasters may be thought of as the fire chief, school principal, town alderman, restaurant owner, hairdresser, and minister, or rabbi all rolled into one. To achieve the highest possible level of service, broadcasters understood they needed to become a reflection of their community. As part of their mandate from the FCC, they were required to actively seek out the needs of their fellow citizens and how broadcasters could help resolve problems plaguing the community. "I think you have to be a good citizen in that community. What do I mean by that? I think you have to help the community and get involved with worthy causes," says Dennis Swanson. To plug themselves into the community, local broadcasters would regularly participate in local events, charities, and civic functions.

As "good citizens," broadcasters have raised billions of dollars and immeasurable awareness for countless charities throughout New York. Making money off the public's airwaves comes with a price, reminds Marty Beck: "Public service may seem unimportant to many people, but it has to be done. It's our job. We've been given the right to broadcast over the airwaves and to make a lot of money while doing it. We should always be finding ways to give back, we really should."

It's probably no accident that many New York broadcasters have taken leadership roles in the Broadcasters' Foundation, a highly respected national charity that assists down-and-out broadcasters in need when life turns difficult in their waning years or due to illness or the death of a spouse. Beck is just one of the New York State Samaritans who have adopted the Foundation. Others include Ed McLaughlin, Dick Foreman, Gordon Hastings, Phil Beuth, Joe Reilly, Phil Lombardo, Jim Delmonico, Bill O'Shaughnessy, Jim Champlin, Tony Malara, and Nick Verbitsky.

Long before the Internet, broadcasting served as the primary "connector" among individuals within a community. Its promotional power combined with its reach proved to be a powerful tool in helping local charities get their message out. Unlike newspapers, radio and television possessed an emotional element in their storytelling. Listeners could hear the pain in the trembling voice of a disaster victim. Viewers could literally see how their donations are spent. It forms a powerful bond between those in need and those who wanted to help a fellow citizen. New York broadcasters turned over their microphones countless times to those in need over the last 50 years, promoting blood drives, flood disaster relief, fundraisers for terminal diseases, and getting kids off drugs, to name just a few. They regarded their duty as broadcasters to be a conduit in making their communities a better place to live.

During the 1980s, Jim Duffy "reinvigorated" the handling of public service announcements (PSAs) at the ABC Television Network. While the obligation to serve the public had always been fulfilled to an extent, he felt that PSAs "always got the back of the hand" or was viewed as "something you just had to do." He helped co-found Project Literacy, which would become one of the most renowned public service efforts in the history of broadcast television. The campaign was built around the concept that "It was never too late to learn to read." In partnership with PBS and National Public Radio (NPR), messages were run on both television and radio to focus on the literacy problem in America. All divisions of ABC were involved from the top down to make the effort a success. To bring greater attention to the cause, then First Lady Barbara Bush became the spokesperson. ABC aired the literacy campaign in September 1986 through the summer of 1992. Duffy looks back on the program as one of his proudest achievements and a sterling example of how broadcasting can have a positive effect: "I'm proud of it because it was unprecedented and literally brought millions and millions of new readers out. It actually increased the skills level in this country. The fact that we could reach into 100 million homes with some intimacy on a continuous basis enabled us to make a difference. You can change patterns . . . and we certainly did that with literacy."

Broadcasting could almost be regarded as a ladle, gently stirring a pot of goodwill in almost any community. No one understood this better than Jim Delmonico, the long-time general manager of WRGB-TV in Schenectady. For him broadcasting and helping his community were one and the same: "Broadcasting is a wonderful mechanism to raise money. People want to become part of it. . . . If you ignore the community, you're a darn fool. You ought to be out of the business." His most successful charitable program, "Melodies of Christmas," raised money for a child cancer care program at Albany Medical Center. The station underwrote the entire annual production, arranging for local kids from the area to sing as the Empire State Youth Orchestra played carols.

All the sponsorship money for the program went directly to the hospital. According to Delmonico, the program has raised almost $4 million. One year a woman made a whopping $1 million donation to the charity. The station also organized other promotions to raise additional funds. They partnered with Grand Union, a supermarket chain, to get people to return bottles to local stores, sending all the money from the deposits to the charity: "The more charities we worked with, the better business seemed to get for us. It just kept going around and around, coming back to us. It was a wonderful way to reach out to the community."

To help get kids off drugs, Barry Lillis, a weatherman at WGRZ-TV in Buffalo, founded a charity called "Kids Escaping Drugs." He envisioned building a halfway house where kids could go to get off drugs. To raise money for the new charity, he organized a radiothon and a telethon, asking all the radio and television stations in western New York to participate. Merrill Rosen remembers participating in that event and how successful it was for his stations: "Our two little radio stations way down in Jamestown generated more money than any of the big stations in Buffalo or Rochester. The only reason for that was not only were we voices in the local community, but also our fellow citizens paid attention to us and believed us. That's the way it's been all these years." An indication of how the Jamestown station earned that trust resides with their announcers. Jim Roselli, the station's longest-serving announcer, has been there for over 50 years. Their morning man, Dennis Webster, has been with the station for over 30 years, and his father was on the air at WJTN before him.

Each year since, WGRZ-TV in Buffalo has run the telethon to raise money for the charity. According to WGRZ's local sales manager, Don Angelo, millions of dollars have been raised over the past 25 years. Local advertisers have also lent their support to the telethon. Every penny has been used to build a campus in West Seneca, a suburb of Buffalo, where teenagers can find help getting off drugs or to stop drinking. They can even seek assistance and counsel for family problems. The teens live right on the campus and go to school for a year as they try to turn their lives around.

Traveling farther east into the heart of New York, the youth of Syracuse are also not without their problems, explains Jim Delmonico's son, Joel Delmonico, vice president and market manager for Clear Channel Radio Syracuse: "There's a violence 'issue' here, and when kids are shooting each other, they get all the press. They get all the attention. I'm looking at the good kids, who don't get the attention, and thinking what could we do about it?" Last year he developed a program to help teenagers get jobs and to provide them with the connections he took for granted growing up. Working with a dozen local businesses, he launched a youth employment program: "We told the businesses that what they got out of it in media would be worth way more than what we were asking them to put into it." His long-term vision for the project is for it to become a "feeder" program for hiring talented minorities.

Rather than focus on just one or two local charities, WOR-AM in New York has recently developed a campaign called "Operation Good Neighbor." Each fiscal quarter the station picks one organization to help, says vice president and general manager Bob Bruno: "We spotlight an organization we believe deserves to be recognized and applauded. Then we put our 50,000-watt voice behind that organization." WOR has drawn attention to many different types of efforts, from a battered women's shelter to saluting the troops overseas. "It is a way for us to reinforce our local connections to the community."

Many times, broadcasters react spontaneously on their own, acting as a catalyst in the community. The immediacy of broadcasting is particularly attuned to developing a quick response to a tragedy. Ed Levine, a broadcaster in Syracuse and Utica, recalls an incident in which a couple of firefighters were killed in the town where he lives: "I walked into the fire station just as a private citizen. You could just feel the grief there. It was almost palpable. I asked the firefighters if they needed anything. A lot of the wives and families in these types of situations have little protection here when it comes to the necessities of everyday living. I told them we would talk the next day about raising some money." Within 48 hours, Levine had a radiothon on the air: "Now, radio being as competitive as it is, Clear Channel decided that it was also going to do a radiothon. In the end we raised $50,000, they raised $50,000, and the families got $100,000."

Diversity

Another necessary ingredient to best detect the pulse and instincts of a community is through diversity. According to Dennis Swanson, mirroring the needs and wants of the community is more than just turning on the transmitter: "Diversity is critical to a broadcaster's success, and their programming should reflect the marketplace they are serving. That is only going to come from a diverse workforce."

Beginning in the 1960s, broadcasters became more aggressive about mirroring their communities. When Paul Dunn was first hired by R. Peter Straus to head up WTLB in Utica, he says one of his first orders of business from Peter Straus was to hire an African American: "There wasn't a single African American in the entire Utica/Rome market working in broadcasting. He told me that needed to change and that I was the one who was going to change it." Dunn ended up hiring Fred Reed Jr. at the tender age of 19. He went onto to become a DJ and was later program director at WNEW in New York, according to Dunn.

One of New York's first African American broadcast owners was Andrew Langston. He learned his craft at the venerable classical New York station WNYC. In1968 he applied for an FM frequency in Rochester, and his station, WDKX, began broadcasting in 1974. He saw ownership as an opportunity to give African Americans a voice, as well as a platform to give back to that same community. "I think we did more in the market to help make people more aware of the problems in the community and how to get involved to help meet those challenges," says Langston. The sounds of WDKX were reflective of the music tastes of African Americans, like rhythm and blues, as well as jazz. In fact, the call letters represent the deep connection Langston wanted to build with the African American community in Rochester. The "D" stands for Frederick Douglass, the "K" stands for Martin Luther King Jr. and the "X" stands for Malcolm X. Throughout the long application process and the launch of the station, he worked with African American businessmen, religious leaders, and politicians to secure their help to ensure that the new station was attuned to the needs of his audience: "I told them I want to be successful, but in order to be successful, I needed support from people like them."

In addition to minority groups, half the American population was also sparsely represented in the early days of broadcasting. Women were relegated to administrative positions for the most part. Jane Barton, a former reporter for *Variety*, covering broadcasting in New York State, was one of the women fighting for greater equality in broadcasting. She also served as a representative for American Women in Radio and Television (AWRT). Her positions brought her into contact with almost every station in the state. She recalls how little women were thought of: "You were supposed to be an executive to be a member of American Women in Radio and Television. All the traffic directors were women. That's an important job, scheduling commercials, but they were treated merely as clerks. They actually handled all the traffic for each station, their bread and butter! That always irritated me."

Women began to enter the broadcast profession in larger numbers in the 1970s and 1980s, particularly in gatekeeper roles. Nancy Widmann would be one of those women to open doors for future generations of her gender. She was the first woman to ever hold every position in which she found herself at CBS. She was the first woman hired in sales at CBS Radio, the first female general manager, the first to run a station group, and the first woman president of CBS Radio (actually the first woman to hold the title of president of anything at CBS). She quietly paved the way for other women: "I didn't do it in a kind of public forum. What I had to do, and what I did, was in a much more private way. I promoted women and I made sure we had women on our sales force. In some ways I just had to order it."

Maire Mason was one of the many women Nancy Widmann took under her wing: "I kind of followed Nancy through CBS. When she was named general manager of WCBS-FM in the 1980s, it suddenly became a normal idea for a woman to become a general manager at CBS." Mason regards Widmann not only as a mentor, but also as a pioneer. Widmann understood the double standards that lay before women all too well, and offered Mason advice on how to handle herself both inside and outside the office: "She taught me how to hoot with the owls and soar with eagles. She told me I could go out all night, but that I better be the first one in the office in the morning." Women not only had to fulfill the duties for which they were hired, but also had to overcompensate, because they knew someone was always looking over their shoulder. Women have come a long way in broadcasting, but new challenges still lay ahead for today's women entering the business: "It's still not clear sailing, but young women have the ability to choose between a career or raising a family. My generation was fighting for the ability to make that choice," says *Radio & Records* publisher Erica Farber. It's probably emblematic of the times that today most sales staffs are largely made up of women.

The English language has never reigned exclusively over New York's airwaves. For many immigrants, broadcasting, particularly radio, has offered a connection to their homeland far away, as well as with their brothers and sisters in their adopted country. Over the last 50 years it was not uncommon to hear Polish, German, Italian, Greek, Yiddish, or a number of other languages over the airwaves of New York. These "ethnic" and multicultural programs reflected enclaves of new immigrants living within the established local cultures throughout the state. Some of those legendary producers and hosts of "heritage" programming include Lou Greenwood, Martha Ley, and Elsie Maria Troija Walter reaching out to German Americans. Bill Shibilski spoke to Poles. "Uncle Floyd" Vivino, Louis Miele, Nat Carbo, and Joe Farda were just a few of the Italian voices on the airwaves. Many New Yorkers were soothed by the Irish brogues of Tommy Smythe, Jim McGinty, John Riordan, and Adrian Flannelly. The melodic and tranquil sounds of the Caribbean were brought to New Yorkers by Bobby Clarke, Ken Williams, Herman Singh, Maria Thomas, and Carl Moxie, to name just a few.

The 2000 census confirmed what many already knew—Hispanics were entering the United States at an unprecedented pace. Their population numbers were exploding, surpassing African Americans as the country's largest minority. Long before this trend, Malin Falu became a comforting voice for her fellow compatriots on the radio in New York City. Working for a variety of Spanish-language stations over the last 25 years, Falu is best known for her nighttime broadcast "Hablando con Malin" ("Speaking with Malin") on WADO-AM. She has traveled the world covering stories for her listeners, concentrating primarily on Latin America and the Caribbean. She has been described as a wonderful role model who has served her community with dedication and dignity. Her sweet voice is full of conviction. Milan has not been merely a passive observer, but also a dynamic broadcaster seeking solutions to the problems facing her community.

The Fourth Branch of Government

The genius of American democracy is the intricate system of checks and balances found at each level of government to protect against the abuse of power. The executive and legislative branches of the federal government must act in concert to pass and enforce new laws and are never permitted to act alone. The judicial branch works to interpret those laws. It is the freedom of the press, however, that provides the last line of defense, helping to maintain vibrant democratic discourse. Over the last 50 years, New York broadcasters have vigorously exercised their right to free speech under the First Amendment. They have simultaneously borne the awesome responsibility of keeping a watchful eye on government, in addition to raising the voices of average citizens in the representative bodies elected to protect their interests.

Government officials haven't always appreciated the determination with which broadcasters took their role as defenders of free speech. Paul Dunn remembers having a few "run-ins" with one of Utica's mayors, Ed Hanna, who was notorious for making outrageous statements. On one occasion the mayor made an announcement that the city of Utica had received $750,000 from the U.S. Department of Housing and Urban Development (HUD) for a new development project. "We learned to always question whenever he announced something, so we called HUD and they told us the appropriation was not three-quarters of a million, it was only a quarter of a million," says Dunn. He immediately went on the air with it and Hanna called him, screaming that Dunn got the story wrong: "We double checked and he was actually right. We were wrong, but so was he. We had an interview with someone from HUD and they apologized to our listeners and told them it wasn't a quarter of a million, it was a *half* million." Hanna called Dunn again, demanding that he apologize to him on the air. If Dunn didn't, he threatened to call the FCC. Dunn refused, calling his bluff: "A couple of days later, my attorney in Washington called, telling me, 'Paul I don't think you can do anything wrong in the future. Your mayor called up the FCC. They told the mayor that your station had bent over backwards to be fair and he had no complaint coming.' Whereupon the mayor called the FCC representative a few choice names."

No one in broadcasting is a more passionate defender of the First Amendment than Bill O'Shaughnessy. His nationally recognized work on behalf of freedom of speech stretches far beyond his realm in the Golden Apple, the confines of Westchester. He does not always appreciate some of the most offensive and obscene uses of the broadcast medium, yet he will vigorously defend a person's right to be heard. O'Shaughnessy relentlessly promotes public discourse and would be the first to put a microphone in someone's hand who finds himself in opposition to any comment he may have made on the air. "Talk about passion. He is relentless in insisting on the full application of the First Amendment for everybody, even for people commonly thought of as 'objectionable.' They may be people of poor taste. They may be repulsive, but they possess the right to free speech as far as O'Shaughnessy is concerned," observes Governor Mario Cuomo, himself an ardent supporter of the First Amendment.

The most significant benchmark in testing the bounds of the First Amendment in broadcast media involved the CBS documentary "The Selling of the Pentagon," in 1971. The piece took issue with the increasing cost of taxpayers' money for public relations activities by the so-called "military-industrial complex" to shape public opinion in favor of the Pentagon and the military in general. It was a controversial topic already swirling around the nation's capital, but the real dispute surrounded the methods CBS used to recreate certain key interviews and speeches depicted in the documentary.

In the spirit of the Fairness Doctrine, CBS re-ran the documentary a month later. Immediately following the broadcast, CBS aired opposing views from Vice President Spiro Agnew and Secretary of Defense Melvin Laird. CBS News President Richard Salant provided a rebuttal. Still unsatisfied, Congressman Harley O. Staggers (D-WV), chairman of the powerful House Committee on Interstate and Foreign Commerce and of its Special Subcommittee on Investigations, issued broad subpoenas demanding that the documents and other materials used in the production of the documentary be produced before Congress. CBS responded by providing the film and complete script of the broadcast, but refused to provide other requested material, including outtakes and source documents.

Dr. Frank Stanton, president of CBS, appeared before Staggers' subcommittee, claiming he had "a duty to uphold the freedom of the broadcast press against congressional abridgment." He argued that such an issue would not arise with the print media "because broadcasters need government licenses while other media do not, but the First Amendment permits such an intrusion into the freedom of broadcast journalism, although it admittedly forbids the identical intrusion into other press media." Testifying for more than four hours, the articulate Stanton still refused to turn over the requested documentation.

Frank Stanton's argument about the difference in treatment by the government in regard to the broadcast media versus the print media would be validated when the Supreme Court voted to allow the unrestrained publication of what would become known as "The Pentagon Papers" after *The New York Times* published the first installment of the papers three months after the initial airing of the CBS documentary. Staggers' committee requested that Congress cite Stanton in contempt, but Congress failed to muster the necessary votes. A month later, Representative Hastings Keith (R-MA) introduced legislation to prohibit broadcasters from "juxtaposing or rearranging by editing" an event, a key argument made by Staggers for the release of materials used in the production of the CBS documentary. The legislation never made it to the House floor for a vote. The whole ordeal would be considered an important victory for broadcast journalism in its fight to defend the First Amendment. Still, Mr. Staggers, by trade a "right of way" agent from Mineral County, West Virginia, would not relent.

The trade press would rally around the cause of Dr. Frank Stanton and William Paley, the founder and chairman of CBS. Don West, a former senior editor at *Broadcasting Magazine*, remembers the intensity with which Stanton held to his ideals: "Stanton remains to this day an absolutist and would fight to the death, I suppose, for the right of all people to say whatever they want to say." Sol Taishoff, the founder of *Broadcasting Magazine*, was a kindred spirit of Stanton's when it came to freedom of the press. He espoused the "American Plan" of commercial broadcasting, arguing that state-run media enterprises should be avoided at all costs in the name of freedom of speech. Taishoff, opposed to the Fairness Doctrine, became the "alter-ego" of the government, defending purveyors of poor taste and radical views all in the name of free speech. According to his son, Larry Taishoff, he once received "one of the nicest letters" from Reverend Carl McIntire, an ultraconservative evangelist known for spreading anti-Semitic views. The letter read what "a good friend Sol Taishoff was to him" for defending his right to free speech in the editorial pages of *Broadcast Magazine.*

Bill O'Shaughnessy would throw the full weight of his relentless conviction to defend free speech by helping organize the trade press in defense of CBS, and for that he would be thanked personally by Mr. Paley himself. "I got a call one day here at the station," recalls O'Shaughnessy. "I picked up the line and the voice on the other end said, 'Bill, Bill can you hear me? This is Bill Paley.' I responded, 'Mr. Paley?' He continued, 'I am about to get on a boat to sail for Europe with Babe, but I just wanted to let you know we won, and future generations will thank you for what you did for the cause of freedom.'" O'Shaughnessy gave the credit to Congressman Ogden Reid, who led the fight against Staggers on the House floor, and to the trade press, citing Les Brown of *Variety* and Don West of *Broadcasting Magazine.*

John Tabner remembers Stanton coming to speak to NYSBA shortly after the showdown with Congress. As at many NYSBA meetings, there were a lot of politicians in the crowd, including Walter Mahoney, New York State Senate majority leader from Buffalo. As a standard practice, Tabner was asked to review Stanton's speech. In light of the fact that there would be a lot of politicians in the audience who didn't hold such a favorable view of the broadcaster's response to the recent Congressional proceedings, Tabner recommended toning down the speech. All NYSBA members who discussed the speech with Tabner were from CBS, with the exception of Merl Galusha from WRGB-TV, the NBC affiliate in Schenectady. Tabner remembers being told that the word from CBS was that no one ever changes Dr. Stanton's speeches. During Stanton's address, Mahoney got up and walked out in disgust. Later on, Mahoney's people asked if NYSBA had its counsel review the speech. The lone voice in a crowd of CBS executives, Merl Galusha, piped up, "They sure did."

A Voice in the Darkness

In times of crisis, broadcasters frequently assume a mantle of leadership to which they were not elected. Acting almost as a temporary surrogate "government agency," they direct their communities to safety during floods, blizzards or unthinkable tragedies, like the attacks of September 11th. In short, they become the lifeblood of the community in which they serve. While the federal and state governments have the authority to use broadcast signals directly via the Emergency Alert System, more often than not the awesome responsibility of guiding the public through trying times is left to the reassuring voices and familiar faces of local broadcasters.

"When we had the blackout in the Northeast two years ago, that was a shining moment for WOR. We were basically a candle in the dark for our listeners," recalls Bob Bruno. For all the remarkable technological advances of the last two decades, it is the mobile battery-powered radio that remains a voice in the darkness and a connection to the outside world when all other forms of communications are silenced by electrical power outages. WOR's staff would go beyond the call of duty, doing everything to keep their coverage on the air. "We were off the air a total of, I think, 30 seconds while our transmitters shifted, but we stayed on the air through that entire ordeal," says Bruno. They depended on a generator on the roof for their source of power. "We're up on the 23rd floor and it's up on top of the building, about 25 floors up. We actually had people bringing up five-gallon jugs of fuel, and as you can imagine it was tough to walk back down after awhile, much less walk back up 25 flights carrying that heavy weight." What impressed him most of all that day was how his staff stepped up to the challenge: "The people listening don't get to see the 'hamsters on the wheel'. . . the people on the other side of the radio, running all over the place, doing more than what they have to do. Many of us merely walk through our jobs every day. Then you see us under pressure and you realize the level of skills, commitment, and intelligence we're able to bring to a situation, no matter how dire it is. It makes you very, very proud."

Nor'easters, hurricanes, blizzards, and severe summer thunderstorms have made Paul Sidney of WLNG a familiar voice to those living on the eastern end of Long Island. He acts almost like a de facto employee of the local electric company when the power goes out: "I take calls to help people get their electricity back. I ask them, 'Where's your power out?'" He literally connects callers with the utility workers out in the trucks: "The power company out here used to be LILCO, now it's NYFA. The guys in the LILCO trucks would listen to us and call us up, asking, 'Hey, where was that call you just took from?' We became almost like a public utility." For Sidney, getting the power turned back on for just a few houses on a single street is just as important as getting the power back on for the whole town, an indication of the deep connection he has with each one of his listeners.

In the Eye of the Storm

Weather calamities have the potential of simultaneously delivering individual personal hardships a thousand times over, sweeping local broadcasters into their emergency role as a vortex of information. Tony Malara, once the general manager at WWNY-TV in Watertown, remembers realizing the true potential of local broadcasting during the great Blizzard of 1977: "I understood the power of broadcasting when I would sit there and say to myself at Syracuse University, 'Why are thousands of people calling, asking for a record to be played on the

radio?' At first, it was kind of fun to watch all that happen, but the real importance of local radio came to me in that blizzard." Images of downtown Buffalo
completely buried in snow flashed around the country, earning it the reputation
as the nation's "snowiest city." It would become the first snowstorm to warrant a
federal disaster area declaration. Eight-foot drifts at the Buffalo Zoo enabled
three reindeer to walk over the fence and wander around the city.

Up in Watertown, Malara's station, WWNY-TV, became the nerve center for
many of the communities located in rural areas. During the first couple of days
of the storm it was virtually impossible to get around. Many citizens in outlying
areas lived in mobile homes, virtually trapped inside by mountains of snow.
Even the winter training exercises for 2,200 troops at Fort Drum had to be can-
celled because of the storm, recalls Malara: "Through my 'political' contacts, I
got those troops released to help with relief efforts in our county. Even the
county civil defense director was snowed in. The radio and television station
handled emergency calls for medicine and food. Then the Marines would take a
helicopter to the homes of these callers, jump out, and snowshoe to the home
where the call came from. The Marines would have to shovel the snow away just
to get to the front door." After the storm, the U.S. Marine Corps presented
Malara with a plaque making him the only honorary field marshall in the history of the U.S. Marine Corps!

Jim and Keela Rodgers would find themselves in a similar situation during a
severe ice storm in upstate New York in the late 1990s. They became a clearinghouse for their communities' basic needs, says Keela Rodgers: "If somebody ran
out of firewood, they would call both the radio station and the Red Cross. The
Red Cross would then call us and say, 'So and so is out of firewood, can you see
if there is anybody who would like to donate or deliver firewood?' Then we
would make the announcement and someone would call in half an hour later
letting us know they had five cords of wood to spare." Soup kitchens would also
use the station to put a call out for food. Then they would call back to let the
Rodgers know when they had more than enough provisions, so the station
would stop requesting donations. Not only does broadcasting act as an orga-
nizer of relief supplies in times of crisis, but also acts as a catalyst for bringing
the community together to help themselves. Almost three-quarters of Rodgers'
20,000 listeners were directly affected by the ice storm. For weeks afterward, the
impact of the storm would still be felt, as residents struggled to live without
power in the dead of winter. "There were people around here who were out of
electricity, really cut off for weeks. I can't tell you how many people said we were
their only connection with reality," recalls Jim Rodgers.

Making personal sacrifices also comes with the territory when broadcasters
need to make themselves available to their community. Crises reveal their role as

a "necessity" and one of "convenience" for members of the community. In these tense situations broadcasters regard their work as a "duty" rather just a "job," explains Larry Levite, former owner of WBEN-AM/FM in Buffalo and now the publisher of *Buffalo Spree* magazine: "You know, in a snowstorm, we didn't have to ask our staff to stay over, they just knew what they had to do. It wasn't just a 'job' to them."

Amos Finch and Myra Youmans, former owners of WDLA-AM in Delaware County, also understood that big news events weren't "conveniently" scheduled during their hours of operation. Their regular broadcast day ran from 5 a.m. to 10:15 p.m. at night. A few years ago, tornados were predicted to move through their listening area, so they decided to stay on the air, well past their sign-off time. They broadcast until 3:30 a.m., when the danger had past. "When we got word the tornados might be hitting the area , we told people to stick with us and we would stay on all night if necessary. Even though the tower kind of leaned a few times, which was right at the studio location, we stayed on the air. We had quite a bit of damage in Delaware County. A lot of buildings were destroyed, trees blown down, but fortunately no one was killed," recounts Finch.

Human Tragedies

Assuming the role of being the bearer of bad news is never an easy one, but New York's broadcasters have borne that responsibility with exceptional dignity time and again. More often than they would like, they have brought their listeners and viewers to those neighbors or loved ones who found themselves in the center of unspeakable tragedies or anguishing scenes of social unrest. Many times, radio or television are the only sources of information about the safety of a family member or neighbor. The revered Leavitt Pope, long-time president of WPIX-TV in New York, remembers the sinking of the *Andrea Doria* in 1956 off the coast of Nantucket, Massachusetts, to be a particular heartbreaking event for many New Yorkers: "There were a lot of people from New York on it. We got hold of an amphibious airplane and flew out to sea and got a lot of shots of the *Andrea Doria* as it was sinking. We brought the footage back to New York and had it on the news that same day. Later on we covered the survivors as they came in along the docks on the Hudson River." It would be one of the first times a New York television station had the ability to air footage of a major news event outside its viewing area on the same day.

Upstate in western New York, the Attica Prison riot would grab national headlines in 1971. According to Bill Brown Jr., former owner of WBTA-AM, his station was first on the scene with reporters: "43 people were killed, including inmates and hostages. We were the closest station to the riot, just 11 miles away."

The four-day revolt involved over 1,000 New York State Police, and 11 of the 38 hostages tragically died. In the days following the riots, several hundred radio stations requested WBTA's reports, sharing this important "local story" with the rest of the nation.

Like most states during the 1960s, New York was no stranger to demonstrations, marches, and social unrest. The shooting deaths of four students in 1970 at Kent State University in Ohio touched off student protests all over the country, including the main campus of the University of Buffalo. It was one of John Zach's first big stories as a young reporter at WKBW-AM: "I was working the overnight shift at the time and I was about to go home at around 10 a.m. All of a sudden, a call comes over the police radio that the students are marching down Main Street toward Winspear Avenue, carrying torches, and they're complaining about the state police." He decided to see what was going on for himself and ended up working the story all day, until early in the evening.

His coverage described the scene that day for the rest of Buffalo: police attempting to slow down the advance of countless students and trying to disperse the unruly crowd. As the scene grew more confrontational, police started firing canisters of tear gas. John Zach's live coverage would be interrupted as a result: "My live on-the-air report ended when a tear gas canister was thrown back in our direction by one of the students. It landed in the news truck and bounced all over the inside. I started coughing until I just couldn't talk anymore, so that's how my report ended. Jim Fagan, who was probably the number-one, consummate radio reporter in Buffalo at the time, came up to me that day and said, 'To top you, I'm going to have to kill myself.'"

9/11

Hurricanes, riots, snow storms, floods, economic crises, and countless other events will become clouded with the passage of time, but there is one event that will forever be seared into the minds of all New Yorkers. The events of 9/11 forced broadcasters to dig deep within themselves, rising to the occasion to provide calm, information, and guidance to the communities they served. Everything their community had ever asked of them and their license required of them provided broadcasters with the resolve to conduct their duty on that unthinkable September morning.

On that day, broadcasters would cover the first foreign attack on the American mainland in almost 200 years. A stunning, dramatic, gratuitous display of evil would leave thousands of New Yorkers dead. Broadcasters were first charged with the task of telling the world what little they knew as events quickly unfolded. In doing so, they would risk their lives, and unfortunately some would even give their lives. Steven Jacobsen of WPIX, Channel 11; William Steckman of WNBC, Channel 4; Gerard (Rod) Coppola of WNET, Channel 13; Isaias Rivera and Bob Pattison of WCBS, Channel 2; and Donald DiFranco of WABC, Channel 7 were engineers busily maintaining their stations' towers and transmitters on top of the World Trade Center so the the horrific events that would end their lives could be shared with the world.

While the country became paralyzed by shock in the days and weeks after the attack, the role of broadcasters shifted to help organize relief efforts, to provide hope, and to console. The network news divisions provided an unprecedented 96 hours of continuous coverage, foregoing millions of dollars in advertising revenue. Andrew Heyward, president of CBS News, called Neil Shapiro, president of NBC News, during the first hours after the attacks, suggesting that the networks share all their footage and overlook their rivalry even for just a day.

Two weeks after the attacks, the four major broadcast networks took another unprecedented step of working together to organize a prime-time telethon, "America: A Tribute to Heroes," to raise money for victims and their families. The simultaneous broadcast on CBS, ABC, NBC, FOX, and several cable networks raised more than $30 million.

No one will ever forget Mayor Rudolph Giuliani's impromptu, "on-the-run," press conference with broadcast journalists to assure New Yorkers that the city government had the situation well in hand. His command center became compromised as a result of the attacks, and the mayor himself survived a close call as the Towers collapsed. The mayor would use another broadcast venue, "Saturday Night Live" on NBC, a couple of weeks later to let New York and the nation know it was "OK to laugh again."

Broadcasters would also attempt to guide America through a national discussion to reflect on the country's basic values and define what the nation stood for, as Americans took their first tentative steps in a world forever changed. To help curb potential violence against Muslim Americans and Arab Americans, and to celebrate the diversity of America, the Ad Council produced a simple but powerful PSA called "I Am an American," broadcast on all the networks, showing people of all races, ages, and creeds.

Ernie Anastos spent the first day, for over 12 hours, covering the story from the CBS Broadcaster Center in the WCBS-TV studio. He has covered his share of stories from war zones, but nothing could prepare him for what was left of the World Trade Center: "I would say without a doubt the biggest story I've been on, and the most personal story, was 9/11. I mean . . . I remember that so vividly in my mind. I went down to the scene the second day. When I got there, the authorities allowed me to see some of what was going on. I mean it just moved me so much. I couldn't believe where I was. It did not feel like New York City. I've been to Nicaragua, I've been to El Salvador and other areas where you can see the effects of war, but this was something I had never seen in my life."

Initially people would be glued to their television trying to determine if they were watching some horrible movie or if what they were seeing was in fact true. The story eventually turned to radio, as people needed to pour out their emotions, "I sat before that microphone for about 10 hours. We opened it up and it became a forum, and people talked about their fears," remembers Bill O'Shaughnessy. He turned over his airwaves to countless callers on that day. There were some who had yet to hear from loved ones working in the World Trade Center, those who needed to express their outrage at this attack on our country, and still others who tried to help make sense of a seemingly unexplainable event. Politicians and civic leaders were also on hand to address the frightened residents of Westchester, the Bronx, and Long Island. Mario Cuomo was on the air, recounting the first terrorist attack on the Twin Towers in 1993, when he had an office there as governor. "The genius of WVOX was evident on 9/11. I was only a typical broadcaster on that sad day . . . doin' what comes naturally," says O'Shaughnessy.

It is sometimes difficult to refer to 9/11 as broadcasting's "finest hour," when most broadcasters would humbly agree they were simple performing their duty during the country's darkest hour. Thankfully, events like 9/11 aren't necessary to demonstrate the greatness of broadcasting on a daily basis. For the most part, broadcasters serve their communities in countless, uneventful ways, from letting listeners know if they need to take an umbrella off to work in the morning or by inspiring their community to raise funds for a victim of a tragic fire or simply encouraging citizens to live a healthier lifestyle. Those grievous attacks on September 11, 2001, did, however, demonstrate the multilayered role broadcasters play in society and in local communities across America. They gave us comfort as we grieved. They let us help those in need. They reassured us of our American values. They gave us the courage to fight back. They breathed life back into New York City's shaky economy. Most importantly, they reminded us of the strength and hope that can be drawn from uniting together as a community.

4

The Pioneers: Building Broadcasting in New York

> "We didn't buy our station thinking we were going to become million-aires, although we did very well for ourselves."
>
> —Pat Tocatlian, owner of WSLB and WPAC, Ogdensburg, New York

At the time NYSBA was founded, the broadcasting industry was filled with a spirit of entrepreneurialism. The barriers to entry were still manageable enough for anyone to simply secure a loan from the local bank to buy a station and be-come a broadcast owner. Most who entered the profession never expected to make a killing. "When I got in the business, the phrase 'mom and pop' was used to describe the broadcast business. I like that description. These were broadcast-ers, not necessarily businessmen. They were the businessmen of broadcasting, the guys who started by their boot straps," said Jim Greenwald, former Katz Media chief executive officer, describing what a typical broadcast owner was like prior to the age of deregulation and consolidation.

Spending most of her career on the corporate side of the business at CBS, Nancy Widmann admires the range of skills individual owners possessed: "What I loved about some of the smaller broadcasters is that they did every-thing. They built something from scratch outside the corporate environment. The corporate confines don't give you the total skills you need to survive as a business owner." More often than not, owners made decisions by the seat of their pants. They learned their craft through trial and error and from each other.

The majority of NYSBA members through at least the 1980s were individual owners. Gathering together each year against the historic backdrop of Saratoga or along the quiet banks of Lake George at the Executive Conference provided a forum to exchange ideas and solve business problems. The Executive Conference itself was borne out of a desire by broadcasters to assemble seminars to learn how to tackle the latest trends shaping the industry. For the most part there was no established "guide book" on how to build a radio or television station in the early days of the Association. Obstacles were overcome by the sharing of knowledge facilitated by organizations like NYSBA.

The Trials and Triumphs of Ownership

Building a local broadcast operation was unlike starting up most small businesses. It was relatively complex, involving a multitude of decisions to be made by the owner in a wide variety of disciplines, including technology, sales, programming, finance, and labor. Starting out on your own can be a daunting task, especially when there is no instruction on how to sustain an instrument of communication at the local level. As Pat Tocatlian was starting off, she remembers drawing inspiration from Jim and Keela Rodgers, owners of WNBZ in Lake Placid: "Jim Rodgers was an inspiration in that I'd look at him and say, 'He keeps on going . . . and he's all right.' I'd say to myself, 'Go ahead. You can keep going too.'"

Little did she know that the Rodgers were having a tough slog, too. "I found that a radio station in a small town for us was sort of like a boat with a hole in it, into which you kept pouring money, hoping to plug it up. We paid off a sizeable debt only when we sold the station," comments Jim Rodgers. The Lake Placid station served 20,000 listeners covering a wide area from Saranac Lake to Lake Placid to Tupper Lake to Plattsburgh.

Why did some broadcasters feel it necessary to become owners? For Andrew Langston of WDKX in Rochester, it meant an opportunity to be able to do more for his community: "I've always believed as an owner you can do more than those who weren't owners. Your opportunity to grow your own business was all up to you and your abilities, so I gave it my best shot."

Others decided to become an owner to spread their creative wings. It enabled them to execute their personal vision of how to entertain or inform their audience. A fixture in broadcasting for over 50 years on Long Island, Jack Ellsworth cherished his days as an owner: "As an owner you can do any thing you like. The world is in your hands. I programmed my station with something like 9,000 selections. I picked all the music and rotated that many songs. We had a great library, and I stuck to it rigidly. All the guys who worked for me had to follow music sheets I put together." For more than 30 years, Ellsworth worked for WALK, rising to become president and CEO of the company. When the station was sold in 1981, he bought his own station, WLIM, which stood for "Long

Island Music." He ran that station for more than 20 years before being exhausted by the relentless pressure and demands of being an owner.

Prior to deregulation, a typical broadcaster usually bought just one station, making it a tightly knit part of the community. Some would own multiple stations, but they were then prevented by the FCC from owning more than seven radio stations or five television stations. Phil Spencer was one of these individual owners, returning to his hometown after the Korean War to pick up his career where he left off: "When I got out of the Army, I came back to Gloversville for a few months, and then I got an offer to come to WCSS in Amsterdam in 1953. They offered much better pay and more responsibility. I was the program and news director. By that time I was also married and wanted to have a family, so this was a better job for me personally." A couple of years later, Spencer unexpectedly came into some money. An owner of a liquor store in town sat on the board of directors of Spencer's company. While visiting the store, Spencer got to talking to him and mentioned his new-found wealth. "He told me I had a good future and I was management material. He asked me why I didn't buy stock in the company. I told him I wasn't aware there was any stock available."

At the age of 27, Spencer decided to pursue the opportunity to take his career to the next level. Encouraged by his conversation with a member of the board, he decided to approach his direct boss about buying some stock. He was immediately rebuffed. Feeling threatened by Spencer's intentions, his boss informed Spencer that he alone had an option on the stock, which prevented the young broadcaster from buying it. "Within two days I got a letter, praising me to high heaven, telling me what a great employee I was, but that everybody who works at the company had to live in Amsterdam. I was still living in Gloversville at the time. They never told me to move before. In fact, I never even missed a day of work. He basically fired me and gave me three weeks severance pay."

Feeling dejected but not deterred, Phil Spencer decided to go for the big time: New York City. A few months after landing an on-air gig in New York, he got a call from the attorney representing WCSS, asking him to came back to the station as general manager. Spencer played hardball this time, demanding the opportunity to purchase every available share of stock. They obliged his request. "I invested a good share of what I had. That was in 1956, and over the years I kept buying stock. At one time, we had 70 stockholders. I kept buying them out, and when people passed on I bought their stock. Ultimately I gained control of the station, and from there I grew the company. We were one little station when I took over, and we ended up with five."

He bought his next station in Oswego, up near the Canadian border. He would also purchase WIPS, an FM station in Ticonderoga, also up in the North Country, by submitting a competing application for the station. It was losing money and was on its fourth owner. He knew he could do a better job running the station based on his success with WCSS. Spencer recalls defending himself at the FCC hearing: "I represented myself, and the administrative law judge told me to get a good lawyer because nobody represents himself. I told him I was well aware of the law, so he decided to give me a chance. The other side had a darn good lawyer from a big firm in Washington. I was doing a good job, but I knew I was putting my foot in my mouth in a of couple places. The judge would encourage me, saying I was on the right track. Their lawyer got up and said, 'What the hell is going on here? This guy's too cheap to get a lawyer, so you're helping him out?' The judge started to laugh, and relented. He didn't help me anymore, but he allowed me to continue to represent myself." The hearing went on for a few days, when the judge finally told both parties to seek a settlement over lunch. After some haggling, Spencer emerged victorious.

Jerry and Sasha Gillman originally decided to move to Woodstock as an escape from the hectic life of New York City in the 1970s. Jerry worked in public relations, and Sasha was doing publicity for a theater in the city. As Jerry was setting up their stereo for the first time in their new Woodstock getaway, he wasn't sure if he set it up right: "When I was all finished, I turned to Sasha and said, 'It doesn't work, I can't even find a local station.' Then I realized after a while that there *was no* local station." Gillman was astonished, particularly because of the rich musical heritage of Woodstock: "Woodstock is a music community. Most people associate it with the rock festival, but the Woodstock Chamber Orchestra has the oldest continuous classical series in the United States. When we first came, kids were allowed into bars with their high school teachers because of the jazz in the bars up here. Of course, there are probably a dozen famous rock musicians who live up here too." These two accidental broadcasters would build one of the most eclectic collection of radio programs on WSDT, described by their peers as "cerebral" and "cutting edge."

Many people who enter broadcasting are drawn to the excitement of the "programming side," totally unaware of the "business side" that makes the programming possible. This was the case for Ed Levine: "I wanted to be a disc jockey. This whole thing I do now . . . I didn't even know this part of the business existed when I got into it. The fact that you sold advertising, had accountants . . . , and that this was a business based on cash flow didn't matter to me then." Over time Levine says he transitioned from the "art of radio" to the "business of radio." As he grew older, he was tired of moving around and thought if he became an owner, he would be able to lay down his roots somewhere. He started attending seminars to learn the ropes on the business side: "I remember the first time I heard the term 'mezzanine financing' in the mid-1980s, I was totally thrown." As he started building his first station, he sought out the advice of Bud

Wertheimer, a sort of financial guru in the industry. He basically served as a mentor to Levine, helping him understand the language of business. "I didn't know what he was talking about, much less follow his advice. I really didn't understand what he was saying half the time." Levine literally started from scratch, constructing the building for WKLL in Utica, his very first station.

As if building his first business in an industry as competitive as radio wasn't challenging enough, his first full year of operation would be 1991. The country was going through its first recession in a decade, and it would be the first time radio revenues declined in 30 years. Fortunately he didn't have a lot of bank debt. Levine's company was privately financed by a "classic" angel, who had the patience to see Levine's vision through those tough times: "I didn't think it was a valuable lesson at the time because it was so painful, but when I went to secure some significant financing in 2000 to refinance this company, our investors were really impressed with what we had gone through in 1991 and survived it. They figured I must at least be persistent." He put his first station on the air for just $165,000.

The rules of the game have changed since building that first station in Utica because of consolidation, says Levine. "It definitely changed our model eventually, in that it became a 'grow' or 'go' world. You're either thinking about growing the company or you're thinking about selling it. Remaining static was not really a smart position." He believes it is no longer possible for someone to build a company as he did in the current business environment: "I'm pretty confident that the company I built in Syracuse, Utica, and now Albany couldn't be replicated today." Like broadcasters of yesteryear, he just wanted to make a comfortable living: "I didn't do this for money, cash flow, or valuations. I did it for a much simpler reason, to have control of my own destiny."

Long before Percy Sutton became involved with broadcasting, he was already passionately working on behalf of the African American community in Harlem and Manhattan. Broadcasting was not merely an opportunity to serve his community but rather an extension of his vast activities to help advance the cause of his neighbors. He is a Renaissance man of the modern era: an accomplished attorney, businessman, politician, human rights activist, technologist, and broadcaster.

Sutton's career is intertwined with the historical milestones of African American advancement during the second half of the 20th century. He served as a combat intelligence officer in World War II with the Tuskegee Airmen, the fabled all-black fighter group that fought with honor and distinction in North Africa and Italy. He served as legal counsel to civil rights leader Malcolm X and argued cases before the United States Supreme Court. During the 1960s, Sutton was elected to the New York State Assembly, introducing legislation in the areas of housing, higher education, and abortion. In 1967, while holding the office of

Manhattan borough president, he founded the first National Caucus of Black Elected and Appointed Officials, along with California Lieutenant Governor Mervyn Dymally. Their efforts helped thousands of African Americans get elected or appointed at all levels of government throughout the country.

In 1971, Sutton, along with a group of investors, formed Inner City Broadcasting, buying WLIB-AM in New York the following year. WBLS-FM was added two years later, quickly becoming one of the top-ranked stations in the country. Sutton was credited with coining the term "urban radio" and was a pioneer of the new format. The company went on to acquire additional stations in large markets throughout the country, as well as making investments in cable. Like so many broadcasters, ICBC is a family business. In 1990, Sutton's son, Pierre "Pepe" Sutton, was named chairman and chief executive officer. In a recent speech honoring the Sutton family's remarkable contributions to the broadcast industry by the Broadcasters' Foundation, Phil Lombardo, chief executive officer of Citadel Communications, described ICBC as "a beacon of innovation, leadership, activism, and commitment to the community."

Hal Jackson was also part of the group that helped build Inner City Broadcasting. He was the first African American radio sports announcer, calling Howard University's home baseball games and local American Negro Baseball League games for WOOK in Washington, D.C. When Jackson moved to New York in 1954, he earned the distinction of becoming the first radio personality to broadcast three daily shows on three different stations. His shows offered a mix of jazz and interviews with celebrities. It was estimated that he had 4 million daily listeners at the height of his on-air career.

Long Island's only commercial television station, WLNY-TV, Channel 55, was founded just 20 years ago by Mike Pascucci and Marv Chauvin, symbolizing the "new" money being invested in broadcasting by individual owners. Not only is it Long Island's only commercial television station, it is also one of the last independent television stations in America. David Feinblatt, the dynamic current general manager of WLNY-TV, left the radio world in 1995 to join the station as sales manager. After just a year, he became the general manager, savoring the privilege of working for one of the last independent television stations in America.

Corporate Roots Grown in New York

In 1954, a private group of investors led by Frank Smith and the legendary anchorman, commentator, and explorer Lowell Thomas purchased Channel 41, an obscure UHF station in Albany. They raised $700,000 and paid $250,000 for the station, assuming $250,000 in debt. Thomas Murphy was hired as general manager of the station. Smith and Thomas would go back to their stockholders twice, requesting $150,000 each time, before the station became finally became a profitable venture three years later. The FCC had allocated only one VHF station, WRGB-TV in the Albany market, because of the hilly terrain, eventually adding several UHF stations to compensate for gaps in the broadcast service area. WROW-TV, Channel 41 (later to be renamed WTEN-TV), was one of them. As a UHF station, they would struggle, because most television sets at the time couldn't even receive a UHF signal. This, however, was the birth of the highly regarded Capital Cities Broadcasting, which would later expand its empire to include newspapers and ABC.

Tom Murphy had no idea he was building a company that would one day buy one of the major broadcast networks, the American Broadcasting Company. "We were just trying to survive week to week," Murphy humbly says. According to Phil Beuth, Murphy's first hire, Murphy set his sights high right from the very beginning: "I used to tease him and say, 'Tom, you have 11,000 shares and I only have 300.' He said, 'Don't worry, we're all going to get rich. We're going to build the best company in the business, Philly.' He always called me 'Philly.' He told us we were going to build the best company in the business and we did."

Even today, Tom Murphy is modest about his success: "We were fortunate enough to get in a very good business right at the beginning of it. For the next 40 years, the television station business was a wonderful business to be in." As their margins steadily increased, they would use their free cash flow to buy additional stations. FCC rules limited ownership to just five stations, so they sold off stations to acquire new ones in larger and larger markets. Once that strategy had been exhausted, they turned to newspapers and magazines. They bought the prestigious Fairchild Publications, run by the fashion arbiter John Fairchild, the father of *Women's Wear Daily* and *W* magazine.

By the mid-1980s, Capital Cities represented roughly 8% of the ABC Television Network's total coverage, with affiliates in Philadelphia, Houston, Buffalo, Hartford-New Haven, and Raleigh-Durham. As deregulation rolled through the industry in the 1980s, CapCities' strategy for growth would change when the FCC expanded the station ownership cap from 5 to 12. Murphy knew that once he was able to buy up to 12 stations, he wanted to buy ABC. Leonard Goldenson, the founder of ABC, was getting on in years and was seeking a way out, recalls Murphy: "We knew ABC quite well, and I think we developed a reputation for being good partners, so that's how I was able to make that deal with Leonard Goldenson in 1985."

Murphy quickly discovered that running a network was much different from running a station: "The margins are lower and all the risk is taken by the network, not by the affiliates. There is also a substantial 'fail rate' with prime-time programming." A decade later, The Walt Disney Company, the giant entertainment conglomerate, would acquire Capital Cities/ABC.

Albany would nurture the growth of another broadcasting company, borne out of a partnership between a car dealer and a broadcaster. John Kelly was general manager of WPYX in Albany and oversaw 11 other radio stations throughout the Northeast, owned by a flamboyant Philadelphia-based broadcaster, Herb Scott. In 1980, Scott died and Kelly was asked to run the company for the Scott family. A couple of years later the company was sold to Hollywood icon Merv Griffin for $15 million. Incidentally, Merv Griffin hired Carol Reilly some years later to run WPYX and WTRY in Albany.

Prior to the sale of the group, John Kelly had organized a contest to give away a car at a dealership owned by Jim Morrell. Their relationship would grow as Morrell increasingly became aware of broadcasting as a valuable business opportunity, and Kelly was looking for a new challenge now that the Scott stations had changed hands.

Both he and Morrell found their opportunity, and they decided to buy a couple of stations in Albany. At this time, Kelly said broadcasting really took off: "The demand was just unbelievable." They closed on their first station in 1987, under the name "Albany Broadcasting." "When we took over WFLY, it was floundering, but we turned it around, making it number one," recalls Kelly. They would go on to buy two more stations in Albany, as well as stations in Westchester and the Hudson Valley.

As the company expanded, it was incorporated as Pamal Broadcasting, taking the first letter of the middle names of Morrell's four children. The stations were eventually organized into clusters, so the stations in Albany would continue to operate under the Albany Broadcasting name. Morrell has been very satisfied with the company's growth ever since: "We are limited only by our own personal financial wealth. We either borrow money or we inject the company with cash, so we've done as well as we can under the circumstances." Today Pamal Broadcasting owns 27 stations in New York, Massachusetts, Vermont, and Florida, making it one of the largest private broadcasting companies in the country. John Kelly retired in 2001 as president of Albany Broadcasting to oversee the campus radio station at Siena College as part of the development of its broadcast journalism program.

Born out of an antitrust suit to break up NBC's Red and Blue television networks, the American Broadcasting Company became the "third network" in 1952. It would struggle for years before finally finding its stride in the 1970s. "Not only were we the upstart, we were the fourth network in a three-network race," quips Jim Duffy, former president of the ABC Television Network. As local television stations sprang up across the country, CBS and NBC were the most sought-after affiliations because of their powerful programming lineups that were virtually guaranteed to bring in large audiences, thus advertising dollars.

ABC had its work cut out for it, explains former ABC Television president, Wally Schwartz: "Programming and distribution were the keys. The other guys always had more money and they could make the necessary investments. I think they probably had better people, too, from a programming standpoint. They had also been at it longer, and I think they just did a better job than we did for a long time." When Duffy took over sales for ABC in 1963, it had only 143 stations, while CBS and NBC each had 200-plus stations. When he became president of the network in 1970, his primary goal was to level the playing field in terms of distribution: "We had an all-out drive to increase our affiliate lineup, and we did. In a period of some four years, we had 77 stations change. We went after basic CBS and NBC affiliates and enticed them over to ABC. In doing that, not only did we even up the number of stations in terms of actual numbers but also in terms of the quality of our station lineup."

While working to sign more stations, there was also a strong effort to improve the quality of programming on ABC. According to Duffy, they focused on being as creative and innovative as possible: "From a programming standpoint, we tried to stand out in as many areas as we could to attract advertisers, but also to attract affiliates. We saw sports as an area we could do well in. In 1960, Roone Arlidge came in as president of ABC Sports and launched 'Wide World of Sports.' He also won the rights to the Olympics and got 'Monday Night Football' on the air." Their dual effort paid off, launching ABC into the number-one position during the 1970s for the first time in its history.

William Paley, David Sarnoff, and even Allen B. DuMont have all received their rightful share of ink through the years as pioneers and builders of networks. The entrepreneurial efforts of John Kluge, a food broker from Maryland who went on to found Metromedia, are worthy of note when discussing the achievements of these titans, at least from a financial standpoint. Kluge ran his businesses by concentrating on identifying high-growth, cutting-edge opportunities and less on investing in prestige and glamour or waging battles to defend free speech.

John Kluge began building his company in 1956 after taking the sizable returns he made from his investments in the food business in Baltimore to buy the former DuMont stations. While he saw the high-growth potential of television, he felt it was too late to try to start another network. Despite relatively small audiences, he built the largest and most valuable group of independent stations in the United States by keeping operational costs low.

In the late 1960s, Stuart Subotnick joined Metromedia, eventually rising to chief financial officer and Kluge's right-hand man. After working with him for well over three decades, Subotnick respectfully describes Kluge as the most un-usual person he has ever met: "He is innately intelligent, meaning he can size-up situations. He can identify potential, and he has the ability to see around the corner. He has vision. Some people have those things and never act on them." Subotnick believes most people don't act on these instincts because they are too cautious. This is not to say Kluge was not cautious, but Subotnick believes that if Kluge could gamble the house on the right idea, he would definitely gamble the house. A couple of times the gamble didn't pan out, admits Subotnick. Metromedia lost millions buying a niche magazine called *Diplomat* in the late 1960s and later crafted plans to launch a fourth network, but failed. Kluge's methods are driven by financial acumen, explains Subotnick: "The guy is cre-ative, absolutely brilliant, and a risk-taker. When you put all those characteris-tics together, you've got a very unusual individual." In the mid-1980s, Kluge, Subotnick, and two other partners took Metromedia private. The other two partners were eventually bought out, leaving Kluge and Subotnick working to-gether on their own for the last 20 years.

For a period of time, Metromedia controlled television and radio stations in several major markets, including New York and Boston. Their roster of ex-ecutives included well-known and respected station operators like Bob Ben-nett on the television side and John Van Buren Sullivan, who ran the mighty WNEW-AM in New York City. Metromedia also had its own rep firm headed by H. D. "Bud" Neuwirth. For the most part, Kluge was recognized more for his abilities to see lucrative investment opportunities than for his statesman-ship as a broadcaster. Metromedia eventually retreated from station owner-ship. Over a period of 30 years, Kluge had built a group of independent stations that would fetch nearly $2 billion when they were sold to Rupert Murdoch in the mid-1980s.

Born in Utica, Dick Clark would go on to become the most recognized disc jockey in America. His phenomenal success as an on-air personality and pro-ducer aside, he was eventually drawn to ownership, much like Ed Levine. In the late 1970s, Nick Verbitsky pitched the idea of having Dick Clark host a "count-down" show to compete with Kasey Kasem, the most popular Top-40 count-down show host at the time. It took some convincing. Clark was hesitant because he felt radio was too much work for too little payoff. Unlike Kasem's show, which stations paid for, Clark's would be offered to stations as barter, with half the advertising going to Verbitsky and Clark. He eventually agreed, so "Dick Clark's National Music Survey" went on the air in the early 1980s. "It was a huge success," notes Vertibitsky.

Not long after, the success of the show helped Clark cast aside his reserva-tions about the radio business. Verbitsky remembers Clark proposing the idea of going into business together: "We were having dinner with our wives on a Sunday night in Manhattan at a place called Primavera on First Avenue. Clark says to me, 'I think we should be doing this for ourselves. We should start our own company. I'll put the money together and you'll do the heavy lifting. We'll be partners.'" Verbitsky knew Clark saw a huge opportunity in radio, so United Stations was born in 1981. The company initially focused on syndicated programs. In 1985 they bought the RKO Network, adding news and sports programming to their offerings. Eventually they merged with Transtar, bringing 24-hour formats to the table. In 1992, the company was sold to Westwood One. "We had stayed out of the business a couple of years because of a noncompete clause, but we started the same company again in 1994." Much to the dismay of Mel Karmazin, the new company was also named United Stations, recalls Verbitsky. Karmazin's Infinity Broadcasting managed Westwood One, which had acquired the original United Stations.

The new company no longer provides finished programs to radio stations but rather supplemental information for program directors to help enhance their format. "We gear everything we do to suit the needs of the radio station and the program director. Then it's up to them to take it and use it in the form they need to garner a larger share of audience in their market," explains Verbitsky. For example, country-music stations subscribing to their country service receive a 12-page document at 3 o'clock every morning, outlining everything they need to know about country music that day.

Getting Television on the Air

For all intents and purposes, television was still a brand-new medium in the early 1950s. As with every new medium before and after, getting the public and advertisers on board took some time. Even building a station in the number-one market wasn't without its challenges, recalls the long-time and greatly respected president of WPIX-TV, Leavitt Pope: "There weren't an awful lot of sets around in those days. I believe there were fewer than 100,000 receivers in the entire New York metropolitan area when we started. The big problem was money . . . getting enough backing from advertisers to get into the black. It took us several years to get up to that stage." WPIX was then owned by the *Chicago Tribune*, which also owned the *Daily News*. Upon securing their license for a New York television station, Pope was hired by the *Daily News* to help get it off the ground. "Since I had been in the U.S. Signal Corps and was a ham radio operator, they thought I knew something about broadcasting, which I obviously didn't," quips Pope. He would go on to become one of the foremost experts in television broadcasting, learning how to run most of the station's operations from the time it went on the air. He ended up serving as president and chief executive officer of WPIX for his last 20 years in the business.

From its earliest beginnings, WPIX would remain an "independent," without a major network affiliation. Most owners launching stations at the time regarded an affiliation with a network as instant validation, necessary to quickly attract advertisers. Pope never regarded being independent as a handicap:" We made our own decisions and bargained with various people to buy programming. From what we saw of the network affiliates in those days, their lives weren't any easier. We operated as an independent for the next 40 years or so."

Out in the western tier, the *Courier-Express* newspaper in Buffalo had applied for a license to operate a television station in 1945, after its archrival, the *Buffalo Evening News*, did so. They eventually dropped the idea as "unfeasible." Alan Kirchhofer, the president of the *Buffalo Evening News*, was a recognized innovator in the newspaper industry. Despite his own reservations about the new medium, he put WBEN-TV (now WIVB-TV) on the air in 1946.

In the early 1970s, the *Courier-Express* applied once more for a television license, but after a change of heart, it sent a letter to the FCC declining the offer. When the license became available again, Al Anscombe, vice president and general manager of WKBW-AM at the time, convinced WKBW-AM's owner Reverend Clinton "Doc" Churchill to apply for it. Then another daytime radio operator in Buffalo applied on top of them. Seeing the error of its decision, the *Courier* decided to submit another application. A total of five applications for the license were submitted before the FCC would finally make a determination.

Representatives of each of the companies came together to see if a compromise could be reached. A partnership between all or some of the companies to launch the new television station was proposed. Churchill, the owner of WKBW, the big, booming radio powerhouse, was the most well-known broadcaster in Buffalo but was also regarded as a "rabble-rouser" by the business community, according to Anscombe. He was an evangelist, and Anscombe remembers he really had it in for one of Buffalo's banks: "Every time there was a foreclosure, Doc would put it on the air. He would say so-and-so bank was at it again and they've just taken a house from some more poor people." Incidentally, the call letters "WKBW" stand for "Well Known Bible Witness."

During a meeting of the rival applicants, the question of who would run the new organization arose. Someone suggested that Reverend Churchill should run it because he was the biggest name in town. Anscombe recalls that the *Courier-Express* would have no part of it if Churchill was in charge, so it withdrew its application.

The talks broke down, so Anscombe knew WKBW had to go it alone. The FCC ended up awarding the license to the *Courier-Express*. Anscombe got hold of the letter the *Courier* sent to the FCC declining its original application for the license. He had it published in the other local papers and sent the letter to the commission. Seeking to avoid further embarrassment, the FCC reversed its decision and awarded the license to Anscombe and Churchill in 1970.

The station automatically became one of the "big three" in Buffalo when it became an affiliate of ABC. Although ABC was not a strong network at the time, admits Anscombe, it was a still a network with potential. Faced with the monumental task of building a television station, Anscombe remembers getting invited to lunch at the prestigious Buffalo City Club by Alfred Kirchhofer, head of WBEN and owner of the *Buffalo Evening News*. Intrigued, he accepted the invitation. "We sat down and he asked me, 'What do you know about television?' I told him, 'Not a darn thing.'" Kirchhoffer made an offer to help out Anscombe—not necessarily because he had pity on Anscombe, but to protect his interests: "He'd just as soon see me be successful because the *Courier* would have moved in immediately if we lost our license." Kirchhoffer helped Anscombe hire a couple of consultants and spent five days a week at WBEN learning how to run a television station. A decade later, WKBW-TV was sold to Capital Cities for $14 million.

In the mid-1980s, another Buffalo broadcaster would get a shot at building a new television station in the same market. Don Angelo was hired by Tim McDonald, chief executive officer of TVX Corporation, to leverage his skills in broadcast sales by building WNYB-TV, Channel 49. "A once in a lifetime experience, you know. Not many people get the chance to start a television station from scratch," notes Angelo. He and his colleague, Bill Salzgiver, were in charge of every detail, from building the physical structure to hiring staff and buying furniture. Miraculously they went on the air September 7, 1986, after starting from nothing just six months earlier. "It was a blur how fast it went up. The thing that makes this story really interesting in broadcast history is the fact that we got right to the brink in August and Tim McDonald called the two of us down to Virginia Beach for a meeting."

McDonald wanted to know how to make the station stand out in the community. After some brainstorming, he suggested going after the broadcast rights to one of the local sports franchises. "Knowing the market, the only sports franchise I thought might even listen to us was the hockey team, the Buffalo Sabres," says Angelo. McDonald liked the idea and told him to contact Mitch Owen, president of the Sabres: "Before you knew it, McDonald was flying to Buffalo to meet with the owners of the hockey team. The meeting was at 10 in the morning, and he said he wanted to meet privately with the owners and their attorney." When the meeting was over, McDonald called Angelo on his cellphone and asked him to drive him to the airport: "We're driving to the airport, and I said,

'How'd the meeting go?' He says to us, 'I've got good news for you guys.' Of course, we had different expectations about what he was about to tell us. He says, 'I sold the television station!' Bill and I were both in shock. He continued, 'Oh, this is going to be great for you guys. I actually sold the station to the owners of the Buffalo Sabres.'" With just four weeks to launch, Angelo was in disbelief: "We got to the airport; he shook our hands and said, 'Good luck guys. Goodbye!' He got on the plane and we never saw him again."

The next week Angelo and Salzgiver had a meeting with their new bosses, Seymour Knox, the patriarch of a great Buffalo family and owner of the Sabres, and Mitch Owen. They were still getting everything ready to go on-air, but the new owners decided to go with a different look. Angelo was also informed that the station would now be carrying 40 Sabres games each season. "We got to the beginning of September and had our scheduled sign-on date. We threw a reception, and at 7 o'clock at night on September 7, we pressed a button to turn on the transmitter and we were off and running." Soon after sign-on, they became the first Fox affiliate in western New York. They called the station the "New York Superstation, WNYB-TV."

Deals and Transactions

New York's broadcasters executed a wide variety of innovative strategic decisions as their businesses grew that shaped the broadcasting industry as a whole. Many of their investment philosophies tracked that of other industries, whether seeking a specific rate of return or to balance their portfolio of businesses.

In the early 1980s, small and medium-sized businesses were still required to put up collateral, such as real or personal property, in order to secure a loan from a bank. As the broadcast business developed, the value derived from the tangible assets of a broadcast station—like the building, broadcast equipment, and transmitter—was no longer enough to meet the investment demands of broadcasting's fast-paced growth at this time.

Today's investors have come to realize that the true value of a broadcast station is its license and its ability to generate future cash flow. Albert L. Wertheimer (known as "Bud" in the industry), former owner of WVOR in Rochester and the Lincoln Group, became one of the leading advocates to help change how bankers viewed broadcasting as an investment opportunity. Twenty years ago, bankers wouldn't take a broadcast license as security because it wasn't personal property, so Wertheimer decided to circulate the idea of "cash flow funding" among New York's banks. The basic concept was to grant loans to broadcasters based on a business plan of future cash flow. It was a sea change in how financial institutions came to understand broadcasting as a business.

Wertheimer remembers the wide chasm he had to cross to get bankers to buy into this new concept: "They asked me what my promotion budget was for the following year. I told them I had a $250,000 budget. The department head at the bank nearly fell off his chair. He said, 'But you don't make $250,000.' I responded, 'Yes sir, I know, and unless we spend the $250,000, we won't make a dime.'" In time he managed to change a few minds, particularly among younger managers who were more open to new ideas than their older counterparts.

Soon bankers started taking interest in his research. They poured over his marketing plans and ratings charts, and wanted to better understand his programming strategies. Instead of concerning themselves with what types of physical assets a radio station owned, their focus shifted to its marketing plan and an assessment of its competitors. "Once they got into it, it was show biz! They got very involved with the concept, and there's a number of banks around the country that had a terrific experience with it. I was involved with about 32 different radio deals using this approach, financing them through banks one way or the other," says Wertheimer.

The value of a broadcast television station had as much to do with it is promotion plan as it did with its network affiliation. Prior to the 1970s, CBS and NBC were the two strongest networks and thus the most desirable for affiliation. Their programming drew the largest audiences and provided huge lead-ins for local programming on their affiliates. The majority of a local television's station revenue was drawn from selling advertising during local programming, and the same is still true today, the bread and butter of the station.

In 1980, Jim Delmonico and Tony Malara orchestrated one of the most talked-about affiliate swaps in television history. Delmonico was vice president and general manager of WRGB in Schenectady at the time and Malara had been recently named president of the CBS Television Network. WRGB was not only one of NBC's strongest affiliates, but also carried huge sentimental value as NBC's very first affiliate.

Delmonico knew the affiliation was a sacred cow, but CBS was offering him a deal he just couldn't refuse: "Nobody wanted to do it, but I got a guarantee to increase our compensation by $3 million. We got $3 million more in network compensation, which increased the value of the station by $30 million and made it possible for us to sell it for $57 million. CBS also agreed to give us promotional money—$650,000 the first year, $450,000 the second year, $350,000 the third year, and a guaranteed 10-year, "no-cut" clause. This meant making $30 million for doing absolutely nothing." Of course, each network wanted to be number one in each market, and WRGB was the number-one station in the Albany/Schenectady market for years.

The relationship between Malara and Delmonico had its roots in their involvement with NYSBA, when Malara was still working at an obscure television station in Watertown. The personable Malara was eventually courted by CBS to help manage affiliate relations. Always seeking to boost the profile of CBS's affiliates, on becoming president of the CBS Television Network, Malara contacted Delmonico to ask him what it would take for him to switch to CBS. Delmonico decided to play hardball. He told Malara he would be picking up the best station in the market. "Your news numbers will skyrocket because ours are so strong," Delmonico recalls telling Malara.

WRGB was the first station outside the metro New York area to do a local one-hour newscast. Everyone thought Delmonico was crazy at the time, but he knew better: "We started to concentrate on news, because that's where the money is if you're purely local. We bought a big General Motors mobile home, a magnificent unit we could park anywhere. We put in a studio, and wherever there was something going on, we were there." Around the time of the negotiations with CBS, WRGB's operating profit margin was over 40%, and each of their newscasts was number one, according to Delmonico.

The two broadcast executives finally agreed on a deal. Just as they were putting the finishing touches on their agreement, Delmonico told Malara there was a "slight problem." Approval of the deal had to go all the way to the top, to the chairman of the board of General Electric. Malara couldn't believe it. He thought the deal might fall through. After some last-minute negotiations, the deal was approved in the end. Malara recalls celebrating with Delmonico: "I flew up to Albany and I met Jim at a hotel. We signed the deal and then called room service to celebrate, but it had already closed. I ended up getting somebody in the kitchen to send us up some toast and cheese, and that's how we celebrated."

In the early 1980s, new tax legislation recently passed by Congress offered corporations a new "creative" source of funding, whether that was the intended spirit of the bill or not. The new law permitted companies to acquire the tax benefits of other companies. For example, one company could buy another company's depreciation investment tax credits. The purpose of the legislation was to help ailing companies that may have been leaning toward bankruptcy.

Stuart Subotnick of Metromedia, always seeking a financial edge, immediately saw the benefits of the new legislation: "It was a significant opportunity." He swung into action, buying airplanes, boats, and machinery. He gained some notoriety when he purchased $100 million worth of New York City buses and subways: "For a small, little company, I bought close to $600 million worth of assets. I got the depreciation from those assets and immediately got the investment tax credit." At the time, General Electric was the only other company that acted on the benefits of this new law, buying over $1 billion of assets itself, according to Subotnick. Hundreds of millions of dollars were raised in the process for Metromedia. This new source of funding was used to launch Metromedia into the nascent cellular phone business in 1983.

Selling Airtime

The average person on the street may simply label broadcasting an "entertainment" or "media" business. From a purely business point of view, it is actually a sales business. The audiences attracted by broadcast programming are sold to advertisers to market their messages. The size and makeup of the audience determines the value of the advertising sold. Plain and simple.

The best-kept secret most broadcasters are all too happy to reveal is that most senior managers come up through the sales ranks, not the programming side. "Yes, there is a great need for talent, both on the air and behind the scenes, but the truth of the matter is that the overwhelming majority of managers come out of sales. You will never hear this being told to university students, because it's just not sexy enough," notes Dick Novik.

The fundamental need to constantly improve sales techniques would become one of the unifying factors among NYSBA members. Of the deep portfolio of services NYSBA has offered to its members over the last 50 years, sales seminars and training workshops are among the most popular, as has already been noted. While NYSBA members were always eager to listen to the advice of sales motivators brought in by Joe Reilly, many devised their own unique sales strategies to be shared with their colleagues.

Anyone in broadcast sales will tell you the sales process is just the same in a small market as it is in a large market. Tony Malara says the only real difference is the number of zeros: "When I was selling radio time in Watertown, my spots were $4.50. When I was selling time for television in Watertown, the standard spot was $45. As I started opening up offices in Canada and our programming stayed on all night for our Canadian business, I was getting $450 a spot. When I went to CBS, I was involved in setting the price for the 30-second spot during the last episode of M*A*S*H, for which I was vilified in the advertising trade press. It was $450,000 a spot! All you do is add zeroes."

This was one of the lessons Malara would hammer away at with his network sales people. The risks and rewards may be higher at the network level, but the basic challenges remain the same. "You get paid $300,000 in one market and $30,000 in another, but relatively speaking, the problems are the same," points out Malara.

Sales in any industry is tough because of the overriding fear of rejection. When Bob Ausfeld got into the business at WPTR in Albany, the practice of sales was still pretty nuts-and-bolts stuff: "I took the job and got a $150 weekly draw. I was given the Yellow Pages and told to go out and sell. I went out there and started selling and talking to people. It was tough." Most broadcast sales-people quickly learn, however, that sales is not just a numbers game. In broad-casting it is also about helping clients develop "solutions" for their "problems" to close the sale.

What makes sales in broadcasting even tougher is its intangible quality. Broadcasters often joke about selling "air" because they are selling airtime. Be-yond the size of an audience and its approximate demographic makeup, broad-casters relied on their persuasive abilities to capture the imagination of their clients. Radio is often referred to as "the last turf on which an entrepreneur can run," unlike television where advertising is sold strictly based on ratings. For many years, local broadcasters positioned themselves against newspapers as they competed for local ad dollars. Gillman recalls using a technique he picked up from a NYSBA sales seminar: "I would ask potential clients if they knew what Winston's slogan was? The answer would be, 'Winston tastes good like a ciga-rette should.' We pointed out that it's been more than 25 years, at that point in time, since that advertising has been on the air. Then we would ask them what they remembered about an ad in yesterday's paper."

In addition to catchy jingles, broadcasters highlighted the immediacy of radio and the emotional qualities of television, making them both very power-ful media in their own right. Today radio is touted as a medium tailor-made for targeting audiences. Both radio and television are also marketed as the best methods to reach local audiences. To help clients better understand the target-ing potential of broadcasting, Frank Boyle used the "bandwagon effect" as a radio broker at Eastman, pointing out past successes to potential clients: "What we would try to do is use the success stories of related retailers on our air or in radio in general. We told them the reason they use radio is so that they can tar-get their ads to a specific demo, because each radio station has a different format and each radio station appeals to a different age group or a socioeconomic structure." Among the many national and regional advertisers that built their brands in radio were the tiny Good Humor Ice Cream Company, headed by the marketing whiz David J. Mahoney, later head of the huge Norton Simon con-glomerate. Some others included Howard Clothes, Robert Hall Clothiers, Mod-ell Sporting Goods, and the Curry Auto Group.

Understanding a Client's Needs

The most effective sales strategy over the years has undoubtedly been the ability of broadcasters to understand the needs of potential clients. This was a lesson Andrew Langston learned selling insurance, before he became a broadcaster in Rochester: "How do you sell insurance? You sell it by owning it yourself." Langston brought that philosophy into broadcasting by joining local civic organizations as a back channel to discovering both the needs of citizens as well as the needs of local businesses.

Gordon Hastings enjoyed enormous success in the both the radio and television representation business at Katz Media, selling airtime on behalf of broadcasters. Not only was he attempting to sign up new advertising clients, he was also selling his representation services to broadcasters themselves. He attributes his sales success in part to taking the time to understand the mindset of individual broadcasters themselves, not simply the demographic makeup of the market where their station was located. "We had to satisfy the particular uniqueness of their market, as well as the uniqueness of their ownership. One must understand that when we were doing business back in the 1970s, the majority of television and radio stations in America were owned by individuals. They still had the family names over the door. You were talking to the person who had put that television station—or in some cases, that radio station—on the air. There was no anonymity in the business," says Hastings.

For other broadcasters, approaching a potential client meant learning its business from the inside out. Some would actually send their sales staff to conferences and seminars in a variety of industries—including banking, healthcare, and the auto industry—to understand how to better meet the needs of their clients. Broadcasters learned to speak their clients' language, learning each industry's particular jargon. They also came to understand the unique marketing metrics and sales goals of each business sector, helping design more effective advertising campaigns. As radio became more segmented, broadcasters were quick to learn that "one-size" *does not* fit all in terms of promoting clients' products and services.

Adrienne Gaines, general manager of WWRL-AM in New York City, pounds a similar philosophy into her staff, reminding them that if they are going to be successful, advertisers need to be successful first. She trains her staff to act as more of a confidante than salesperson: "Learn about the product. Be able to talk about leather vs. polyester. Understand whom you're pitching. Sample the product. Go in days and weeks before to a bakery and pick up a few things and create a story. Tell them, 'I had some friends over last night and we sampled some of your poundcake, and everybody was asking where we got it from.' One conversation like that will lead you into the door." Gaines also educates her clients on the inner workings of how broadcasting works. She even encourages them to cut part of the spot themselves. She believes it helps them grasp the power of broadcasting while giving a personal touch to their marketing efforts. David

Ogilvie, the patron saint and towering icon of Madison Avenue, once advised, "When all else fails . . . have the client do the ad!"

Unfortunately, from time to time, even the most seasoned sales veterans break a cardinal sales rule, like not taking the time to understand their audience or client. More often than not, the result is failure, bringing overly confident sales reps back down to earth. Maire Mason recalls making that very mistake not all that long ago. She was convinced that her 50-plus audience at WCBS-FM must be interested in losing weight, so she decided to pitch the Essex Weight Loss Center based in Fort Lee, New Jersey. CBS had generally steered away from such advertisers because of the slew of potential liabilities involved, explains Mason: "We had very strict guidelines on weight loss products and weight loss claims. CBS was very concerned about any kind of liability that we could pass on to our listeners." The web was just coming into being at this time, so she managed to get approval for the ad by having a disclaimer posted on the station's website.

Essex finally agreed to air some spots, promising to double up on their advertising every week they hit an effective target. Mason didn't think the campaign could lose. She thought she hit paydirt: "We were ready to go. We had the top guns on this thing; Harry Harrison, Ron Lundy, and Cousin Brucie were going to do live reads. We didn't want to make people feel uncomfortable about themselves. We just wanted to help them get rid of their little extra chunk of fat in a very light and funny way." After the first few spots ran, she expected the switchboard to light up, but to her surprise there was only a minimal response. She couldn't figure it out: "I went to concerts, and there were lots of fat people in this demo. Whichever event we did, all the people there were fat, so I thought they would listen to Cousin Brucie and want to lose weight." The response rate didn't pick up, so Essex stopped advertising. Still perplexed, Mason decided to take a few listener calls to ask them herself if they would consider Essex Weight Loss. She quickly learned a hard lesson; she had her audience pegged all wrong: "They liked who they were. *I* thought they should be thinner. *They* did not think they should be thinner, so therefore it just didn't work. These middle-aged people were just more comfortable with who they were than younger people. I was stunned."

In the quest to form a deeper connection with their audiences, broadcasters have become more focused over the last two decades with regard to the audience they intend to serve. Often called "segmentation," broadcasters, particularly in radio, have carved out a specific niche and then super-serve it. Ramblin' Lou Shriver always knew what he liked, so he built his radio station around country-western music. He believes the future of radio will continue to be about serving a specific niche: "I don't want to have the largest market share, just my own small piece of the pie." When he was starting out, he quickly realized not even his passion for country-western music would be enough to be a success in radio. His station was one of the first country-western formats in the Northeast. Understanding what it was like to broadcast outside of what was perceived as "mainstream programming," George "Hound Dog" Lorenz took Shriver under his wing. Just as the Hound Dog's career was about to take off, he showed Shriver how to sell. Today Ramblin' Lou proudly shares his sales philosophy: "As I always say, I sell results, not ratings." From beginning to end, his entire sales process is gently moved along by his personal touch. After reading his sponsors' commercials he always adds, "Tell 'em Lou sent you." He understands that advertising is typically the last bill a small business owner can pay, so he kills them with kindness: "If you are too heavy handed they won't pay, but if you are nice they always end up paying."

Deals Sealed on a Handshake

The "personal touch" may sound like an anomaly today, but it was simply how business was done throughout much of broadcast history. There was a time when a handshake was all a broadcaster literally needed to close a deal, says Jim Greenwald: "I would shake hands with the buyer of an advertising agency and thank him for his $20,000 order. I would write up the order and the station would confirm. This was all before any papers were signed. It was a 'trust me, trust you' business. Everybody trusted everybody else. There was never, ever a problem."

The mores of small-town life permitted Jim Rodgers to finalize all his deals with just a verbal agreement, just as Greenwald was able to do: "In 35 years I had one business, with whom I asked to sign a contract. The rest of them were all verbal agreements. The guy I made sign a contract called us up twice after making a verbal agreement and canceled on us. After that I just insisted he sign a contract, but everything else was done on a handshake." Broadcasters could rely on just a handshake because they were a part of the communities they served and personally knew their clients. Many of them were lifelong residents of their community. Their business relationships weren't based on numbers and contracts but rather on words, handshakes, and their own sincerity. Broadcasters practically invented a new form of contract: They always called it "an agreement" with a TFN, "till further notice," end date. "This way the pressure is on us to deliver" went the chant.

Recognizing that their success was directly tied to the health of the local economy, broadcasters took a genuine interest in helping out small business owners. After all, they were one too. "I always felt they were working as hard as I was to make a living, so I tried to get their advertising, but did it in a way that their advertising wasn't running their business," explains Jim Rodgers. He and his wife, Keela, created sponsorship "opportunities" to accommodate small business owners, who weren't necessarily a huge source of revenue for their station. "We took care of the little guy. Some of my accounts had just two or three spots a week," says Keela Rodgers.

Local businesses are regarded more as "partners" than "clients," in the view of Don Angelo. His philosophy reinforces the idea that the financial health of local broadcasting is directly related to the economic health of the local community. It's not just a nice-sounding sales pitch, but something he truly lives out in his business life. Practicing what he preaches, he once helped save a local furniture company in Buffalo from financial ruin: "Rose's Home Stores, they're a local family-owned appliance and furniture chain. They really grew to a point where they were a big-time player in the market, competing with the big 800-pound gorilla national chains. We've worked with them for over a decade. They had a disaster a couple of years ago. One of the stores caught on fire, which just devastated it. It was their biggest and newest store. Everything was ruined, and in the process, one of the employees died in the fire."

The owner was deeply distraught. Unsure if he was going to be able to bounce back from the fire, he considered going out of business. To help, Angelo's station, WGRZ-TV, ran thousands of dollars of advertising, free of charge, over a three-month period. "We did whatever we could to work with him, to support him, and to try to get him back on his feet. Today, that store has re-opened, and he's planning on opening another store in the Galleria Mall right here in Buffalo. He's getting healthy again, and his business is thriving."

Broadcast Sales Strategies

Unlike inventory in other industries, anything that isn't used today can't be sold tomorrow in broadcasting. It just disappears. An old boss of John Kelly's once described broadcast inventory as "an elevator that goes up and down every single day." As a result there is always a danger of undervaluing broadcast inventory. Over the years, broadcasters have devised a variety of techniques to get fair value for their airtime. Drawing on his background in programming, Ed Levine believes in carving out niches to drive value for his sales efforts, much like Ramblin' Lou Shriver: "Very simply, revenues chase ratings, not the other way around. If you have ratings, then you have an audience, and you'll find your revenues. In the end you need to do creative, unique programming." He says he's been creating niches around specific audiences for advertisers to buy into, rather than the commodity type of selling he has seen the industry trend toward.

The simple management of how airtime is used also helps increase its value. "Starving" inventory or reducing commercials is one method. Reducing the supply will increase the demand price for each available spot. Jim Rodgers believes that the abandonment of the original FCC guidelines on advertising has contributed to the commodity-type selling today: "I stuck to the original rules. When I was selling spots, I think you could have 18 minutes an hour of commercials. There's no such rule anymore. I never believed in doing any more than double-spotting at the most. Now you have blocks of five and six commercials back to back!" Most broadcasters of Rodgers' era hold the same philosophy, never airing commercial breaks longer than two minutes and limiting each break to no more than three commercials. They also never countenanced playing two advertisers of the same category, like car dealers, in the same commercial break, never mind back to back. More often than not, each advertiser is given a measure of "exclusivity" without fear of having its competitors' commercials airing in the same break.

Many veteran broadcasters deride the current practice of selling airtime as a "commodity" simply based on price. Most of them enhanced the value of their revenues by delivering tangible results to their clients, not just a mass audience or particular demographic alone, as many stations do today. Rochester broadcaster Bud Wertheimer also helped pioneer another concept, called "demand pricing," to increase the value of each commercial spot. Basically, the price of the unit rate increased as it got closer and closer to its airdate: "We were pricing the morning drive at, let's say, $46 six weeks out. If it was bought just one week out, that $46 rate was up to $62. Here's the funny thing; if we raised that rate to $47 six or eight weeks out, the rate would rise to $70 if it was bought just one week out. This occurred because of the pressures of demand. Frankly, as you kept raising the price, the pressures of demand kept you sold out." This approach to pricing would also keep commercial loads down, appeasing the listener, as well as increasing the awareness of an advertiser's message. "I'd rather not be sold out than lose on price," says Wertheimer. "It's pure supply and demand. Today there is an unlimited amount of inventory." Wertheimer's stations in Rochester and Buffalo at times may have only had a 10 share but commanded 20% of the local ad dollars using this strategy. They had the lightest commercial loads in town, but demanded the highest unit rate.

From an industrywide perspective, Gary Fries, president and chief executive of the Radio Advertising Bureau, sees a growing trend toward "accountability" in radio advertising and a move away from "commodity" selling. "Today a chief marketing officer of a major corporation could not survive if he or she could account only for 50% of the value of his or her broadcast advertising buy. It all leads to the marketing buzzword "return on investment" (ROI), and that's the driving factor," explains Fries. With each passing day, there are more and more emerging technologies to help advertisers track the return on every dollar spent on broadcast advertising. In the early days of broadcasting, all an advertiser needed to know was that a program attracted the majority of the viewing or listening audience at a given time. Today every piece of demographic data is scrutinized.

Thinking Outside the Box

Managing inventory certainly had its role in helping to make advertising messages more special or valuable, but it was the innovative sales campaigns broadcasters devised for their clients that truly delivered remarkable results. One Christmas, Pat Tocatlian pitched an idea to a local furniture store to build some foot traffic: "I suggested putting a Christmas tree in the store and have all the customers put a tag on it with their name. Then the store would draw tags off this tree the week before Christmas and they would get a prize. In the meantime, our station would promote the contest like crazy." The owner liked the idea, but he didn't have a Christmas tree, so Tocatlian brought hers to the store and put tags all over it. It was a huge success and an example of how to capture the imagination of a client.

Long Island broadcaster Paul Sidney is all too familiar with Tocatlian's sales techniques, broadcasting his show live countless times on location at local businesses and events. He believes that broadcasters today rely too much on numbers: "Not every broadcaster pays enough attention to their advertisers; they just go by statistics. They may be number one, but they have no idea how many people they brought into a store to buy the goods."

It goes without saying there was some healthy competition between broadcasters, particularly in the same market, but they also frequently shared ideas on how to make their business better. Phil Spencer recalls learning about an unexpected new category of sponsors: "A friend of mine in Newburgh used to carry obituaries on the air, paid for by undertakers." His friend told him he made $7,000 a year in obituary announcements. Always open to new ideas, Spencer decided to start running obituaries and selling funeral services himself. His first year, he made $6,000 with obituaries. "I had a waiting list for sponsors to get on. I was sold out." He also ran a diverse collection of ethnic programming, including Lithuanian, Polish, Italian, and Puerto Rican. He reached out to the churches in each community to sell sponsorships for his obituaries. "Friends of mine—broadcasters driving on their way through from Buffalo, Syracuse, Rochester, and Albany—would come through listening to my station and say, 'What the heck are you doing? I heard obituaries, I heard polkas. . . .' I would tell them, 'You want to take a look at my books. . . . I'll show you what I'm doing.'"

Managing a public radio station doesn't relieve Alan Chartock of the responsibility of sales. "We've had our battles, but Alan has done an unbelievable job. I don't know very many public broadcasters who can raise the kind of money he can raise," comments John Kelly. Last year the station raised $600,000. Chartock explains his tactics: "I noticed that the wackier I got on the phone drives, like if I played 'The 2,000 Year Old Man' or read *The Little Engine That Could*, people would respond to it. If you make fund drives interesting, people will come." While he has a regional network of stations, his coverage is still relatively small compared with that of New York City, but that hasn't prevented his station from finding its way among the Top-20 public radio stations in the nation in terms of fundraising.

In the 1970s, rather than looking at broadcast and print as mutually exclusive, Gordon Hastings helped pioneer the concept of "cross-platform" selling. "We did it very early on. We called it the 'media mix.' Not only did we package radio and television, but we also packaged radio, television, and newspapers together." Approaching sales in this manner enabled Gordon to highlight the strengths of broadcasting and how those attributes could complement print advertising. The Katz research department developed frequency programs to show advertisers how they could increase their "unduplicated reach" by spreading their advertising buy more equitably across various different media rather than weighting their budget more heavily toward one or another. Hastings offers an example: "We would go into a major department store in a local community, and we'd say, 'Look, we understand you're spending 90% of your budget in the local paper, but let's just show you what happens if you take this budget and reallocate it among newspaper, radio, and television.' Then we would show them how many more unique people they would be reaching as a result."

Promotions and Remotes

"The reason I do so many remotes is to get to the people. It's not that I give great big prizes away. In other words to me it's an image-maker. Of course we make money doing the remotes or I wouldn't do them. We do a lot of public service remotes, too," shares Paul Sidney on his enthusiasm for broadcasting his show on location within his local community. Broadcasters frequently produced live radio programs called "remotes," onsite, at county fairs, malls, fundraisers, and many other local events outside their usual studios. Sidney still averages between 200 and 250 remotes a year. Special promotions and remotes have been and still are the foundation from which radio and television stations market themselves. They are the primary vehicle to break through "the clutter" and to bring broadcasting closer to the people, as noted by Sidney.

These stunts, gimmicks, and shenanigans showcased the creativity of broadcasters from both a business and programming perspective, but all of it should be viewed as a move toward the listener and viewer. Broadcasters frequently teamed up with a local car dealer to organize a contest to give away a car. Through the years, car dealers have typically represented the largest share of local broadcasters' total revenues, up to a third in many cases. Pat Tocatlian recalls conducting a contest with a local car dealer that didn't turn out quite the way it was supposed to: "A local Plymouth dealer had a giveaway. You had to put your hands on the car . . . and the person able to keep his hands on the longest would win. In the end I think the owner of the dealership gave away $1,000 to each of the last contestants left because *he* couldn't wait any longer. I mean he didn't even get to give away the car because *he*, himself, was so tired and wanted to go home!"

Remotes often were used as a special service to take care of a broadcaster's best clients. Caprino's, a local furniture store in Jamestown, would be one of WJTN's most important sponsors. In the 36 years of their relationship, Jim Roselli estimates he has done well over 1,000 shows on location at Caprino's.

Promotions were Al Anscombe's secret weapon for building radio and television stations: "My background is in promotion, that's why we were so successful with Channel 7. We would hide the keys to a Cadillac in a mailbox, and we'd give clues where people could find them." When he took over WKBW-AM, the owner, Reverend Churchill, was losing approximately $300,000 a year. Relying on good service and promotions, Anscombe turned the station around. After his first year as manager, the station broke even. The following year it made a profit of $300,000.

As Jim Delmonico built up WRGB during the 1960s and 1970s, the novelty of television had yet to wear off. People were still fascinated and ecstatic if they saw someone they knew on television. "I used to send the news guys out every day and tell them I wanted each crew to get shots of people walking in and out of drug stores or whatever. We'd tell people that if they saw a guy with the camera peeping out of a van, they were going to be on television that night," says Delmonico. His station would use the footage as "bumpers," just before commercials or during the open and close of their newscasts throughout the day. People called to ask when they might be on. They were told they would just have to watch or they could request a tape. It was an ingenious way of personally interacting with individual members of the community and making them feel the magic of broadcasting. In recent years, as today's children have grown up with many different media outlets, Bill Jaker, a producer at WSKG-TV in Binghamton and co-author of *Airwaves of New York* with Peter Kanze and Frank Sulek, observes that people now have a much more pedestrian view of broadcasting:

"When I started in this business, if you were going to put somebody on television or radio, they got all excited. They take it in stride now. Many times I'll walk into somebody's home along with the crew, setting up the lights and cameras and start moving things around. It really doesn't faze them."

Delmonico also used a variety of other simple gimmicks that ingratiated WRGB's brand into his community: "We used to buy T-shirts with the NBC peacock on them before we switched affiliations and had Channel 6 on the back. Every school kid in Schenectady was wearing those shirts, and we were getting free promotion. We bought them for a buck each. We would also send balloons to the school with Channel 6 on them . . . inexpensive things like that, but they would get us a lot of attention."

The best-produced promotions not only help market a station or drive revenue for a sponsor but also actually create a local event for a community. Each year Ernie Anastos' stations upstate in the Saratoga region take the idea of producing remotes a step further by actually organizing bridal fairs, health fairs, and children's fairs. They are community events that help small businesses showcase their wares while establishing the radio station as the voice of the community. According to Anastos, the larger goal is to create a bond with local citizens: "We sponsor these events during the year at different shopping malls. It's very important to be part of that community because once they know you're the voice and source for information on a local level, there's a connection."

Management Philosophies

The management philosophies and labor practices of radio and television owners and executives were guided more by common sense than overly complicated management theories devised by business schools. For many, management simply meant treating their employees, clients, and community with respect, taking the time to listen and addressing their needs.

From its humble beginnings, Capital Cities' management approach was very straightforward, explains Phil Beuth: "We really believed there were no short cuts in the television business. Capital Cities was a 'clean' company. It started right at the top with Tom Murphy. I helped him write a speech in 1960 based on the theme 'You get no second chance at CapCities.' If you embarrass us in any way or bring any kind of embarrassment to the company, or yourself, you're gone." Beuth said over the years CapCities would lose a few people because of that policy. It would become a trademark of how business was to be conducted. Beuth said the company was also guided by a kind of unwritten mission statement: "When you do well, you should do good." CapCities employees came to believe that if they did "good" for their communities and clients, they would do "well" for the company's bottom line. The legendary financial "Sage of Omaha," Warren Buffett, a CapCities director, was frequently quoted as saying, "The only thing missing on CapCities' balance sheet was its integrity."

Passion is a vital component in the management philosophy of Adrienne Gaines. It is the energy source that runs through all her transactions and relationships, creating the bond between her team and the people they serve: "I believe in passion. If my managers don't have any passion for their job, they can't work for me. They've got to exude passion and a really strong work ethic." She believes it is the secret weapon to help broadcasters cut through the monotony of today's media landscape. "That's going to be the challenge going forward, the ability to exude that passion to our local listenership. If that all works, then the advertising piece will work. It will help keep the value of our advertising very high."

In sales it is important to stand your ground and be tough when necessary, otherwise the value of the advertising you are selling will be diminished. There were many situations in which the affable Tony Malara had to get tough, but for him it was equally important to listen to an opposing viewpoint: "When you left my office or a meeting with me, you may not have liked the response or the conclusion, but there was never any doubt in your mind as to how I felt. My first obligation was to make sure I listened." He admits that as he acquired more and more influence and rose through the ranks of CBS, the temptation to impose his will also increased. He constantly reminded himself to listen first. Earlier in his career, a colleague would advise him how to open up his ears: "Don't say 'but.' When somebody's talking to you and you say 'Yeah . . . but,' you're dismissing his or her point of view immediately. What you should be saying is 'and,' to be more inclusive of their point of view." Thereafter, Malara recalls saying "and" quite a lot.

Many managers also did their best to make themselves available and keep in touch with the needs of their staff or clients. To encourage open communication among his employees, Dick Novik always believed in leading by example: "As a manager, my door was always open. What I found is that regardless of being upstate or downstate, people are always coming into your office and talking about the most important thing on their mind . . . and that's their own problems."

There is nothing more important than creating a sense of teamwork in broadcasting. Maire Mason has found that building teams in radio is one of the most rewarding aspects of her career: "I like the whole idea of building a team, having your team 'colors' so to speak. You know . . . radio is very fragmented, so you need something that's cohesive among your group. You go out there and it's very competitive. It reminds me a lot of college basketball." Each individual member of a broadcast operation has his or her part to play on the court of informing or entertaining the audience. Without programmers and producers there would be no reason for people to tune to a radio station or television channel. Engineers are needed to maintain the broadcast signal to deliver programming to millions of receivers. Without the sales staff, there would be no financial support for the entire operation.

Teams, however, only truly thrive when managers have complete confidence in them and know when to get out of their way. "Hiring the best possible people you can find and giving them the authority to do their job is what we did. I really enjoyed that. I got a great deal of satisfaction out of seeing our people grow in their responsibilities and in their performance," remarks the great Tom Murphy on his management style.

At a young age, Frank Lorenz found himself in control of his father's radio station when "The Hound" died suddenly in 1972 at the age of 52. Many in the business counted Frank out, predicting he would have to sell the station within a year. In his heart of hearts, he knew he had to keep the station going because of everything his father worked so hard to build. He says he found success simply by having confidence in the people he hired: "I identified my strengths and weaknesses and hired the right people. I ended up having good counsel, and everything just fell into place."

John Kelly used a similar technique, never being afraid to delegate. Broadcasting has its fair share of high-powered egos, but that just wasn't his style: "I've met a lot of people in this business who are geniuses but who impose their will on everything because they think they know everything. I never really pretended I knew very much, so I would always get good people and let them do the job."

The very best managers understood that not only was it important to stay out of the day-to-day tasks of their employees but to give them a sense of "ownership" in the overall vision of the company as well. Jim Greenwald quite literally did just that, giving Katz employees a chance to participate in the success of the company: "We certainly felt that if an employee owned a piece of the company, he or she would work harder. He or she would be part of the action." During the 1980s, the company did very well financially. It did so well, many employees started to retire, cashing in their stock. Eventually Katz ended up paying out the same amount to its retirees as it was taking in. Ironically, they had to abandon the program over time because the more financially successful the company became, the more money it cost them.

Stock options, profit sharing, and other employee ownership programs weren't the only methods available to give individuals a sense of ownership over their daily work life. At ABC, Ed McLaughlin held the view that the role of senior management was to provide a road map for the company, but to let individuals decide on the best vehicle to arrive at the final destination: "One of the reasons I loved working at ABC is that if you had an idea you could bring it to New York headquarters or bring it to your superiors and lay it out for them. If they agreed, they supported you 100%. There was very little second-guessing. They would give you a timetable, and you knew it would be realistic. If you were successful, they applauded and reimbursed you. I think that is important, to be working under conditions where you can really accomplish something." Of course, this management philosophy comes under pressure, admits McLaughlin, when a company is unable to take financial gambles or is very short-sighted.

When it comes to managing change, broadcasters have typically chosen one of two paths. Either they resisted it, as many AM stations did with the advent of FM, or they accepted it, as television broadcasters did when they switched from film to tape. As former CBS radio executive Nancy Widmann puts it: "You choose to see change coming or you don't." Too often, tried and true methods or formulas have lulled broadcasters into complacency. The most successful broadcast managers have understood that their focus should not be on mastering the intricacies of the business model du jour but rather in looking for the best way to serve the changing needs of their audience. Wally Schwartz has seen his fair share of managers unable to make the transition: "I've seen a lot of guys who are perfect for their job for a time but weren't quite sure how to make the transition. Change in broadcasting is not like pulling down a shade. It doesn't happen overnight." Managers who choose to see change coming will be able to take the leadership position in a new paradigm rather than wasting their time jockeying for position in the old one.

On the whole, New York broadcasters, through the years, have striven to make a comfortable living *and* to run financially healthy companies. Broadcast management isn't something that can be taught out of a book but is rather a collection of experiences and examples gathered through the years. The most successful managers in broadcasting are those who have a deep understanding of themselves and their values. Their sense of what they are willing to compromise on and what they aren't is what guides their overall decision-making process. All too often, broadcasters merely follow each other. Some say it's a "copycat" business. Once you understand who you are and where you want to go, the rest becomes clear. Ralph Guild, chief executive officer of Interep, recommends taking risks: "Be willing to take risks; don't just go by the book and do the same stuff over and over again." The great achievements of New York's broadcasters over the last 50 years that have served as a beacon to push broadcasting to even greater heights, are born from taking chances, not from embracing mediocrity. For individual broadcasters, the road less traveled has undoubtedly provided many exciting and colorful experiences that few other career paths can offer, as countless New York broadcasters can attest.

5

The Mission: Informing and Entertaining

> "Announcers who broadcast to an audience are like an artist with a paint brush; they paint a picture in the minds of the people listening to them."
>
> —John Zach, announcer, WBEN-AM, Buffalo

In the eyes of the audience, programming is like the tip of an iceberg in broadcasting. It conjures up memories in the minds of New Yorkers of sharing their daily routine with on-air personalities, eating their breakfast, driving off to work, or settling in for a relaxing evening with their "invited guest." Most are blissfully unaware of the inner workings that make radio and television possible, mundane but necessary things like tower maintenance, advertising sales or newsgathering. They judge broadcasting simply by what they see or hear, as well they should. Even the most seasoned broadcasters can't help but get caught up in the excitement when the larger-than-life faces and voices of New York broadcasting pay a visit to NYSBA's Annual Meeting and Executive Conference. Over the last 50 years some of those luminaries included Dan Rather, Charles Osgood, Chris Matthews, Larry King, William B. Williams, Maureen O'Boyle, Jane Pauley, Rush Limbaugh, Tim Russert, and Geraldo Rivera.

Radio and television entertain and inform audiences, but the subtleties of their characters have forged different and distinct relationships with listeners and viewers. "Radio is a more ambient, a more ongoing part of our lives, whereas television is more appointment driven," observes David Hinckley, radio reporter for the *New York Daily News*. Radio has often been referred to as the "theater of the mind," as broadcasters masterfully guide listeners through their own unique version of a story. In its earliest days, television was described as "radio with pictures." It evolved to become more of a passive medium than radio, but had the unique advantage of enabling the audience to become an immediate eyewitness to history.

Both radio and television have extended human companionship to those who have become withdrawn from society for whatever reason. For others, broadcasting occasionally serves as "background noise," keeping the listener or viewer company with familiar chatter. Jerry Gillman, former owner of WDST in Woodstock, believes true broadcasting is about listening, not hearing: "As far as programming is concerned, people turn on the radio and tune in to what they want to listen to. Not to 'hear' but to 'listen.' Hearing is background noise, while listening is something you specifically want. That's how we built a very successful following."

New York's first generation of broadcasters was offered no guidebook on how to create programming in the embryonic mediums of radio or television. They were forced to draw on their training from vaudeville, the theater, film or the concert stage, translating their talents as they established the boundaries of these new mediums. By the 1950s, the second generation of broadcasters began to emerge, building on the foundation laid by the first generation. In the opinion of WSKG-TV producer Bill Jaker, it was this second generation who were the most effective broadcasters: "They nurtured their own talent. All the techie stuff they had to worry about, like which camera was on, which microphone was on, or how quickly you could move on camera, became second nature. As a result, they were able to direct their own personalities, fine-tuning them to the nature of broadcasting. It is a gift that has to be nurtured."

Reinventing Radio Formats

The number of hours of network radio programming peaked in 1954. By the end of that decade, network radio, as it had been known, became history. Radio was blindsided by the overnight success of television. At first, popular radio shows were simulcast on television, eventually making the full transition to the new medium. The last radio soap operas went off the air by 1960. Popular variety programs like Arthur Godfrey on CBS and Don McNeil's "Breakfast Club" on ABC were among the last golden embers of network radio. By 1956, there was more news programming than any other format on radio, providing an indication as to the future of the medium. President Dwight D. Eisenhower's initiative to build thousands of miles of highways at this time also provided a glimpse of how radio's role would change. Americans were madly in love with their cars. They embraced the new "on the go" culture, and radio was the medium they would take along with them. By 1960, almost 70% of all cars had a radio.

Without the programming resources of the networks to draw on, individual radio stations were forced to become more self-reliant than they had ever been. They would turn to local news and their own home-brewed music programs for survival. Radio networks still offered hourly news updates and coverage of breaking news, but local stations supplemented their coverage, using "rip n' read" copy from wire services, as well as their own local news coverage. Many stations used an MOR or "middle of the road" music format in an attempt to provide something for everyone. The strings of Mantovani and the lush, romantic ballads of the Jackie Gleason studio orchestra found great currency on the airwaves, along with the Ray Conniff singers. *Radio & Records* publisher Erica Farber, explains: "Most radio stations 25 years ago used formats that were much more general. A Top-40 radio station was not only listened to by a teenager but by the mother of that teenager as well. Today it's much more segmented, so you don't have just one, big format."

The rise of FM in the 1970s broke those MOR conventions, turning radio into a segmented medium as stations began to identify themselves according to specific formats like news, talk, rock, jazz or country-western music. The segmentation trend encouraged a greater diversity of programming in radio, points out Farber: "Within the music format, they became much more targeted, resulting in more diversity of programming. There was a truer reflection of the demographics in individual markets as well—not only mainstream demographics but also those of African Americans, Hispanics, and Asians, reflecting the real population of urban areas in particular."

It would take almost 40 years for the superior technology of FM to unseat the AM band as king of the dial, but looking back, many broadcasters will argue that AM lost out to FM because of programming, not simply because of advanced technology. Many AM stations failed to keep up with the times and were slow to meet the changing tastes and sensibilities of their audience.

Some AM broadcasters chose to meet the FM challenge head on, developing new programming techniques to prove that people tune in for programming, not merely because of a variation in technology as between AM or FM. FM radio tended to gravitate toward music-based programming, taking advantage of its superior sound quality compared with AM. To keep their ratings up, programmers at FM stations focused on their "quarter-hour maintenance." The "Average Quarter Hour" (AQH) is defined by Artbitron as "the number of users tuning in for at least 5 minutes in an average 15-minute period of time (quarter hour) during the reported time period." Basically, program directors tried to determine how many "quarter hours" people listen to each day, as well as how many people were tuned in at a given time during the day. To do so, stations would "tease" or promote the upcoming music set or program segment in the next quarter hour.

They would also mix their music in such a way as to not drive people away. All this was done to keep up the all-important "quarter-hour maintenance."

AM was a slightly different animal by the mid-1980s in that most of its programming was sports and news. Talk began to emerge as a format as well. As programming changed on AM, some broadcasters developed an alternative to "quarter-hour maintenance" to better accommodate the nuances of AM programs, called "cumulative maintenance." For example, if an AM station was broadcasting a baseball game, as soon as the umpire called the last out, that station would lose most of its audience, unless it had another baseball game on. Essentially, AM stations were constantly building and losing, building and losing their audience throughout the day. This, of course, was before the advent of talk radio. Instead of promoting the next show, AM broadcasters began to cater to their listeners' tastes by promoting other shows in their lineup that would appeal to them. If it was during a sports broadcast, sports-related shows airing later that day or even throughout the week would be promoted.

After consolidation, Interep head Ralph Guild believes radio has actually become less segmented: "Before consolidation, a lot of individual broadcasters within the same market were experimenting with new formats. Now the formats are determined more frequently by a national program director." For example, there may have been two different rock stations in the same market with a slight variation on how the same genre of music was presented, but now there is probably only one rock station in a given market. Erica Farber explains: "The days of head-to-head, direct-format competitors are gone for the most part, especially in a cluster where most of the radio stations are owned by the same group. Some people will argue that because there is a lack of direct competition within a particular format, the excitement or uniqueness of that format could suffer a little bit. I think that is a valid point."

Guild doesn't believe that all programming has necessarily become "cookie-cutter," as many of his peers would argue. However, he does think there is a lot less experimentation today. "Organizations are bigger now, and they have more resources to determine which formats are more likely to attract listeners. The business is more formularized today because of computers and the vast knowledge base of music research. We just know more than we did 20 years ago."

Developing Television Programming

Technology would exert a large influence over how television was produced in its earliest forms. For example, most programs were broadcast live, giving viewers an almost theaterlike viewing experience. In 1953, almost 80% of programs were live before the transition to tape began in the 1960s. Popular formats like variety hours, dramas, comedies, and music were plucked right from radio. At that time, most of the programming was produced by sponsors, advertising agencies, and local stations, not by the networks.

As production costs began to skyrocket in the 1960s, program development shifted from advertisers to the networks. Originally produced local programming would also fall into decline. By 1960, local stations across the country reduced their live local programming from 22% in 1955 to 11%, and increased network schedules from 48% to 61%. Local stations produced a wonderful smorgasbord of programs, including children's shows, public affairs programs, news broadcasts, and special coverage of local events. Jane Barton, a former reporter with *Variety*, recalls when local stations even created local programming specifically aimed at women: "Almost every station had a half-hour women's show. For example, in Schenectady, Martha Brooks had her own program for 40 years. She was on since the beginning of television. The stations took those women for granted because they had to do *all* their own producing, packaging, and selling."

As time went on, local television stations not only came to rely more heavily on the networks for programming but also resorted to syndicated programs and old films to fill their off-network hours. This was particularly true of many UHF and independent stations that had fewer resources to create original programming and no network affiliation to rely on for programming. Prior to the 1970s, as popular "off-network" shows (programs already aired on the networks) went into syndication, most affiliated stations turned their noses up at them, thinking no one would want to watch something they already saw. They couldn't have been more wrong, notes former Katz Media executive Gordon Hastings: "When M*A*S*H went into syndication in 1976, who bought M*A*S*H? The independents bought it. Guess what happened? It became the birth of independent television as we know it today."

Metromedia, owner of one of the largest independent television groups, knew the odds were stacked against it in terms of building a fourth network. However, it saw the potential of syndicated shows as an alternative strategy, says Stuart Subotnick: "We counterprogrammed the networks by acquiring such programs as 'I Love Lucy' and 'M*A*S*H' against the networks' news and prime-time programming. We wound up creating a significant audience that way."

According to Hastings, the syndication of M*A*S*H generated dramatic results for independent stations: "It took independent stations from hash marks in the ratings books and catapulted them into the marketplace." As this trend gained momentum through the early 1980s, Katz Media decided to build another firm dedicated to representing independent television stations called "Katz Independent Television Sales." As more syndicated programming became available, it now had a place to go. Independent television stations would evolve from running old movies no one wanted to watch to airing first-run programming and affiliating themselves with emerging networks like FOX, UPN, and WB in the 1990s. Fledgling cable networks would borrow the programming strategy of independent television stations by airing reruns throughout the 1980s, becoming formidable competitors to the broadcast networks by the turn of the century.

The Role of Broadcast Journalism

News and public affairs programming provided by New York's broadcasters was one of the most obvious expressions of their duties and responsibilities as dictated by their licenses. News coverage also provides the most direct link between broadcasters and their audiences, particularly at the local level. More often than not, news is more intently consumed by the audience, compared with entertainment programming, because it directly affects their daily lives. Whether listening to traffic reports, the weather or the results of a local bond referendum, people have depended on broadcasting as a source of immediate local information. It provides a sense of belonging to a larger community, as well as providing urgent information or even comfort in times of crisis.

Over the last 50 years there have been a variety of approaches on how best to cover the news, from experimenting with new formats to defining the boundaries within which broadcasters should involve their editorial opinion in news stories. As radio's entertainment programs were derailed by television in the 1950s, radio became more and more reliant on local news programming as it found its new voice. Radio legends like Edward R. Murrow and Eric Severeid would make the move to "radio with pictures," the new visual medium of television. At this time, network television news programming was limited to 15-minute updates broadcast each evening. By 1963 the networks extended their daily news broadcast to half an hour. Walter Cronkite on CBS competed with NBC's Chet Huntley and David Brinkley. ABC didn't find success with its own anchor team until 1970 when Harry Reasoner left CBS to team up with Howard K. Smith.

As with other professional journalists, broadcasters constantly struggled with decisions about which stories to cover and the extent to which they should be covered. While at WBEN-TV, Bill McKibben's news judgment was rooted in making his coverage as reflective of his community as possible: "I used to say to people we are nothing but a mirror. We mirror what is interesting to the community. We can tint that mirror a rosy color, but as soon as I change it, nobody's going to watch anymore. Nobody's going to listen. I think that's still true."

A set percentage of nonentertainment programming was once required by the FCC on all broadcasters' schedules. Typically, this came in the form of news.

Most stations used a general format or played music. For Utica broadcaster Paul Dunn, knowing where to schedule news in his programming lineup to meet the FCC requirement was always a challenge. His mentor R. Peter Straus taught him: "Since everybody has to have news, even if your audience wasn't tuning in for the news, the better the job you did as a newscaster, the better your audience would be for it." Dunn took pride in his news coverage. As owner of WTLB-AM, his news department consisted of four people, four more than most stations today. On one occasion, while having lunch with the editor of a local paper, the print journalist accused Dunn of costing him too much money because of the radio station's extensive news coverage: "I asked him how so, and he responded, 'Well you assigned a reporter to cover the county office building recently, so now I have to go hire a reporter to do the same thing. I said to him, 'Isn't that too bad?' Who wins? Obviously the public wins."

Many broadcast journalists viewed their role as an objective participant in the process of allowing the audience to become a witness to history and to make judgments for themselves. Print journalists had only words and an occasional grainy picture to rely on to recreate the atmosphere surrounding an event, increasing the possibility of their own personal judgment creeping into their coverage. In broadcasting, on the other hand, there is less opportunity to misquote or misinterpret an event. For these reasons, former Senator Alfonse D'Amato has always preferred communicating with New Yorkers via the broadcast media: "One of the incredible things about broadcasting is it gives you an opportunity to be heard in an uncensored manner."

In the present age of 24/7 news coverage, it is hard to believe that television news was once limited to just a daily 15-minute newscast by the networks. Local news programming is now the primary driver of revenue at local stations. Economic pressures have fostered the explosion of local news over the last decade, with some stations programming as much as seven hours of local news a day. Shell Storrier questions the wisdom of so much local news: "WKTV-TV is the only television station that does local news in Utica, but they do it from 5 p.m. until 6:30 p.m. Is it really necessary to do an hour and a half of news in Utica, New York? Many would agree in the affirmative."

Covering the News

In a rural community like Batavia, just to the east of Buffalo, the major news broadcast of the day went on at 12:30 p.m., when all the farmers went home for lunch. WBTA had only one news editor to compete against the local newspaper's team of reporters. The news editor at WBTA nervously waited for the local paper to come out at 1 p.m., recalls Bill Brown Jr., former owner of WBTA: "If the news editor didn't cover the right stories, people would read them in the newspaper that afternoon, then it was a *really* bad day for him."

In the age of satellites, most local broadcasters today depend on satellite feeds for much of their news programming. There was a time when local broadcasters like Jerry and Sasha Gillman had their own eyes and ears to the ground, working on behalf of their community. To keep their finger on the pulse of state and national affairs, WDST had its own stringers (freelance reporters) in both Albany and Washington. Its dedication to news would pay off handsomely in the form of a scoop of a lifetime, explains Jerry Gillman: "When President Reagan was shot, there was only one reporter in the hospital, WDST's reporter. When our guy heard the news that Reagan had been shot, he figured out which hospital they would be going to and got there before the motorcade. He got into the hospital and was the only one on the scene."

WDST made its coverage available to all the other NYSBA member stations. It wouldn't be the last scoop they shared with their fellow broadcasters. Jerry Gillman does recall an instance in which there was a public station that didn't take to his philosophy of sharing the wealth: "We had a scoop of some sort, which I always made available to NYSBA members. I got a call from a public radio station, and they wanted to know if they could have it, too. I said to them, 'Can I use any of your programming?' They said to me, 'Certainly not.' I said, 'Then I guess you know my answer, too.'"

According to Albany public broadcaster Alan Chartock, the rivalry between public and commercial stations in terms of news coverage is less intense than it was when he arrived on the scene over 25 years ago in 1979: "Commercial broadcasters didn't think it was fair that we should be able to receive underwriting and federal funding when they saw us as direct competitors." Through the years, tensions between public and commercial stations have eased. "What we're finding is that we never hear commercial broadcasters complaining about us anymore . . . *ever*," says Chartock. He believes their objections have been quieted because of the evolving landscape of radio: "I think one of the things that's happened is that we have taken an even larger role in news and public affairs at a time when commercial broadcasters have shifted their focus elsewhere. Our news division alone has 10 people. This would be unheard of at a commercial station." Some in the industry also point to NPR's sharp rise in the ratings over the last few years as an indication of its commitment to local news programming.

Innovative News Programming

One of the most revolutionary approaches in news programming was the development of the "Eyewitness News" format by Al Primo to promote diversity within a community. He first experimented with the concept at KYW in Philadelphia in 1965. In those days, if someone's hand so much as appeared on television for just a matter of seconds, he or she was entitled to a talent fee. As a result, to keep costs under control, televisions stations could afford only anchors, not reporters. When Primo reviewed the American Federation of Television and Radio Artists (AFTRA) contract on his arrival as news director of KYW, he noticed a clause that stated that any member of AFTRA could write, report, and appear on the air with his or her own story without any additional compensation. After verifying his assumptions with the station's lawyers, Primo set out to create the first "beat system" in broadcast television. KWY was already using the title "Eyewitness News" in its broadcasts, but it would be Primo who finally gave it real meaning.

Within a couple of years of his arrival at KYW, he received a call from WABC-TV in New York to become its news director. WABC was facing tough times, poor ratings, and meager revenues. Its general manager Dick Beesemyer was looking to shake things up. Primo demanded the ability to hire and fire *any* member of his staff. Beesemyer agreed, as long as he could turn the ratings around. Once again, Primo reviewed the AFTRA contract. In New York there was a clause referred to as the "break line of pay." For those paid under a predetermined salary range, they were paid talent fees for any on-air work. For example, if the break line of pay was $30,000, everyone making less than that would be paid talent fees. Everyone above that salary would not receive additional compensation. Primo was determined to bring his "Eyewitness News" concept to WABC. To get around the clause, he started hiring staff just above the break line of pay. This enabled him to hire a bunch of on-air reporters without having to pay additional talent fees. Of course, this would be the beginning of the upward spiral of high-priced on-air television news talent. At least initially, Primo was able to hire the cream of the crop from markets like Boston, Philadelphia, and Baltimore for fairly reasonable salaries, just so they could have a shot at the big time in New York.

Creating the beat system was just the beginning of the changes Primo would introduce to local television broadcasting in New York and then around the country: "One of my proudest achievements was a memo I sent to the staff at WABC, stating that 'Every story that comes back to the station will have *people* in it.' I wanted every story to have a personal angle and real people talking about the event being covered. I didn't want the reporters going out to a fire and interviewing the police or fire chief. I wanted them to interview the people who lost their belongings and homes. That was the key breakthrough."

There would be more dramatic changes. Primo wanted his reporters to reflect the people they were covering. When he arrived in New York City, that certainly wasn't the case at the local television stations across the board: "When I came to work in New York, everybody on the air was a white Anglo-Saxon Protestant male. Everybody was tall, handsome, blonde, and beautiful. However, when I walked down the street to work, there were black people, Hispanic people, Jewish people, Italian people—a great ethnic mix of the universe surrounded me." Suddenly it occurred to him to put reporters as "representatives" of these people on the air. He put Melba Tolliver in the anchor seat for the 11 o'clock news. She became one of the first African American women to hold that high-profile role. He hired Roseanne Scamardella and told her to keep using her real name, instead of simplifying it, as was the common practice among talent. She would become great fodder for the comedians of "Saturday Night Live," who regularly parodied her. He hired Geraldo Rivera, the first Puerto Rican on the air in New York. "These anchors and reporters became a television family everybody could identify with. It didn't make any difference what your ethnicity was, you saw somebody like you on television. Nobody ever did that before. It was a big change."

Primo would also go after stories that weren't typically covered by local television. He went for human interest stories often overlooked: "I was coming to work one day and I went past St. Patrick's Cathedral, and there was a huge crowd with a marching band and men in uniform. I said to myself, 'What is going on?' It turns out it was a funeral of a policeman who had been killed two days prior. I called our desk and asked if they were covering the story. They responded, 'Oh, we don't cover those stories.' I told them I wanted a crew and a reporter down there right now. We aired the story, which was full of pomp and ceremony.... We had pictures of the widow and the kids crying. They had never put that stuff on TV before."

During his first few years at WABC, Primo's competitors ridiculed him, calling the new format "gimmicky." Their conventions would not allow them to view it as "real journalism," and many derisively dubbed it "Nit-wit-less News." As WABC's audience began to grow, Primo had all the validation he needed when the station finally launched itself into the number-one spot in New York. The competition took notice, paying Primo the highest form of flattery by copying his ideas. In an age now fascinated by technology and live shots, Primo still believes that the best stories still reside with the people: "The lesson of "Eyewitness News" is that you must cover stories as they affect people because people tell stories better than any reporter can, no matter how well trained."

Another member of the WABC on-air team at that time was Ernie Anastos. After turning down higher-paying television anchor jobs in New England, Anastos decided to take a job with WABC-TV for much less pay. He was fulfilling his dream of working on-air in New York. After just three months on the job, he was paired with Roseanne Scamardella on the 11 o'clock news, making him the first Greek American television anchor in America.

From those early days as a reporter and anchor in New York, Anastos recalls covering the death of Nelson Rockefeller as his most memorable story: "I always remember that being a very special kind of moment, especially since he was such a strong, vivid figure in New York. He was such an interesting person who had made so many contributions to the State of New York, to the country, to the world, and to his family." Anastos was the first reporter on the scene. He watched the former vice president and governor pass him as he was brought into Lenox Hill Hospital in New York, where he was pronounced dead.

New York broadcasters would introduce several other innovations in news programming. Even before the networks began airing their 15-minute newscasts, WPIX in New York City was already airing a half-hour local newscast. Con Edison, the local power company, served as the original sponsor of the news broadcast. "We started local news from the first day we went on the air. We had a newscast at 6:30 p.m. every night with John Tillman. We always did at least a half hour, and then they grew to an hour later on," explains Leavitt Pope, former president of WPIX. The station would have as many as eight news crews out on the streets of New York on any given day. Keep in mind, this was still in the days of film that had to be taken back to the station to be developed and edited by hand!

At the time, WPIX was owned by the *New York Daily News*. Pope believed it was the entrenched news culture of the company that made the management so supportive of the station's pioneering efforts in television news programming: "Being in a news environment, which our parent company had been for a number of years, we thought we could do a pretty good job. We ended up with a very good audience and got a lot of positive feedback from the people who watched our news." Serving a coverage area with 3 governors, 6 senators, and more than 60 congressman, Pope saw news and public affairs programming as an obligation, a duty to carry out on behalf of the public.

When Bill McKibben arrived at Channel 4 in Buffalo, the station's news broadcasts were in tough shape. CBS was severely disappointed because its highly rated programming was giving the station very strong lead-ins for their 6 and 11 p.m. news, but their ratings still suffered. The network wanted action, so CBS commissioned a survey of all the on-air personalities in Buffalo, recounts McKibben. The results of the survey were disheartening. Channel 4's anchors were dead last in popularity and believability. To make matters worse, the station kept rotating its anchors, never giving the audience enough time to form a connection with them.

There was one interesting exception in the survey results, noted McKibben: "Surprisingly, the two top guys on the list were two of our three sports guys. The sports guys were allowed to write their own copy because they were in a separate union from the news guys, who never wrote a word of what they said on the air." Based on this information, McKibben decided to switch things around. He reassigned the top sports anchor on the survey list to one of the news anchor spots. The second most popular personality on the list was Channel 4's sports reporter, who had just started covering the Buffalo Bills. McKibben now scheduled him to cover sports everyday as the main sports anchor. The station's weekend weatherman ranked higher than the weekday weatherman, so McKibben switched their positions. The end results were staggering, says McKibben: "We went from a 7 share at 6 p.m. and an 8 share at 11 p.m. to a 48 share in both slots in one book! We also did a lot of promotional things and started treating news in a more exciting way."

Tony Malara is fondly recognized by his peers as "fun loving" and "jovial," but he was also blunt and tough when he had to be. He frequently said what was on his mind, an endearing quality to the CBS executives who took him out of Watertown. He recalls, however, a particular instance in which his honesty and conviction left him with a lot of explaining to do to his "big boss," William S. Paley, the legendary founder of CBS. Malara was still a relative newcomer to the organization as vice president of affiliate relations: "In 1979, we had a situation in which Mr. Paley wanted to create a national late-night newscast at 11:30 p.m. for CBS. At the time, the local stations were doing all kinds of programming on their own in late night. We were doing pretty well."

Malara was invited to an executive meeting presided over by Mr. Paley to share the affiliates' views on the merits of whether to launch a late-night newscast: "Mr. Paley used to sit at this oval table in his conference room, and whenever you had a meeting with him a chart had already been given to him, so he would know where everyone was sitting." As the meeting got underway, Paley directed a question to Malara. "We started going back and forth. All of a sudden, it became the 'Bill and Tony Show.' He was saying, 'Yes, but,' and I was saying, 'Yes, but.' We were really involved. I could see my boss out of the corner of my eye starting to sink right under the table. I got a little nervous and realized I was mouthing off to a pretty big group of people, but they had asked me for my opinion." At one point, one of Malara's superiors tried to interrupt to get Malara out of the hole he was digging for himself, but Paley told Malara to finish his thoughts. "I was so emboldened that after he made another point, I looked at him and said, 'Mr. Paley, you don't understand!' Just as soon as I said those words, I thought, 'You idiot, you just told one of the icons of the broadcast business he doesn't understand.'"

Dead silence fell over the room, says Malara. Once again one of his superiors tried to take back control of the conversation. At this point, Malara was all too keen for a way out from his last comment: "I just wanted to crawl under the table. Mr. Paley then says to me, 'Well, make me understand.' We continued our conversation. When we were done, he looked at me silently and then he said, 'Very interesting. Very thoughtful, but you're *wrong*.'" After a few more meetings, Paley was eventually dissuaded from launching a late-night newscast. "I got hell from my bosses for being so mouthy, but I also got a nice little note from the great Paley, telling me he appreciated hearing a fresh view from a young person."

Unfortunately for Malara, the issue wouldn't die there. While at a conference in San Francisco a few months later, he received an urgent call from Gene Jankowski, the president of the CBS Broadcast Group: "He told me ABC had just announced an 11:30 p.m. news program on the hostage crisis in Iran, and Mr. Paley is not very happy. He wants us all back in his conference room to explain again why we all thought a late-night newscast was a bad idea." Malara hopped on a plane and returned immediately to New York. "This meeting was just dreadful. Mr. Paley never yelled or screamed, but he was firm and he could be very cutting. He said, 'Are they just stupid or is it possible they all know something that you don't know?'" After another few meetings the top brass at CBS convinced Paley their original decision had been the correct one. "He thought we made more money in prime time, when in fact we were making more money in late night at that time because the costs of the programming were so different. We proved that ABC never made money on late night. 'Nightline' has been terrific for them, but they've never had a very profitable late night."

Whether or not residents of Jamestown went to bed watching "Nightline," they most certainly spent their Saturday mornings listening to Dennis Webster on WJTN. For over 50 years WJTN has broadcast its "Saturday Morning Breakfast Party" live from various locations throughout Jamestown and environs. Currently, they pack a local Friendly's restaurant, announcing birthdays and anniversaries on the air, as well as allowing any local individual or organization to promote upcoming events. A few years back, Merrill Rosen, the general manager of WJTN, wanted to try taping the show so people could hear themselves on the radio the following Sunday morning. He quickly came to understand not to tamper with tradition, learning that the airwaves truly do belong to the public: "Everyone thought it was a great idea except our listeners. We told them we were just testing the concept. Our live audience went from 75 people down to a dozen or so people for three weeks straight. We decided to go back to live every Saturday morning, and our attendance went back up to 75 people every week. There are things that really don't belong to the radio station. They belong to the community."

Broadcasters on the Scene

As home to the headquarters of all the major broadcast news networks for both radio and television, New York has had to inevitably share countless broadcast legends with the rest of the country. Americans woke up to Charles Kuralt on "Sunday Mornings," wept with Walter Cronkite when President Kennedy was assassinated, rejoiced with Tom Brokaw during the fall of the Berlin Wall, waited to see how Barbara Walters was going to bring the latest "it" celebrity to tears, cheered for American athletes with Jim McKay at the Olympics, and "saw" the poetic Charles Osgood on the radio.

There are also countless broadcast legends who are known only within the boundaries of the State of New York but are in no way any less important to New Yorkers. In most cases, they are perhaps even more important because they are neighbors and members of the same community. Their personalities and parochialisms reflect the character of the community they so dutifully serve.

Last year Ed Dague retired from broadcasting after spending his entire career in Albany. He held the distinction of working for all three television affiliates in the capital region. He started his career at WTEN, then moved on to become an anchor/reporter at WRGB. In 1984 Dague went to WNYT, where he remained for the rest of his career. Steve Baboulis, general manager of WNYT, credits the station's turnaround in the 1980s in part to Dague: "He really helped us set the stage to be competitive. He brought an intelligence to our newsroom that you just can't duplicate. He really made reporters ask questions of themselves and in their interviews, so that we could have an intelligent approach to the news." The full transformation of WNYT came together when Dague was teamed up with Chris Jansing, who is now shared with the rest of the country as a correspondent and anchor for MSNBC.

As for Baboulis, he got his start in Albany at WNYT (then known as WAST) as a news intern: "One night between the 6 o'clock and 11 o'clock newscasts, a producer walked out and quit. They needed some help and they stuck me in there. I guess I did a decent enough job. They were pretty impressed." He has lived his entire professional life at WNYT, an anomaly in a business known for moving around to get ahead. His proudest achievement is being part of the evolution of WNYT from being an also-ran 25 years ago to becoming number one in the market. "My philosophy has always been to make sure at the end of the day we are always serving the viewers. The license we operate under is a privilege. The main goal is to serve the viewer and their community interests."

Buffalo produced a pipeline of news talent second only to the Big Apple. Regarded as the "dean of Buffalo radio news," John Zach has been a model in news broadcasting. He went for an audition at WKBW-AM in 1961 and was hired by Buffalo broadcast legend Irv Weinstein. He admits to having a rocky start: "I was a liability to the staff; I wasn't a newsman. I was constantly missing important details in stories; I was not a good writer. I was constantly driving Jim Fagan nuts. He was already a consummate newsman and I probably gave him the gray hairs he has today." After a few months Zach got the hang of being a broadcaster and his lifelong passion blossomed. He hopes he is remembered for writing in the vernacular and introducing the language of the common man to broadcasting: "It was my belief that people wanted to listen on the radio to the same language they used in their daily lives. If they do hear that, sooner or later they're going to recognize it and identify with the person behind the microphone. It's just using common, everyday words on the radio."

Les Arries, another Buffalo icon, will be remembered for many pioneering achievements. He began his career at the dawn of television with the DuMont Network in 1946. He helped develop Merv Griffin's talk show and syndicated the "Mike Douglas Show." In Buffalo, however, he holds the distinction of being the longest-serving general manager in that market, running WIVB-TV (formerly WBEN-TV) from 1967 to 1989. Bill Brown Jr., from nearby Batavia, reflects on Arries' contributions to broadcasting: "Les was a visionary. He was a top television broadcaster. He was highly regarded in the industry." Arries sought to both enlighten and entertain his fellow citizens. He launched a weekly tournament of knowledge among scholars called "It's Academic." In 1971 he experimented with an hour-long newscast on WBEN-TV, hiring CBS Pentagon correspondent Steve Rowan as anchor. Five years later, his "First Team News" at 6 p.m. returned to a 30-minute format.

Arries was also immersed in the activities of NYSBA, serving as president in 1974-1975. Members remember him as "an inquisitor," someone unafraid to engage governors or senators on contentious issues facing broadcasters. Arries was also a powerful figure in Buffalo civic affairs.

"People turned on the radio not to hear the news but to hear Mike Cuneen with the news," memorialized John Kehelle, a reporter for *The Oneonta Star*, after Cuneen's death in 1974. Mike Cuneen was vice president and general manager of WDLA in Walton. He enjoyed a friendly rivalry with Kehelle, but the two were forever dedicated to keeping the citizens of Delaware Country well informed. "He loved scooping the local newspaper *The Oneonta Star*. 'You'll hear it now and read it in the morning,'" Kehelle once wrote of Cuneen. Thousands listened to his broadcast each morning. He was known for sprinkling birthdays, facts from the almanac, and bits of history in between local and national news stories to maintain the interest of his listeners.

Cuneen would serve as a mentor to many, including Amos Finch: "Mike was a good man to work for. He was very fair and had a lot of patience. Even if you screwed up a few times, if he could see you had potential, he'd stick with you." Like other consummate broadcasters, everyone in Delaware County seemed to know Mike Cuneen, and he seemed to know everyone. Finch recalls how active he was in the community: "He spent a great deal of time attending everything that happened, whether it was political, a retirement dinner or whatever else was going on."

Known as the "Dean of Syracuse newsmen," E. R. "Curly" Vadeboncoeur was unarguably the most legendary figure in Syracuse broadcasting. He began his career as a reporter for the *Syracuse Journal* in 1920. After the paper merged with the *Herald* a few years later, he decided to switch to broadcasting. He had already been exposed to radio, doing a Sunday night broadcast on WFBL called "City Editor" while at the *Journal*. He landed a job at WSYR doing the noon news and soon became known for his colorful commentaries each day.

He used his role as a broadcaster to fight for his community. He successfully fought against a city sales tax, but years later, to his dismay, it eventually found its way back into city hall. He brought the frontlines of World War II home to his neighbors, filing reports from the Pacific theater for a month. He eventually became president of the Newhouse Broadcasting Corporation, the owner of WSYR-AM and WSYR-TV. He signed on WSYR-TV, Channel 3, in 1950 and presided over its operation until it was sold in 1980. As he was becoming more involved with management in the 1950s, he slowly relinquished his on-air duties but continued to offer lively analysis of returns each election night.

In some respects, Mary Margaret McBride was the "Oprah" of her day. Her popular radio program on NBC offered an alternative to soap operas, delving into topics beyond the running of the household. At its peak, her show attracted as many as 8 million listeners each day. The show was an attractive forum for advertisers. She helped make brands like Bohack's, Dolly Madison Ice Cream, and Cut-Right Waxed Paper household names in their day. Her persuasive abilities "doing the products," as she referred to the sponsored portions of her show, led one of her advertisers to comment: "That woman can sell anything!" She provided useful information for women and wasn't afraid to tackle concerns of the modern woman: unwed mothers, marriage, and careers. She pioneered the magazine format used by many talk shows today, interviewing both notable guests and average women about their own lives. Choosing not to marry, she was a symbol of the emerging modern American woman, crafting an identity outside the traditional roles of women at the time. During her last years, Mary Margaret broadcast from her retirement home overlooking the West Shokan Reservoir on WGHQ in the Hudson Valley.

During the 1970s, New Yorkers came to know Roger Grimsby's and Bill Beutel's innovative style of presenting the news as "happy talk." Both anchors felt the term was belittling. Their banter was frequently parodied on "Saturday Night Live." Grimsby opened each broadcast with the familiar greeting, "I'm Roger Grimsby. Here now, the news." He signed off by saying, "Hoping your news is good news." The two were paired together for 16 years on WABC-TV starting in 1970, helping to redefine local television news forever.

When Sue Simmons teamed up with Chuck Scarborough in 1980 at WNBC-TV, little did they know it was the beginning of a 25-year working relationship. Their on-air run together has been the longest of any anchor team in the history of New York City broadcasting—an astounding achievement in a profession known for its revolving door of on-air talent. Simmons got her start in neighboring Connecticut, as a reporter for WTNH-TV in New Haven. She also worked as a reporter for the NBC-owned affiliate in Washington, D.C., WRC-TV. While there, she was the first reporter to interview the Hanafi Muslims, who took over several Washington-area buildings, just after the seizure of the U.S. embassy in Teheran by radical student revolutionaries. She believes "viewer likeability" is what has kept her in the anchor chair so long: "My mindset was always that the camera was a person. I always pictured that person to be my 'hip grandmother'—somebody who had a sense of humor, but on the other hand someone I did not want to offend."

While Roger Grimsby and Bill Beutel were at the height of their popularity, a young Chuck Scarborough joined WNBC-TV in 1974 after reporting for television stations in Mississippi, Atlanta, and then Boston. The station's ratings were abysmal at the time. To reverse its fortunes, executives decided to launch the first two-hour local evening newscast in New York City, from 5 p.m. to 7 p.m. In time, NBC's flagship station became number one in the market for local news. In 2004 Scarborough celebrated his 30th anniversary at WNBC. During all that time, New York City has never failed to excite or inspire him, he says: "It has always been a very exciting place to cover news. Almost any story on the face of the earth is of interest to somebody here. This is such an international city that not only do we have news being generated out here on the streets of the five boroughs, we're also keenly interested in what's going on in many communities around the world because of the city's diverse culture." Scarborough has been honored and recognized for his storytelling abilities many times over, including 28 Emmy Awards! Simmons and Scarborough were among the first inductees into the NYSBA Hall of Fame in 2005.

Irv Weinstein is to Buffalo what Sue Simmons and Chuck Scarborough are to New York City. As the news director of WKBW Radio in the late 1950s, he developed the concept of "rock-and-roll" radio news. He called his news broadcasts "WKBW Pulse Beat News." It's writing style was hip, pithy, and fast-paced. "If it bleeds, it leads," describes the type of coverage Weinstein thought was perfect for radio. In 1963 Weinstein took his act to television, becoming news director and lead anchor of Channel 7's "Eyewitness News." He stayed there for almost 35 years. He is regarded by his colleagues as "the most popular TV personality in the history of western New York."

Advocates for Their Communities

One of the many fronts on which broadcasters fought in their efforts to achieve parity with print media was the right to editorialize. As late as the 1960s, broadcasters were still divided as to whether their licenses afforded them the opportunity to air editorials. One school of thought believed it was inappropriate, regarding broadcasters as mere observers in gathering and distributing news. The opposing view believed broadcasters should have the same privilege as newspapers to take a stand on an issue, while also sharing the airwaves with other perspectives as per the dreaded Fairness Doctrine.

R. Peter Straus was one of the leading advocates in support of editorializing: "We started editorializing on the air before anyone else. It was considered to be against FCC rules. We thought the mission of a broadcaster was to say something important. We've always been into activism and personal responsibility. We weren't going to change the world, but we darn well had to try." When Straus' father, Nathan Straus, purchased WMCA in the 1940s, he was unaware that airing editorials was still illegal. A former New York State senator and administrator of the U.S. Housing Authority in the Roosevelt Administration, Nathan Straus was extremely public minded and saw his station as an opportunity to get the public talking about the great issues of the day. After six months of debate before a senate committee, WMCA won the right to editorialize.

Beginning in 1954, the station began regularly airing editorials. Every Thursday night R. Peter Straus broadcast his editorials and invited comments from listeners. He also believed that editorializing helped stations sound distinctive, adding to their local flavor. In October 1960, WMCA became the first radio station to endorse a candidate for president by supporting John F. Kennedy. Jim Rodgers of WNBZ also saw the broadcast microphone as a tool to help guide important discussions in the community: "I believed it was our responsibility to be unbiased as much as we could, but also to take sides when we thought it was really important. We were aware of the unbelievable power of a local radio station in a local community."

While serving as president of NYSBA, Sam Slate provided definitive leadership for New York's broadcasters on the issue of editorializing when he aired his first series of editorials on WCBS-AM on January 25, 1960: "We delay the start of the next broadcast so that you may hear 'Opinion of the Air' . . . clearly labeled and submitted in the hope that your own thinking on important issues will be stimulated." As with Rodgers, Slate took the view that broadcasting was a force, not just a service. He believed that if broadcasters were to accept full responsibility as defenders of the First Amendment, they had an obligation to express a point of view about the news, as well as offering the opportunity to air opposing viewpoints. Slate's editorials touched on a wide variety of topics swirling around in the minds of New Yorkers at that time, from criticizing the ability of the proposed Lower Manhattan Expressway Project to alleviate traffic problems to the belief that a proposed Korean War bonus for New York State veterans amounted to a political payoff. The support and vibrant opposition to his editorials didn't phase Slate. He just wanted people to think.

During the controversy involving CBS's program "The Selling of the Pentagon Papers," Senator Jacob K. Javits spoke out against congressional scrutiny for the first time at NYSBA's 10th Executive Conference. In his address he urged broadcasters to editorialize: "I welcome editorializing and hope you do more. Be as muckraking as newspapers traditionally have been. Government licensing does not mean government control, even indirect control. News media must be treated alike." As the senate's father of the War Powers Act, Javits's ringing encouragement really emboldened broadcasters to step up and speak out.

As the 1970s rolled along, more and more broadcasters became comfortable with editorializing. "When I started writing them in the early 1970s, it was unusual for a broadcast station to editorialize. As the years went by, of course more and more began to do it. I wanted to give the public a point of view on issues and personalities, all local, of course. We had a local newspaper whose editorials were full of motherhood and apple pie, but you had to read between the lines. I thought the community needed an editorial voice and I proceeded to provide that," recalls Bill Brown Jr. of WBTA in Batavia. He would go on to become one of the most prolific editorial writers in New York broadcasting, producing over 5,000 editorials and winning 16 awards for his work from NYSBA.

Bill Brown III describes his father as a frustrated newspaper reporter: "My father was the antithesis of a broadcaster because he was interested in the community angle of news and opinion. His trademark was his editorials. His editorials were pretty much no-holds-barred. Even the newspaper didn't write editorials that were controversial." His son believes it took an amazing amount of integrity for his father to throw the punches he did, as well as take a few on the chin. However, he never let his editorials get in the way of friendships or sponsors. He just wanted to help people develop their own viewpoints on local issues. People would often comment on Bill Brown and his "red light problems" because of the frequency with which he would discuss the problems with the traffic lights on the Main Street in Batavia: "I likened our Main Street to the nation's longest parking lot," comments Brown. Now retired, he's still at it, delivering a weekly commentary in Batavia called "As I See It."

Dick Hughes would also receive many accolades from NYSBA for his editorials at WPIX-TV. For over 20 years he would oversee the editorial committee at WPIX-TV, as well as prepare many of the editorials themselves. "Dick headed our editorial committee, in which three or four of us participated so we would not be one-sided. We'd try to get all sides of an issue, acting in the best interest of the public," recalls Lev Pope. "I still have an Emmy Award on the shelf in my office that was awarded to the station for one of Dick's editorials." Pope remembers one of Hughes's editorials in particular, which turned into a public service announcement of sorts. "There was an epidemic of what they call rubella, which is measles. It can be pretty harmful to young children and expectant mothers. We started a series of editorials, called the 'Rubella Umbrella,' to persuade people to get their children inoculated against rubella. We used a symbol of a little red umbrella on the air, and we got schools involved to inoculate all the preschool children in New York." Their efforts resulted in a very high percentage of children getting inoculated. They got the health department, the mayor's office, and even the governor of New Jersey to help. "That's something nice we were able to do. You can't always do that, but in this instance we did."

Almost 25 years after Harry Thayer's death, Walter Maxwell still gets comments about his stepfather's famous editorials: "I still get people commenting on them. They talk about the traffic circle, where the Thruway entrance is in Kingston. He called it the 'Black Hole of Calcutta.' Harry would also comment on the county office building, which he named the 'glass menagerie,' because when they built it back in the early 1970s, it was very modern looking. Harry's argument was, 'Hey, we have a historic community, can't somebody design it to fit in with the community?' He's still remembered fondly today." Thayer would broadcast an editorial every day, constantly being quoted in the local newspaper, according to Maxwell: "The newspaper was locally owned, but it didn't do editorials. They weren't so involved in the community as Harry was." Thayer also blasted his fiery rhetorical guns on the lawmakers in Albany. He had some monumental battles with Governor Nelson A. Rockefeller, but for all of Harry Thayer's broadsides, Rocky and he remained friends.

Talk Radio

As early as 1945, Barry Gray had the foresight to get his listeners directly involved with his broadcasts. Using a rudimentary telephone system, he had them call him so he could talk to them live on the air. Despite technical snafus, Gray would not be deterred. He worked for WMCA for almost 40 years, earning the unofficial title, "Father of Talk Radio."

His interview with the popular bandleader Woody Herman would be the catalyst in formalizing what would become the "call-in" radio talk show. He was one of the first broadcasters to say what was on everyone's mind, rather than dance around even the most controversial issues of the day. Warren Bodow, former president and general manager of WQXR and an early WMCA staffer, describes Gray's style: "There was give-and-take and argumentative discussion before talk radio was even invented." His program aired five nights a week, covering topics in business, the arts, politics, and entertainment. It was his pioneering efforts that paved the way for interviewers like Charley Rose and talk show hosts like Don Imus.

"I know people like the editor in chief of the *New Yorker* magazine, who, when they were younger, swore by Long John Nebel," also notes Bodow. Taking a different direction in talk radio from Gray's, Nebel was known for his unusual antics on his late-night talk show during the 1950s and 1960s on WOR. Bodow recalls that the show frequently began with a bunch of New Yorkers from all walks of life talking with Nebel about the cosmos and extraterrestrial beings. He describes the mood as "metaphysical." Nebel was also famous for doing lengthy commercials that went on for three or four minutes. He was a long pitchman before WOR discovered his talents, giving him his own show.

Bob Law fondly refers to the 1970s and 1980s as the "glory days" of black radio when personalities like Frankie Crocker, Vaughn Harper, Enoch Gregory, Gary Byrd, Hank Spann, Gerry Bledsoe, Jane Tillman, and Bobby Jay were rising stars. A civil rights activist, Bob Law caught the eye of WWRL management and was brought on board as public affairs director in 1972. In time he was given his own talk show, "Night Talk with Bob Law," becoming a beacon for Afrocentric issues. The show was eventually syndicated nationally and stayed on the air until about five years ago when he left radio to start a health-food store.

Many African American announcers were either former activists or modeled their on-air persona after the great leaders and preachers of the civil rights era. They did not passively sit in a studio when they were on the air, but rather they performed for a live "crowd." Imhotep Gary Byrd frequently stands during his show, "Global Black Experience," and even turns off all the lights in the studio, relying instead on the light of just a single candle. Many African Americans in New York regard him as a "master communicator," someone continually making a positive contribution to his community. After many years at WLIB, Byrd's show was displaced in 2000, as was the rest of WLIB's lineup, to make room for new programs when the station became an affiliate of the upstart liberal network Air America. Fortunately for him and his many loyal listeners, he found a new home at WBAI-FM.

An indelible imprint will be left on radio as a result of the discoveries by Ed McLaughlin of two larger-than-life personalities. He was tapped to head up ABC Radio's new four-network concept in the 1970s, successfully breathing new life into the network. Paul Harvey was one of the shining stars McLaughlin built the network around. "Hello America!" became Harvey's signature greeting to his listeners at the top of each broadcast. Harvey—with his distinctive dots, dashes, and pauses style—was truly sui generis.

On the sale of ABC to Capital Cities, McLaughlin decided to retire, leaving behind a legacy that would firmly guarantee him a place of honor in the pantheon of broadcasting. His career, however, was far from over. Through a series of circumstances he found himself in the syndication business. ABC had recently decided not to renew the contract of Dr. Dean Adel. McLaughlin worked with Adel from his days at ABC Radio's San Francisco affiliate KGO. They teamed up to start shopping around Adel's medical segments to various networks, launching McLaughlin into the syndication business.

Through a friend, Bruce Marr, McLaughlin was soon introduced to another talent out of Sacramento who was interested in being syndicated nationally. Unknown outside of his market at the time, Rush Limbaugh would forever change the fortunes of Ed McLaughlin and the sound of talk radio. After a meeting arranged by Marr, McLaughlin recalls his initial impressions of Limbaugh: "One of the things that struck me immediately was here was a new voice. I was aware that there was a strong conservative movement in the United States, but it had very little voice. When I heard the kind of response he was getting from his callers, I realized this probably could be that voice. He just had so many elements to his program that went beyond just being a conservative talk show host. He had entertainment elements. He himself was bright, funny, and engaging . . . the things you look for, and he was obviously committed to his political views. At least that was what came out over the air." McLaughlin believed Limbaugh's views were genuine and that there was legitimacy in his credentials: "I didn't purposely go out and find a conservative. What I found was a great radio performer. That he was conservative was a plus in the sense that nobody was addressing that particular audience. It was really more of a marketing strategy than any ideological move on my part."

Sold on Limbaugh, McLaughlin now had to validate his instincts as to whether there was in fact a market for conservative talk radio: "It was a big leap because we both knew his conservative radio style was not necessarily in great demand by stations and advertisers. The biggest challenge was to get him into a major market where I could see if we really had the strength to go forward."

To get him syndicated, McLaughlin first had to get Limbaugh into one of the top-five markets. What better place to test a conservative talk show than in the most liberal market in the country, New York City. Limbaugh went on the air in New York in 1988. "I was aware of some changes that were going to take place at WABC in New York, so we made a deal with WABC. He did a two-hour local show and then went into another studio to do a two-hour national show," explains McLaughlin.

Starting a conservative show in New York City wasn't all that farfetched for McLaughlin. He believed there was an underserved conservative audience Limbaugh could tap into: "I was never as convinced as are many others that the big markets are totally liberal in their political thinking. I was convinced this was also true of New York, because Staten Island, eastern Long Island, parts of New Jersey, and Connecticut were much more conservative than Manhattan. I was convinced Rush was going to be successful."

Limbaugh didn't become an instant success, but as he added more and more stations, he would take the country by storm. WBEN-AM would be one of the first radio stations to put Limbaugh on the air, notes Larry Levite: "We were the fourth or fifth station to put him on, and we must have gotten 500 calls the first day to 'get rid of that schmuck.' The guy who persuaded me it was the right thing to do was a guy named Ed McLaughlin, who was a real smart guy. I went along with him because I agreed with him that this guy was unique, and of course he turned out to be *the* Rush Limbaugh. A year later, if we had taken Rush off, we probably would have gotten *5,000* phone calls!"

A political column titled "Meet Governor Koch" would give rise to an accidental radio program of a more liberal persuasion than Limbaugh's show. Called "Me & Mario," it ran for 18 years. Alan Chartock and Governor Mario M. Cuomo discussed the latest issues facing the Empire State and, of course, traded a few barbs. Chartock had written an article called "Meet Governor Koch" for the *Legislative Gazette*, the state legislative newspaper he founded. He liked Cuomo, but he just didn't think the articulate lieutenant governor stood a chance against the popular New York City mayor in the Democratic gubernatorial primary in 1982. Chartock and a lot of savvy political analysts guessed wrong, as Cuomo beat Koch in the primary and went on to defeat multimillionaire Lewis Lehrman in the general election.

After the gubernatorial election, one of Cuomo's deputies requested a meeting with Chartock. "I thought I was going to die. I went down, not to talk to Cuomo but to talk to his press secretary. I had been told by a close associate of Cuomo's that if he won I'd never be allowed to set foot on the second floor of the State Capitol. You have to know that Mario's a guy who draws his circle wider." During the meeting the phone rings, it's the governor requesting to see Chartock himself: "I go in and I start to talk to Cuomo. He says to me, 'When am I going to be on your show?' I tell him, 'Anytime you want, governor,' as I feel the weight of the guillotine being lifted from my neck. 'In fact,' I told him, 'you could have your own show on all the public radio stations across New York state.' Cuomo responded, 'Done.'"

Chartock's unparalleled access to the governor would be the envy of every journalist in the state, to say the least. To be fair, he taped the show, providing copies of it to be used by other media outlets all over New York. The "Me & Mario" show was heard on a small, discrete network of about 25 stations all over the country as well. In the beginning, Chartock also invited other reporters to participate, while he served as the moderator. Over time, the logistics of getting the show together each week became too much, and it would eventually just be Chartock interviewing Governor Cuomo, giving rise to the namesake of the show, "Me & Mario."

The format was fairly free form, explains Chartock: "He gave me a lot of latitude. Sometimes he would get mad at me. Sometimes he would muff the question. Then he wouldn't show up for a couple weeks, so we would get Alfonse D'Amato to take his place, and he'd come right back. It was great fun." Cuomo had his share of fun, too, at the expense of Chartock. He frequently gave Chartock a hard time about living in Massachusetts and working in New York: "He would say things like, 'We all know, Alan Chartock, how you put your cape on in the dark of the morning as you slip over the New York State line. You take a big, black bag with you, and you take all the money from the state university where you teach, the radio station and the newspapers where you write, and then you slip over the border again at night spending the money in Massachusetts!' I was the one trying to keep up with him. There's no question he's the funniest and most intelligent man I've ever talked to in my life."

As a programmer, Larry Levite liked taking risks. Rush Limbaugh wasn't the only radio program Levite took a chance on. WBEN would also be one of the first stations to carry the radio version of Larry King. "We put Larry King on the all-night show and we took off a very popular local guy because I loved Larry King. Back then, who was Larry King? I just loved his talent. I thought his voice and delivery were great, and he was just an interesting guy on the air. If you were really popular, you were on in the daytime, not at midnight to 4 a.m. He was very successful and, of course, when he went to a daytime radio show we were the first ones to put him on there, too."

For different reasons than Limbaugh, Don Imus was another to break the established conventions of talk radio. The "I Man" would never merely be one to gloss over the news or great issues of the day; instead he said what he meant and meant what he said. His brash, irreverent, direct approach would be a breath of fresh air for many listeners and make Imus *the* voice of NBC Radio for many years. Bud Wertheimer recalls his favorite Imus program: "WNBC is located right in Rockefeller Center. The day the Russians invaded Afghanistan in 1979, he goes down to where all the flags of the world are flying and steals the Russian flag. He announces he's holding the Russian flag hostage and won't give it back until they get out of Afghanistan. Pretty good bit. The next day he goes down and the flag's back up. There's also a guard standing at the bottom of the flagpole. 'They're guarding the Russian flag. What a country!' he screamed on the air. He worked that thing for a year and you listened. You wondered what he was going to do next. That is the beauty of him." The "I Man" couldn't have said it better.

Playing the Standards

Martin Block didn't just play music; he tried to make his listeners feel like they were listening to the band and its vocalist live for themselves. His "Make Believe Ballroom" was an instant hit for WNEW. He was first hired in the mid-1930s to play music in between developments in the trial of accused kidnapper Bruno Richard Hauptmann, who was later found guilty of kidnapping the Lindbergh baby. As he played the music, he created the illusion of a ballroom for his listeners. The show became so popular, WNEW decided to build a new studio for him, complete with a recreated ballroom for his broadcasts. In 1954, he left for ABC Radio and then finished out his career at WOR.

WNEW-AM became a bastion for the great American popular song. Martin Block was followed by Art Ford and other wildly popular DJs who built the station's fame and fortune. Jack Lazare hosted the "Milkman's Matinee" from midnight till dawn. WNEW's stable also included Gene Klavan and Dee Finch in the morning and Al "Jazzbeau" Collins, Pete Myers, Dick Shepard, Bob Landers, Marty O'Hara, Lonnie Starr, Bob Haymes, and Big Wilson. The station was run by the charismatic general manager John Van Buren Sullivan, a classy, vivid figure who dazzled Madison Avenue with his style. It had a news department with five mobile units, plus its own full-time space correspondent, Martin Caidin! WNEW also boasted a cadre of outstanding news writers and commentators, which included Reid Collins, Jim Van Sickle, Ike Pappas, Jim Gash, Rudy Ruderman, David Schoenbrun, Mike Eisgrau, John Dale, and Mike Rich.

During its glory days, back in the late 1950s and into the 1960s, WNEW had an unheard-of 23% share of the New York audience, a position of dominance in the ratings that has never been equaled. Today the number-one station garners about 6%.

By far, the best known of all the WNEW performers was the legendary William B. Williams, a soft-spoken, almost shy DJ who was an icon of New York. He spent over 40 years with WNEW, 30 of them as host of the "Make Believe Ballroom." His signature greeting, "Hello, world," welcomed his loyal listeners at the top of each program. It was William B. who dubbed Frank Sinatra "The Chairman of the Board." The orchestra leader William Basie was "The Count of Basie." Edward Kennedy Ellington was "The Duke of Ellington." He was an avowed advocate of the "old standards," those melodic tunes by Perry Como, Mel Torme, Rosemary Clooney, Lena Horne, and Tony Bennett. Williams was once asked why he rejected "modern" songs. He responded: "These rock groups today, they may be big for three or four months and have a couple of hit records, but then that's the end for them." His theme song was Henri Rene's "You Are the One."

Rock and Roll

During the 1950s, as radio learned to share the stage with television, it quickly found a new voice in rock and roll music. Teenagers were wild for Top-40 formats, as were the record companies, which stood to make a fortune from a hit record. Disc jockeys and broadcast personalities emerged as an integral part of a station's identification and popularity, spawning icons like Alan Freed, Frankie Crocker, and Dick Clark in New York City, and George "Hound Dog" Lorenz, Frank Ward, and Joey Reynolds in Buffalo.

Several New York broadcasters led the way in the development of the rock and roll format. Never one to let an emerging trend pass him by, Al Anscombe was one of those pioneers, fostering the development of the Top-40 format in 1957 at WKBW in Buffalo.

Anscombe hired away Dick Lawrence, a program director, from WBNY-AM, a small 250-watt station in Buffalo. To make that small station stand out, Lawrence overhauled its programming to become one of the first true Top-40 formats in the country.

Anscombe saw the success WBNY had with the new format and recognized its potential immediately. WKBW dumped its broad-based programming lineup of country-western music, religious programming, ethnic shows, and even its network feeds from NBC. The new brand of WKBW would become known as "FutureSonic Radio," a fast-paced Top-40 format.

Prior to the introduction of the Top-40 format on WKBW, the "Sound of the Hound" was broadcast all over the eastern seaboard by WKBW. George "Hound Dog" Lorenz was another Buffalo broadcast legend whose influence extended far beyond New York, and even radio itself. He helped break the color barrier in radio music by nurturing the emerging sound of black music. His son, Frank Lorenz, says his father acquired a taste for black music in his early teens: "He really thought it was a reservoir of talent being overlooked and he pursued it. When you think about it, it was remarkable at the time."

The senior Lorenz would spend a lot of time hanging out with African Americans, absorbing their culture and music. According to Frank Lorenz, when they asked his father what he was up to when he came around to see the neighborhood guys, they used the pet expression, "Hey George, you doggin' around?" His nickname was initially "Tag Dog," but soon he became known as "Hound Dog," his signature. If you listen closely to the end of the Elvis tune "Hound Dog," you can actually hear Lorenz say, "You ain't nothing but a hound dog!"

George Lorenz got his start at WXRA in Buffalo in the late 1940s. He started playing black music, but it didn't last long, says his son: "The station was getting a lot of heat for it and they ended up letting him go." He moved on to WJJL in Niagara Falls as the morning show host, where he continued to experiment with his sound. "He had this black sound, which was going to be the pedestal for rock and roll music in this country. He saw all this coming," says his son.

To properly execute his vision, the Hound Dog knew he needed a larger platform. WKBW in Buffalo, a 50,000-watt clear-channel station heard in over 20 states, was exactly the kind of coverage he needed. He repeatedly approached WKBW with his ideas. Al Anscombe, the station manager, was unsure how his listeners would react to the music Lorenz was playing. However, he did see talent in Lorenz himself: "He was a character, let me tell you, but he knew what he was doing. He knew his music and he was really way up on it." As Anscombe watched Lorenz's ratings climb in Niagara Falls, he decided to take a chance, putting him on the air for two hours a night: "He'd gotten to be a nuisance, but I kept seeing his ratings coming up. I could see what he was doing. One day he came in and I said, 'I'd be interested in you, but I'm not really interested in your show.' There were some parts I really didn't think fit with us. We talked about it, and he said he would 'clean up' his show and make it a little more 'mainstream.'"

Lorenz invented his own fast-paced, smooth-talking language that really revved up his show. "A convertible was a 'ragtop.' The phone was the 'horn.' He had a whole dictionary of slang. It was all his," explains his son Frank. "If he talked about a car, he'd talk about 'wheels.' If he talked about money, he'd talk about 'green stuff,'" recalls Anscombe.

The Hound had more than just vision and a feel for African American music or the ability to invent new hip slang. He was a sales and marketing genius. At first he proposed doing a show for WKBW from 7 p.m. to midnight. Already comfortable selling his own time in Niagara Falls, he offered to forgo a salary at WKBW for a commission on everything he sold. Anscombe finally agreed, first giving him two hours a night, five nights a week. "He had to do the program and pick the records all by himself. If he sold out the 18 spots, I told him I'd increase his time right away. After his first two weeks he had his18 spots sold. I gave him another hour, and then he sold that out! He had a lot of sponsors like Mogen David Wine, Gillette, and a lot of other national spots."

Lorenz also had his own newsletter for his "fan club." He wrote it himself, including a Top-10 list for the newsletter each week. He charged a dollar, just enough to cover printing and postage. He understood it wasn't about the money, it was about marketing. Eventually he would also syndicate his show with WKBW's permission. Lorenz made a dozen tapes of his show each night to distribute to stations in Syracuse, Albany, and Boston, further extending his reach. "As I got older and came to understand him, what I admired most was that he was a bright guy. He had great writing skills, street smarts, common sense, and vision. That's a lot to find in one person. He had all of that, and that's what made him so great," says his admiring son.

His purchase of WBLK-FM in 1964 fulfilled George Lorenz's long-held dream of owning a radio station. It was one of the first FM stations in the country to regularly program African American music. His dream would be short-lived. The Hound passed away unexpectedly at the age of 52. His legacy, however, would be enduring. According to his son, many black artists owed their careers to him: "It was the Hound who started this whole revolution. If you talked to a lot of black artists, they were so happy with him because nobody else would play their music." Shortly after his father's death, Frank Lorenz recalls being paid a visit by Little Richard: "He was playing in town that night and said to me, 'I just wanted to come by and give you my sympathy for your dad. You know, if it wasn't for him, none of us black artists would have ever gotten off the ground. I remember coming down to see him once, and I had a pair of cuff links for him because I wanted him to play my records. He told me I didn't have to do that. He said he would listen to the record, and if it was good he would play it. He did, and he made me into something.'"

After his father died in 1972, young Frank Lorenz found himself, at the ripe old age of 21, with some very big shoes to fill: "I was so shaken by all that was happening, I used to sit in his office and cry every morning because it was just so hard. He was such an unbelievable guy and such a pillar that you didn't think anything would take him down." In those sad, early days of his stewardship, Frank Lorenz

Figs. 35 and 36. Unsure what do with his life after graduating from high school, a young Amos Finch (left) was persuaded to take a job in his hometown's radio station, WDLA in Delaware County. There he met Myra Youmans (right), who eventually became his business partner. They would run WDLA and a couple of other stations in the foothills of the Catskills for almost 45 years.

Fig. 37. NYSBA had no more outspoken advocate than Phil Spencer of Amsterdam. As owner of WCSS and other stations in upstate New York, Spencer was an active member of the Association, always at the ready to defend broadcasters' rights. Here he is being presented with an award by Perry Bascom of WNBC Radio, recognizing his 25 years of service to NYSBA. Spencer passed away in December 2004.

Fig. 38. Harry Novik (left), former owner of WLIB-AM, organizes his notes in preparation for his interview with the great civil rights leader Dr. Martin Luther King. His son, Dick Novik (right), now senior vice president of NYSBA, gets ready to record the interview.

Fig. 39. New York State Lieutenant Governor Stan Lundine presents Si Goldman of WJTN and WWSE in Jamestown with a plaque for his decades of service to broadcasting and the people of western New York.

Fig. 40. Chris Coffin, former owner of WVOS-AM/FM in Liberty, with his wife, Pat Tocatlian, owner of WSLB and WPAC in Ogdensburg. Known for her "straight-shooting" style, Tocatlian was the first woman elected chairperson of NYSBA in 1989.

Fig.41. Richard Foreman sits across from music legend Neil Diamond in the studios of the ABC Radio Network in early 1981. The photo was taken just before recording the interview tracks for "The Neil Diamond Special," a two-hour network special that aired in the summer of 1981. Foreman was vice president of operations for ABC Radio at this time, and shortly thereafter he would go on to form his own media brokerage company, Richard A. Foreman Associates.

Fig. 42. Ellen Sulzberger Straus, shown here as a panelist at an Executive Conference, created the widely copied radio program "Call for Action," to improve consumer awareness. She was also deeply involved with the running of WMCA in New York City with her husband, R. Peter Straus, who also headed the Voice of America.

Fig. 43. Paul Sidney (left) is at the center of it all in eastern Long Island as the voice of WLNG in Sag Harbor. He is pictured here at a NYSBA event, with Julie and Rory LaRosa (center) and Harry Durando (right) of WYNY and his wife Pat.

Fig. 44. Marcia Devlin (right) presents Dr. Marion Stephenson (left) with a silver bowl for winning one of NYSBA's Excellence in Broadcasting awards. Dr. Stephenson served as the president of NBC Radio and more recently served as chairman of the board of prestigious Hartwick College in Oneonta.

Fig. 45. Ernie Anastos is well known as a New York City anchor, currently reporting for WNYW, Channel 5, but he is also an owner of radio stations. Anastos is pictured here in one of his radio studios in the Saratoga region.

Fig. 46. CBS Radio executive Nancy Widmann with Hugh Barr of WSYR and WYYY in Syracuse. Widmann was the first woman ever to hold the title of president of a CBS division.

Fig. 47. Rochester broadcaster Bud Wertheimer shares his financial wisdom at a Great Idea Exchange in the 1980s. Left to right: NAB's Gary Girard, Bud Wertheimer, Larry White of WBUF in Buffalo, and Bob Mahlman Jr. of the Mahlman Company.

Fig. 48. Albany Broadcasting president John Kelly (center) is welcomed to Siena College in 2001 to serve as an advisor to the college's president, Father Kevin Mackin (right), for a new broadcast journalism program, and to serve as volunteer-director of the student-run radio station WVCR. Father Jim Toal is pictured on the left.

Fig. 49. Broadcast heavyweights Jim Delmonico (left), general manager of WRGB-TV in Schenectady, and Levitt Pope (right), president of WPIX-TV in New York City, pictured here in 1977.

Fig. 50. Left to right: owner Rick Buckley; WOR vice president and general manager, Bob Bruno; chief operating officer, Joe Bilotta; and WSEN-AM/FM and WFBL-AM vice president and general manager, Doug Fleniken. Founded in the mid-1950s by Richard D. Buckley, Buckley Broadcasting remains an independent company to this day. Its holdings include the WOR Radio Network and 18 stations in 7 markets.

Fig. 51. ABC Television president, Jim Duffy, makes a "point" at an NYSBA Conference with Paul Dunn, a former broadcast owner in Utica. Duffy retired from ABC in 1989 to become a consultant. Dunn is currently a public broadcaster in upstate New York.

Fig. 52. Left to right: Former WMCA owner, R. Peter Straus, poses with Susan and Jack "On Your Side" Thayer of WNEW and NAB president Eddie Fritts. Today Straus owns a string of local and regional newspapers in upstate New York and New Jersey.

Fig. 53. Former upstate radio owner and Katz Media rep Gordon Hastings (center) and former WRGB-TV general manager David Lynch (right). Lynn Hastings, and the Hastings' son Gordon are pictured on the left. Hastings is currently the president of the Broadcasters' Foundation.

Fig. 54. Left to right: CNN's Lou Dobbs, a keynote speaker at the 2003 Executive Conference, with Scott Herman of Infinity Broadcasting (center) and Nick Verbitsky (left) of United Stations.

Fig. 55. Left to right: Frank Boyle, former president and chairman of radio rep firm Eastman with Dennis Ryan at an NYSBA conference.

Fig. 56. Left to right: As NYSBA chairman in 1988, Jim Champlin of WBLI in Long Island presents Ralph Guild, chief executive officer of Interep, with the Delaney-Cuneen Award.

Fig. 57. The future of New York City broadcasting is in good hands with this bunch! Betty Ellen Berlamino (far left), vice president and general manager of WPIX-TV; Frank Comerford (center), president of WNBC-TV; and Lew Leone (far right), vice president and general manager of WNYW-TV.

Fig. 58. Two-time NYSBA chairman Dennis Swanson poses a question during a breakfast meeting with Governor George Pataki. Eric Straus, former Hudson Valley broadcaster and current owner of RegionlHelpWanted.com, sits on the right. NYSBA president Joe Reilly is seen in the background.

Fig. 59. Having a good time at a NYSBA event, from left to right: Andrew Langston, owner of WDKX in Rochester; Maisha and Barry Mayo (Barry is currently senior vice president/general manager of Emmis New York); Joe Parish of WPLJ; and former NAB chairman Ted Snider.

Fig. 60. Ron Ruth of Transtar (center) converses with WBLS and WLIB vice president and general manager, Charles Warfield (right). The late Herb Scott, owner of radio stations throughout the Northeast, is on the left.

Fig. 62. Dr. Frank Stanton (left), the long-time president of CBS during its years as the "Tiffany Network," is seen here conversing with the legendary founder of CBS, William S. Paley.

Fig. 61. Granite Broadcasting execs stand proudly in front of the studios of WKBW-TV in Buffalo. Left to right: W. Don Cornwell, chief executive officer of Granite; Bill Ransom, president and general manager of WKBW-TV; and Stuart Beck, former president of Granite, now ambassador to the United Nations representing Palau.

Fig. 63. Left to right: Tom Seaver, Phil Rizzuto, and Bobby Murcer proudly display their 1991 NYSBA awards for "Best Coverage of Local Sports," in the WPIX booth at Yankee Stadium.

Fig. 64. Now introducing Ramblin' Lou Shriver and the entire Ramblin' Lou Family Band! In addition to helping their father run WXRL in Buffalo, the whole family regularly performs in Buffalo and makes pilgrimages to the country-western entertainment hub, Branson, Missouri.

Fig. 66. "Do it Frankie, *do* it to it!" rang out a voice to get "The Chief Rocker's" show started. Frankie Crocker is credited with pushing "urban" music in to the mainstream.

Fig. 65. Late in his career Gene Klavan has a "bevy of beauties" all smiles in the studio of WOR in New York City. In an earlier incarnation with his co-anchor Dee Finch, he helped get New Yorkers moving in the morning with his sharp wit for over 25 years on the greatly missed WNEW-AM. Some recognized the brilliant Klavan as one of the first "shock jocks."

Fig. 67. John A. Gambling (left) and son John R. Gambling (right) hang out with Liberace in the studio of WOR. Beginning with John B. Gambling in 1925, the three generations of Gamblings have graced New York City's airwaves for 80 years, an astonishing streak in any business.

Fig. 68. Conservative talker Rush Limbaugh makes an impassioned speech to NYSBA members. Plucked from relative obscurity at a radio station in Sacramento in the mid-1980s by former ABC Radio chief Ed McLaughlin, Limbaugh went on to forever change the sound of talk radio.

Fig. 69. "It's 1 o'clock and here is Mary Margaret McBride . . ." At its peak, her radio show attracted as many as 8 million listeners each day, making her an influential symbol of the modern American woman.

Fig. 70. George "Hound Dog" Lorenz is credited with introducing rhythm and blues, along with other forms of African American music, to vast radio audiences. The dapper "Hound" is pictured here on stage in Buffalo with a young Elvis Presley.

Fig. 71. Long before Barbara Walters, there were influential broadcasters like Martha Brooks on WGY Radio in Schenectady. The "Martha Brooks Show" ran for an astonishing 35 years! She once recorded a promotion for her show, saying, "Martha Brooks is *one* woman whose place is definitely in the home—*your* home. And that's just where you'll find her, too. When you tune into WGY each morning . . ."

Fig. 72. One of Long Island's best-known announcers, Jack Ellsworth (right), is pictured here with his friend of more than 50 years, Benny Goodman (left). Ellsworth is still spinning "the standards" on WALK on Long Island.

had his share of doubters. Most predicted he would be forced to sell the station within 90 days. Drawing on his own instincts, he found his way, running the station successfully into the 1990s, until he sold it to American Radio Systems.

The Hound wasn't the only DJ wooing and winning over Buffalo in the 1950s. He had competition from the latest version of "Guy King" at WWOL. "Guy King" was an alias used by DJs Bruce Bradley, Tom Clay, Frank Ward, and Dick Purtan. They revved up teenagers with the latest sounds and had housewives swooning over classic standards and ballads. Each day "Guy King" would sign off with the familiar tune "I can only give you love that lasts forever and a promise to be near each time you call. And the only heart I own. For you . . . and you alone. That's all, That's all . . ." The song, which was written by Dick Haymes's brother, Bob, became a classic.

Tom Clay gained notoriety in 1955 when he climbed atop the WWOL billboard above the Palace Burlesque building at Shelton Square in downtown Buffalo. He broadcast his show to throngs of screaming teenagers as he repeatedly played "Rock Around the Clock," urging the crowds to "honk your horns, fellas and gals, if you wanna hear that one again!" After bringing Buffalo to a standstill for more than two hours, Clay was escorted off the billboard by the fire department and promptly arrested for his little stunt. Later that year he was off to Cincinnati, before his career eventually headed to Detroit and, later, Los Angeles.

One of the most memorable radio institutions ever created in New York City was undoubtedly WMCA's "The Good Guys." Throughout the 1950s, radio stations across America began to adopt the Top-40 format, playing the most popular songs over and over again. In 1958, WMCA hired Steve Labunski as general manager and Ruth Meyer as program director, two pioneers in the Top-40 format. At WMCA, Meyer evolved the Top-40 format into a "team" concept, in which all the on-air personalities worked together promoting the idea, the music, and each other to build overall buzz.

Joe O'Brien, Harry Harrison, Jack Spector, Don Davis, and Jim Harriott were the original "Good Guys." In 1961 Dan Daniel was hired, and Ed Baer was added soon thereafter, earning the nickname "The Big Bad Bear" because he was the last to join the group. Through the 1960s, WMCA became one of the most popular stations in New York City. The genius of "The Good Guys" lay in their ability to connect with a broad audience. They did everything together: working at record hops, making personal appearances, and even recording an album together. "The Good Guys" were a cohesive team, down to wearing the same suits and sporting the same haircut. Teens were sure to never miss DJs B. Mitchel Reed and Gary Stevens at night, while their parents spent their mornings with the humor of Joe O'Brien.

Approximately 4 million New Yorkers got ready for work listening to Harry Harrison each morning on WABC, from 1968 to 1979. One famous story Harrison often shared was a letter he once received from a woman who gave up listening to his show for Lent as a sign of sacrifice! In doing so, she commented that she started getting up late for work and frequently overslept because she no longer was enticed to get out of bed by his program. At a time when radio was still going after the broadest audience possible, Harrison was able to balance the emerging young sound of Top 40 with bits of news and information for the more conservative taste of adults. Some of his most well-known phrases included "Every brand new day should be opened like a precious gift!", "Stay well, stay happy, stay right here!", and "Harry Harrison wishing you the best . . . that's exactly what you deserve!"

Before landing the coveted morning-drive slot at WABC, he got his start in New York as one of "The Good Guys" at WMCA in 1959. His midday show followed WMCA's early morning personality, Joe O'Brien. One of his best-known features at WMCA was his "Housewife Hall of Fame." Harrison recalls the fun he had with his listeners at WMCA: "We had the greatest promotions. One time we had a picnic. We said, 'We're going to invite you to a picnic, but you're going to have to figure out where it is,' and we gave hints on the air. Thousands of people would show up!"

As AM radio began its decline in the late 1970s, music programs on WABC inevitably faded. Harry Harrison left WABC to join WCBS-FM. He stayed on the air there until 2003, becoming known as New York's "Morning Mayor."

Out on Long Island, Marty Beck also bought into the heart and soul of rock and roll. The format was integral to the building of his stations on Long Island. "It brought legitimacy to the type of programming we were doing. I really felt rock was a lot more than most people thought it was." Beck credits taking a chance on the rock format because of his program director, Jay Mitchell: "Jay was with me at WBLI. He came in one morning and we talked programming. I knew very little and he knew a lot more than I did. I said, 'Jay, look at your age group. Why don't we rock it?' There was no such thing on Long Island at the time. No one ever heard of it. So we rocked and the rest was history. It was a great station and he did a super job." When WBLI-FM was put on the air in January 1971, the first song played was the "Age of Aquarius."

Rick Sklar was another program director who had enormous influence over the development of rock, notes Ralph Guild: "He was instrumental in the early growth of Top-40 radio here in the United States. He was the program director for WABC-AM in New York. In the early days, when rock and roll was really in its hottest period, during the time of the Beattles, Sklar was the guy doing the most creative programming. He got all the big personalities to promote his programs at the stations he worked for. He was just a brilliant guy."

If the title "promotional genius" could be bestowed on just one broadcaster, hands down it would be Rick Sklar. The excitement and cleverness of his buffers and jingles turned WABC into a ratings powerhouse, forcing its competitors to abandon the Top-40 format altogether.

During the 1950s Sklar worked alongside Alan Freed, watching the rock-and-roll phenomenon grow at WINS. He was trained in the art of developing a play list for the Top-40 format. He learned it was better to keep it short, playing popular tunes over and over. Unlike his contemporaries, Rick Sklar would come to base his selections on record sales, not surveys. He learned another important lesson from Freed: never to be lulled by record promoters into the type of pay-ola scandal Freed found himself caught up in. Sklar refused contact with promoters for the most part. Even when they took him to dinner or threw a party for the station, he made sure he always paid.

In regard to promotion, Sklar learned that advertising his programming on platforms outside the station, like newspapers and billboards, was less important than promotion on the airwaves of the station itself. For him, it wasn't about throwing a lot of money at marketing; it was about coming up with a very simple idea to get the audience excited. He picked up this strategy from Murray "The K" Kaufman at WINS. Kaufman was a master self-promoter, pulling crazy stunts like sleeping in a subway station to dressing up as Hamlet, all to draw attention to himself.

When Sklar started at WABC in 1962, he had a shoestring budget for promotions. Some of his first contests at WABC included a "search for an heir to an international fortune" (with a payoff that amounted to only about $400) and a "Secret Agent" contest. The success of these inexpensive but effective promotions quickly advanced him to the position of program director.

When the Beatles came to New York for the first time, Sklar made sure WABC "owned" them, promoting the station as "W A 'Beatle' C." He even devised a contest to design a medal to honor the Beatles, called the "The Order of the All Americans." It was awarded to each of the Beatles live, on the air, by WABC personality Cousin Brucie Morrow.

By 1970, WABC was number one in the ratings. Two years earlier, ABC had finally shut down its old radio network. Sklar was now free to program his entire broadcast day as he saw fit. He branded his station "MusicRadio WABC, 'The Most Music.'" WINS had long since fallen to third, switching to an all-news format. As FM continued its march past AM, WMCA dropped music as well. The high ratings for WABC continued through much of the 1970s. When ABC decided to switch WABC to all talk in 1982, Sklar left to spread his magic as a consultant, traveling throughout the country.

"I did it all. Some I did more than once," responded the late Scott Muni when asked what was the one thing he wanted to do before departing this earth. With a career spanning more than 50 years, there weren't too many events in the world of music in which he didn't find himself part of the mix. Three generations of listeners in New York City knew Scott Muni as "The Professor," teaching millions how to appreciate the nuances of music. His gravelly voice introduced songs from the Beatles to Springsteen to U2. He got his start in the number-one market as one of "The Good Guys" on WMCA-AM, spinning tunes from the Top 40. He moved over to WABC in 1960, before landing at WNEW-FM in 1967, where he truly found his sound, helping to create one of the nation's first alternative stations. His free-form radio crafted at WNEW would influence the next generation of DJs.

Muni was a welcome member in the court of rock and roll royalty, interviewing legends like Paul McCartney, Mick Jagger, and Pete Townshend. His most memorable encounter was with guitarist Jimmy Page. It happened in Muni's radio studio one day. The musician suddenly collapsed to the floor in midsentence, apparently exhausted by days of partying. Ever the consummate professional, Muni put on a record, woke Page up, and finished the rest of the interview with Page lying flat out on the floor.

Not everybody bought into the rock-and-roll or rhythm-and-blues phenomena. In Buffalo, deejay Fred Klestine maintained a devoted following for almost 25 years by offering a mixture of jazz, big bands, cabaret songs, and romantic crooners. Klestine, on WWOL and later on WBNY and WKBW, passed on in 1992 due to a stroke at age 68. However, he's still heard to this day at Cole's Bar in the fashionable Elmwood Avenue section of Buffalo, which plays reruns of Fred Klestine's classy music shows from back in the 1950s and 1960s, commercials and all.

A Rainbow of Music Formats

During the 1970s as black music expanded its presence on the radio dial throughout the country, another format began to grow beyond its roots in the South and West: country-western music. By the middle of the decade, every major market had at least one country-western station. Ramblin' Lou Shriver's love of country music brought the format to Buffalo. It is interesting to note the many parallels and occasional intersections Shriver's career would have with that of George Lorenz. The two formats they dedicated their lives to eventually became among the two most popular formats in the country, and still are today. They would both struggle starting out, but their deep convictions for the music they loved so dearly carried them through.

At an early age, Shriver got hooked on country-western when he spent his boyhood summers in Pennsylvania with his grandfather. In those days, country music was referred to as "hillbilly" music. Shriver's grandfather frequently took him to barn dances where fiddlers would be playing into the night.

He got his start at a station in Niagara Falls, eventually landing an early morning gig at 6 a.m. In time, his show slowly expanded to three hours. His first boss felt that his name didn't sound country-western enough, so he decided to start calling him "Ramblin' Lou," recalls Shriver: "I didn't care what he called me, as long as I was able to get on the air." The show struggled and Shriver had difficulty getting sponsors. He eventually befriended George Lorenz, another young broadcaster trying to break old conventions. It would be Lorenz who took Shriver under his wing to help him learn how to sell, helping him save his show.

Unfortunately the station ended up letting Shriver go. As with Lorenz, Al Anscombe took a liking to Shriver. Anscombe would help give both of these broadcasters a nudge in the early days of their careers. Broadcasting was a small business after all, and he was the station manager of the most influential station in Buffalo. After Shriver was let go, he went to Anscombe for advice. Unable to suggest a station that would take a chance on his format, Anscombe convinced Shriver to buy his own station. "He said he couldn't afford to buy, but I told him I knew one for sale he could afford," says Anscombe. In 1970 he helped Shriver acquire WXRL, a small 500-watt station. He struggled at first, but 30 years later, Shriver has powered-up the station to 5,000 watts, receiving listener mail from as far away as Toronto to the north and Pennsylvania to the south.

In the 1970s, a new format would grab the attention of Interep chief Ralph Guild. It was a sound unlike anything he had heard before: "I found WBLS quite by accident. I became quite a fan of the station at the time. I remember looking through a survey at the time, either Arbitron or Pulse, I'm not sure, and I kept seeing WBLS coming up. I said to myself, 'What the heck is this?' We called them and started repping them. We have represented them ever since." This would be the beginning of the urban format as pioneered by Percy Sutton, the New York powerbroker and former Manhattan borough president. "When I think of Percy Sutton and the urban format, I think it is probably one of the most significant contributions to the radio industry over the last 25 years."

Many stations found success with new formats, but others also found "gold" with the "oldies." Nancy Widmann fondly refers to her old program director at WCBS-FM, Joe McCoy, as the "Father of the Oldies Format." "He did an incredible job of fine-tuning the Oldies format, which is alive and well all over the country to this day. I think one of the things we have to do is acknowledge that it was Joe's format. He really kept it fresh and alive, and he understood it. He brought Cousin Brucie back. He was the first guy to do the Top 500. Now the Top 500 is done everywhere, in every format." Unfortunately, Infinity Broadcasting, the current owner of WCBS-FM, has recently thrown out the long-popular Oldies format for the new free-form "Jack" format du jour that is sweeping the country. The new format is designed to accommodate the changing listening habits of young adults brought on by the music player, iPod. While WCBS-FM, "The Oldies Station," has been wiped from the airwaves, it has found a new home online at wcbsfm.com, where loyal listeners can continue to listen to their favorite tunes from the 1960s and 1970s.

Jack Ellsworth is still spinning the tunes he was listening to on Long Island over 50 years ago. After selling his station, WLIM, in 2001, he wasn't quite ready to throw in the towel. He thought it would be nice to finish out his career where he began broadcasting, at WALK. He was given a daily two-hour time slot and took a commission on all the advertising he sells during the show. "What I'm doing and what seems to be getting a good response is playing the music you just don't hear anymore on the radio," explains Ellsworth. "Not a lot of stations will play standards. They'll mix in other stuff, playing a little Sinatra, a little Ella Fitzgerald, or maybe a little Glenn Miller." Ellsworth, on the other hand, plays the music of these legends exclusively: "What I want to do is keep the good sounds of the Golden Era alive. When I say the Golden Era, I mean the big-band years . . . when we had great singers like Sinatra, Crosby, Dick Haymes, Nat 'King' Cole, Mel Torme, and people like that. They deserve to be heard, and you just can't forget them."

In upstate New York, to get "in tune" with his audience, Phil Spencer went directly to his listeners when he became general manager in Amsterdam, and asked them what kind of music they wanted to hear. "I did something that as far as I know nobody else ever did. I bought a full-page ad in the local paper. It killed me to give them my money, and I did a music survey." Spencer also bought 200 little radios locked into 1490 AM, his station's frequency, and gave them away free to anyone who filled out his survey. He asked them to name their five all-time favorite songs, their favorite male vocalist, favorite female vocalist, favorite vocal group, and the kind of music they liked overall. The response to his survey far exceeded his expectations. Over 500 people participated. He collated all the information he gathered and created music tapes based on what the public wanted to hear, not based on the latest record industry information, national surveys, or record sales: "I knew exactly what this town wanted. My predecessor had no idea. I knew. Is it the station I would have listened to? I doubt it, but I had to put a station on here that the public wanted, and it took off."

"There are Seven Wonders of the World, you're about to be entertained by the eighth . . . do it Frankie, *do* it to it!" That was how Frankie Crocker opened his show on WBLS in New York during the late 1970s and early 1980s. The "Chief Rocker" changed how African American music was played on the radio and made African American recording artists more confident about their music. He got his start as news director at WUFO in Buffalo. By the time he landed at WMCA in New York, the style he became known for quickly began to blossom. Crocker pushed urban music from the fringe to the mainstream.

Before Frankie Crocker, there was "Jocko," also known as Doug Henderson. He has been referred to as the "Black Dick Clark" and the "Father of Rap." As was the case with many emerging rhythm-and-blues DJs in the 1950s and 1960s, Jocko used rhymes like "Hello, Daddy-O and Mommy-O, This is Jocko," or "eee-tiddlee-yock, this is the Jock" to keep the energy level of his show as lively as the music he played. When he came to New York City to do morning drive for WLIB, Jocko continued his show in the city of brotherly love, Philadelphia, where he had crafted his sound. He would later move on to WADO and then WWRL in the late evenings. It has been estimated that his fan club boasted 50,000 members. When he wasn't on the air, he was zooming onto music stages in a rocket ship suspended on wires, enveloped in smoke, rivaling the entrance of the performers he was to introduce. After an unsuccessful bid for Congress in 1978, he dedicated his efforts to promoting his "Get Ready" program for school children across the country. He used rap lyrics to connect with students to teach them math, English, and American history.

Latino Sounds

The explosion of the Hispanic population in the United States over the last 20 years has spread the infectious high-energy sounds of salsa, merengue, and other Latin music over New York's airwaves. Many would agree that Polito Vega gave salsa its first few sparks toward mainstream popularity. He played the first-ever salsa on the radio, called "El Campeon," by Johnny Pacheco. Many musicians like Larry Harlow, a member of the legendary salsa band Fania All-Stars, credit their success to Vega: "If it weren't for him, our music wouldn't even be on the air now. He's really the one who's kept the old music alive all these years. He's always been there for us." His first program, "Fiesta Time," went on the air in 1959 on WEVD-AM. From there he went on to WWRL, WBNX, and, for the last 15 years, he has graced the airwaves of "La Mega," 97.9 FM. Today he is regarded as an institution in the Latino music world and as the keeper of the flame of classic salsa. He is careful, however, never to hold on to the past too tightly: "I have a special show. I have my thing, but sometimes I play new music, too. I combine the new and the old because I don't want to seem too old if I just stay with oldies after oldies after oldies. I'm 66, but in my mind, I'm 25, and that's what has helped me stay on the radio."

Vega's legacy has helped pave the way for other Latino DJs like Manuel "Paco" Navarro, known for introducing dance music into the mainstream in the 1970s and 1980s on WKTU in New York. He was to WKTU what Frankie

Crocker was to WBLS. In 1978 he joined the station from WJIT where he played salsa music. He helped convince station executives to change the format from mellow rock to disco, rebranding the station "Disco 92." His show quickly shot up to the number-one spot. "Paco is my name and disco is my game!" was the nightly greeting he gave to his listeners. A year later, in response to the decline of disco, the station dumped half its music lineup, and Paco survived as the only "disco" DJ, still playing the latest dance music.

Sports and Entertainment

"The key," "the lane," "the top of the circle," and "midcourt stripe" are all part of the vernacular now taken for granted in basketball coverage. They were first introduced into broadcasting by the great Marty Glickman. With his broad New York accent, Glickman became one of the greatest play-by-play announcers in sports. Others of his genre included Mel Allen, the voice of the Yankees, Red Barber, Curt Gowdy, and, in recent years, John Sterling. For more than 40 years, Glickman brought the excitement of New York City's sports teams into millions of homes. He served as the voice of the Knicks, the Giants, and the Jets, but his voice will always be most closely associated with basketball. So sure of his craft, he once said: "Marty Glickman doesn't do color for anybody." While WHN, the station he first worked for when he came to New York, has slipped into history, the influence of Glickman's timeless approach will be felt for generations to come.

In the late 1960s, a little-known assistant program director at WBEN-AM in Buffalo would also make history in sports broadcasting. When Bill McKibben took a job at WBEN, he took his long-time assistant, Linda Arnold Lieberman, with him. Recognizing that her abilities were not being fully utilized, he gave her a promotion, teaming her up with John Patton, WBEN-AM's program director.

As assistant program director, Lieberman was responsible for producing the play-by-play broadcasts for the Buffalo Bills. McKibben was shocked to learn from members of WBEN's crew covering the Bills that the NFL forbade women from entering the NFL press boxes. He didn't think the league would actually enforce such an antiquated policy, yet he received several calls from the NFL organization advising him to reconsider his decision. Even Pete Rozelle, the famous NFL commissioner at the time, contacted McKibben. Undeterred, the broadcaster reminded Roselle that WBEN was a CBS affiliate, so McKibben suggested he be interviewed by Walter Cronkite to explain this policy to the public. Rozelle promptly hung up, and that was the last "official word" McKibben heard from the NFL. Lieberman, of course, would endure a lot of harassment, but those with more enlightened minds like Van Miller, the voice of the Bills, stepped in to make sure she was able to do her job just as her male counterparts.

Clint Buehlman was so popular in Buffalo when he began his career that he even gave Jack Paar a run for his money. John Zach refers to Buehlman as a "consummate broadcaster." He started out at WGR back in the 1930s, during the first Golden Age of Radio. Zach recounts some of Buehlman's wacky stunts that made him so popular: "He would hang over the parapet of a building in downtown Buffalo and describe traffic down below. He would smash the piano in the studio if it was out of tune or if they couldn't get the piano tuner to come in to fix it."

Everyone in Buffalo listened to him. He seemed unstoppable, but WBEN was determined to take Buehlman head on, so they hired an announcer by the name of Jack Paar from Cleveland. Paar was obviously very talented and went on to network fame, but even he was unable to unseat Clint Buehlman. After just two years, Paar left Buffalo's airwaves when he got drafted into the Army.

WBEN decided there was only one course of action left to take: They offered Buehlman a ton of money to come work for the station. In 1943, he started his morning show on WBEN and stayed for almost 35 years. "He is probably recognized as the broadcaster of the century in this community. The younger people don't remember him, of course, but if you ask anybody over 50 in Buffalo about Clint Buehlman, either they listened to him or their parents did. You didn't touch that radio when he was on," explains Zach.

The "Amazing" Bill Mazer was another Buffalo legend around this time. Brooklyn-born and bred, Mazer became the most popular sports announcer in Buffalo in the late 1950s and 1960s before he made the move to the Big Apple, where he worked at WNBC and WEVD. Mazer, now in his 80s, still has a daily talk show near his home in Westchester.

It is rare to find a person who can alone draw a mass audience in radio and television. It is a unique skill, a craft that is developed over many years, to make each listener and viewer feel as if each was the only member of the audience. What may be even more rare is to find a duo, a team, or a partnership in broadcasting that has the talent to weave the audience into their conversation, banter, or innocent off-hand remarks. Jinx Falkenburg, along with her husband, Tex McCrary, helped pioneer "morning chat" on the radio in the 1940s and 1950s. Their show "Tex and Jinx" focused on guest personalities and current events of great importance. Tex played the intellectual, while Jinx peppered Tex and their guests with questions to get at the heart of complex issues.

During the 1950s and 1960s, "Gene Rayburn and Dee Finch" and then "Gene Klavan and Dee Finch" were WNEW's popular morning team. "Rayburn and Finch" broke up in 1952 when Rayburn left WNEW for NBC to work on Steve Allen's local variety show, the precursor to "The Steve Allen Tonight Show." Rayburn went on to become a popular game show host. As Finch's new partner, Klavan was the comic, known for his sharp wit and knack for creating wacky voices for made-up characters like Trevor Traffic, Mr. Nat, Sy Kology, and Victor Verse. Dee Finch was his tried and true straight man. Tame by today's standards, some regard Klavan as one of the pioneering "shock jocks."

Other stellar duos of the day were Ed and Pegeen Fitzgerald of WOR, "Ted Brown and the Redhead" on WMGM, and Peter Lind Hayes and Mary Healy on WOR. Former big-band singer Bea Wain of "My Reverie" fame even had a daily show with her husband, the great voice-over freelance announcer Andre Barúche on WNBC.

One of the most successful and widely imitated "team approach" presentations was Z-100's "Morning Zoo" developed by NAB Hall of Famer Scott Shannon. He first experimented with the concept in Tampa, Florida, at Q105, before launching it on New York's Z-100 in the fall of 1983. In under a year, the show vaulted Z-100 to the top and provided the catalyst for the resurgence of the Top-40 format across America. Shannon has described the "Zoo" as "Saturday Night Live," "The Tonight Show," and talk radio all rolled into one, with heavy doses of parody songs, comedy skits, and biting editorials. His sidekicks, fondly referred to as the "zoo creatures," included Ross Brittain, Jack Murphy, and John "Mr. Leonard" Rio, known for his green leisure suits, cherry red shoes, and the lime-green Pinto he supposedly drove.

Obviously an entertainer first, Shannon also had a knack for delivering thoughtful social commentaries. Like many of his predecessors, entertainment provided a vehicle to get people talking about issues, in addition to being an escape for listeners seeking a brief reprieve from their hectic lives. Today Shannon helms powerhouse WPLJ as program director and co-host of the stations' morning show, "Scott and Todd in the Morning." His partner, Todd Pettengill, got his start in radio at WFLY-FM in Albany. In a recent survey by *Radio & Records*, Shannon was named "The Most Influential Programmer of the Past 20 Years." Don Imus's success is also attributed to his prowess as a shrewd and keen social commentator.

"Whether you like Howard Stern or not, he is just a modern Arthur Godfrey and friends . . . a bunch of people coming in and out of the studio chatting with him," says Paul Sidney, the voice of WLNG in Long Island. Undeniably, those are where the similarities end. As Stern developed his career in broadcasting, he found himself in a world with far more competition than Godfrey ever had to contend with. At a time when societal tastes became more cynical, Stern pioneered the concept of the "shock jock," firmly securing his place in broadcast history. In an interview with Larry King he once said his best listeners were the ones who hated him the most . . . they always waited with baited breath for his next "shocking" act or statement. Stern rarely disappointed.

The millions of dollars the FCC has fined Howard Stern's employers for his antics have had the exact opposite effect of getting him to clean up his act, making him even more outrageous and more popular than ever before. He has been a great political target for those wishing to provide more "wholesome" entertainment for the public. At the same time he has also become the poster child for those defending speech. The conservative tide in the culture wars encouraged some major broadcasters to pull his show from their airwaves in 2004, prompting Stern to bolt for the new medium of satellite radio, which is currently unregulated by the FCC. Some believe Stern's popularity is drawn from his genius in understanding just how close he can take his show to the line of what has been defined as obscene by the FCC. According to Bob Ausfeld, this is what has made him so successful: "What has been interesting is his ability to take it right up to the line. As a listener you have to create what you think he's saying or how you want it to look in your own mind." When Stern moves over to satellite radio, where anything goes, he will no longer be encumbered by FCC regulations. Ausfeld questions how successful Stern will be without that fine indecency line no longer around to hug.

Indecency

Radio and television were born into a more wholesome era than the one they find themselves in today. As the country came of age and stalwart conventions were challenged, broadcasting reflected the changing assumptions of what was in good taste and what was not. When Elvis first appeared on "The Ed Sullivan Show" he was shot from the waist up because his gyrations were considered inappropriate. Fast-forward 40 years to Janet Jackson, who openly overran the boundaries of decency by exposing her breast during the broadcast of Super Bowl XXXVIII on CBS. As the country threw itself into a heated debate about Jackson's actions and the extent to which CBS should share responsibility, pharmaceutical companies continue to fill broadcast airwaves with explicit erectile dysfunction cures viewed by children anytime throughout the day. The boundaries of indecency and the public's perception of what is acceptable and what is not have never been more difficult for broadcasters to navigate.

In 1995, the FCC would shorten the "safe harbor" period by two hours. From 10 p.m. to 6 a.m. broadcasters are permitted to air material that may be deemed inappropriate for younger viewers, or even indecent. After Janet Jackson's "wardrobe malfunction," the U.S. House of Representatives responded to the public outcry to "clean up" radio and television programming by passing the Broadcast Indecency Act of 2004 by an overwhelming 391 to 22 majority. The bill would increase the maximum fine per violation from $27,500 to a draconian $500,000. The Senate is still considering similar legislation and is seeking to regulate programming on cable and satellite outlets as well, which currently fall outside the domain of the FCC. The largest fine ever handed down by the FCC was $1.7 million levied against Infinity Broadcasting for a series of indecency violations by "The Howard Stern Show" in 1995. Since then, to demonstrate its commitment to cracking down on objectionable material, the Commission has actively levied fines against a variety of broadcasters. It fined Clear Channel $755,000 in 2004, the largest single fine ever for sexually explicit material aired on four of its stations in Florida. Young Broadcasting was fined $27,500 for airing a man exposing himself on its "KRON 4 Morning News" show, the second time a television station was ever fined. The first was against a station in Puerto Rico in 2001.

Tony Malara recalls getting thrown off the air in college for an infraction that would barely garner a slap on the wrist today: "I was doing a Grand Opera show on Sunday nights for three hours. On one particular Sunday night, it was supposed to end at 10 p.m. because we had a new show debuting. Everyone, including the dean of the school, was in the studio waiting for me to get off the air. I'm playing 'Aida, the Grand March.' There's no way to fill time after the Grand March." Suddenly the engineer starts tapping his foot on the floor when the song was over, motioning to Malara that he had three minutes to fill. "I thought the microphone was off, so my reaction went over the air. I said, 'Oh, shit!' I filled for three minutes, but everybody in the world heard the 'Oh, shit!'" Phone calls poured in and the station was flooded with mail. Malara, who is today a beloved icon in the NYSBA firmament, ended up getting a fine from the FCC and was kicked off the air for three months.

Most broadcasters took their duty seriously and regarded themselves as an invited guest in their listeners' and viewers' homes. Words that have become part of everyday language were once taboo, recalls Jim Rodgers: "When I first started, the words *rape* or *sodomy* were never used in broadcasting. I always felt we were in your house as a guest, and I didn't want to be inappropriate in your home."

As broadcasting faces increasing competition, some in the industry believe indecency regulations hold broadcasters at a great disadvantage. Others believe that by acting in the public's interest to stay within the socially acceptable boundaries of good taste will actually be an advantage to broadcasters. As Bill O'Shaughnessy reminds us: "It's *not* just about decency and obscenity. It's also, ultimately, about freedom of speech and political discourse." Government intrusion into content is a slippery slope no matter how objectionable the material. Operating in the public's interest will guide broadcasters toward the proper balance of free speech and good taste. As the public's palate continues to evolve over time in terms of how they are entertained and informed, they will no doubt make their feelings known to their congressmen or retain the power to censor themselves by simply voting with their remote or by switching the dial.

6

Meeting the Challenge and Staying Competitive

"It's no longer how many gross ratings points you deliver or your cost per point. It's really all about the return on investment (ROI). Sometimes the largest audience isn't the most effective audience, and broadcasters are starting to recognize that."

—Gary Fries, president and chief executive officer, Radio Advertising Bureau

During NYSBA's first 25 years, competition among broadcasters was primarily defined by the depth of commitment they made to the communities they were mandated to serve and the size of the audience they were able to reach. Over the last 25 years, however, obligations required by broadcast licenses slowly became overwhelmed by the mounting pressure to deliver on the bottom line as broadcasters faced new realities in the marketplace.

A typical NYSBA member in the early days of the Association was an individual owner, indeed, many of the "mom and pop" variety. Today they are an anomaly for the most part. "I've been on the board about seven years now. When I first became a member, there were quite a few guys like me: small, independent guys who owned their own station or even a small, regional group. If you look at the board of directors now, I'm the only guy on the whole board who owns my company. At the same time, I would say there is a good mix of men and women who work for these corporate entities, and they are still broadcasters at heart," comments Ed Levine, former chairman of NYSBA and creator of NYSBA's Hall of Fame.

Owners had no one to answer to but themselves, the FCC, and the public. Today, many broadcast companies are judged by Wall Street analysts on their financial performance alone. Bob Bruno, vice president and general manager of WOR-AM, admits having occasionally to bend to financial pressures:

"I sometimes compromise and I would love to say I don't, but I do at times. I work for an enlightened company, but like every business, it is as bottom-line oriented as they have to be." Even privately held companies like Ed Levine's Galaxy Communications are not immune from the realities of running a business in today's financial environment. Levine does his best to strike a healthy balance. "Some people say, 'have fun, make money,' but I don't believe that, because if I'm not making money, I'm not having fun. Make your numbers, have fun—whether it's revenue numbers, rating numbers, or cash-flow numbers. I still have fun doing this, and I like to think the people in this company are here because they really like to have fun. My joke is we do radio the old-fashioned way, the way it was done prior to 1996," says Levine, obviously proud of his independent, entrepreneurial status.

Several economic trends began to converge in the 1980s and 1990s. The broadcast industry evolved from a mom-and-pop business to one dominated by large corporate organizations. Economic realities also began to erode the decades-old, mass-market business model that had served broadcasting for so long. The rapid pace of deregulation, new competitors, and even the dramatic upstate New York population decline have all had their impact as the broadcasters of the Empire State seek to redefine their relationship with their local communities.

Broadcast Licenses Become a Commodity

Broadcast licenses have long been the sacred foundation of both radio and television, dictating ownership rules, advertising guidelines, and hiring practices. The spirit of these regulations was to ensure that broadcasters were serving their communities to the best of their abilities, while properly using their available resources. After all, these licenses gave them access to a scarce national resource, making broadcasters trustees of the public's airwaves and an integral part of the communities they served.

Responding to a changing, competitive environment, the FCC, led by Chairman Mark Fowler, began to relax ownership rules in the early 1980s. The period between license renewals was extended, the requirement to own a station for a minimum of three years was dropped, and it was made more difficult for a third party to challenge license renewals. In time, the FCC would also raise the cap on the number of television and radio stations an individual owner may possess.

The net effect of these policies over time made broadcasting a more attractive investment than ever before, dramatically increasing the value of the industry. Many long-serving broadcasters couldn't help but feel a little nostalgic for the old days. Many of them became broadcasters for the opportunity to serve, while also making a decent living. Jim Champlin's sentiment is shared by many broadcasters: "We were broadcasters. We weren't really buying licenses with the ultimate game plan to sell them and make a huge profit, because at the time that wasn't really happening. Wall Street hadn't really discovered broadcast at that point." Hometown broadcasters felt their position, after decades of watching over their communities, was slowly undermined as licenses started being viewed more as a "commodity" to be bought and sold rather than as a national treasure to be guarded. Clearly, the notion of the broadcaster as trustee with a fiduciary relationship to the airwaves was coming under increasing pressure.

"When stations started being sold like financial investments, instead of keeping them for three years under the old rules, I think you ended up with people who were interested in making money and weren't necessarily interested in being in the broadcasting business," says CapCities founder Tom Murphy, describing the wave of investors who became attracted to the industry after key FCC ownership rules were relaxed. For most broadcasters, however, the reality of business dealings came with the territory of how to best serve their audiences. Business was only the means to an end. If they weren't making money, they wouldn't be around to serve their community. It was very straightforward. "Bigger" doesn't always mean "better" in broadcasting, according to Bill O'Shaughnessy: "There is no question that the mom-and-pop, hometown-community broadcaster has been slowly replaced over the years by what MBA types call 'asset managers.' The guys who work out of airport lounges with Palm Pilots, beholden to corporate masters a whole continent away."

Many corporate conglomerates have been unfairly derided. They have been an easy target to explain away the challenges broadcasting faces today. It has been estimated that over 60% of all radio stations prior to the 1990s were in the red. Corporations helped bring more sophisticated business practices to the industry and have helped concentrate resources necessary to meet the challenges of tomorrow, such as the multibillion dollar investment required for the upgrade to digital. Ed Levine admits MBAs have become a critical part of the industry over the last decade, but the "vision" should be left up to true broadcasters: "I've got guys like that in my company; they're on my financial team; they're on my investment team; but they're not the CEO. You've got to have them on the team, but you just don't make them the CEO."

Broadcasters once relied on civic leaders, heads of local charities, and other local decisionmakers to help them guide their business. In many cases those guideposts for decisionmaking have been replaced by a myopic focus on the bottom line. Managing large, disparate broadcast empires has made it more difficult for senior management to be in tune with their individual viewers and listeners. As a result, they have become increasingly dependent on balance sheets as their new guide. Former Katz Media chief Jim Greenwald recalls a time when business was conducted on a much more personal level than it is today: "It's not to say previous owners didn't focus on their bottom line, because they did, so they could make a living. However, there was a different kind of client-seller relationship. A different dynamic. You dealt with the principal because he was the owner of the station. Today you may deal with a corporation and your relationship is with only one of the many properties it owns." Of course, there is also the massive pressure exerted by Wall Street to constantly meet revenue targets, and there isn't a line item on a balance sheet to describe how the needs of an audience are being met.

During the mid-1980s, Metromedia decided to take itself private for a variety of reasons, one of which was to alleviate itself from the pressures and scrutiny of Wall Street. "When we were public, I hated to deal with the analysts because I felt they had agendas. Their agendas weren't mine. . . . it is very difficult when the people who are analyzing you and reporting to your investors don't have your vision, don't have your understanding, and look at things quite differently than you're looking at them," says Stuart Subotnick, vice chairman of Metromedia. He came to the realization that it was better to run a media company in the private domain, using alternative sources of funding, rather than depend on the public markets for capital investment.

Evolution of Broadcast Advertising

It is generally assumed that when television started competing for ad dollars, radio immediately started losing money in the 1950s. While national advertisers did pull their money from the radio networks, radio still did well at the local level as its role evolved during this time. To demonstrate the power radio still possessed, broadcasters in New York City worked with the State Department of Agriculture and Markets to run a campaign to promote the consumption of milk in 1962. Over 6,000 radio announcements aired in New York City urging the increased consumption of milk over a six-week period.

Upon completion of the campaign, it was shown that milk consumption increased by nearly 100,000 quarts per day as compared to a decline in nearby New Jersey. Speaking at the NYSBA Annual Meeting that same year, Governor Nelson A. Rockefeller raved about the success of the broadcasters' effort: "This not only demonstrates the power of radio, but also moves us to hope that similar generous campaigns will be applied to other public service efforts affecting the people of this great state." By 1960 local advertising represented 62% of all ad revenues in radio, up from 52% in 1952.

During the 1950s, listening patterns would shift to the morning and evening drive as radio primarily become a mobile, out-of-home medium. This shift helped keep radio listening relatively high. Also, at this time, nearly one-third of all AM stations were losing money nationally. Most FMs were in the red, but their fortunes began to turn in 1975 when revenues rose to over $300 million from just $10 million in 1962.

Television was virtually a gold mine almost out of the gate, but during its first few entrepreneurial years, sales reps had a tough time capturing the imagination of advertisers. Without any audience measurements in the earliest days of television, Utica broadcaster Shell Storrier remembers people constantly asking him: "Well, who's watching?" Not sure how to respond, he posed the question to his boss, and he replied, "They all are." Undeterred, Storrier decided to invent his own local-ratings method, red pushpins. He teamed up with an appliance store and organized a drawing for a free toaster on the air. "We had a ton of postcards, so I took a map of the Utica area and put red dots where all the postcards came from. I put them in a box and carried them around on my sales calls and said, 'Here's whose watching.' That was my ratings service."

Back then most of Storrier's business was from direct contact with clients. Only a small percentage of his business came through ad agencies. Not only did he sell commercials, he also helped write copy, and produced the spots as well. Like Jim Greenwald, he also recalls there was a much more personal approach to business in those days: "A lot of the selling was done at a three-martini lunch or after work; that's how you got to know people."

Television revenues exploded to over $1.6 billion in 1960 from just $454 million eight years earlier. Most VHF stations were in the black within their first couple of years despite the huge investment of around $1 million or more to get the station up and running. UHF stations, on the other hand, were plagued by a variety of technological challenges, keeping them from attracting audiences as large as VHF stations were able to do, and thus advertisers. Most UHF stations wouldn't become a viable business until the 1970s, when they carved out their niche, running off-network and syndicated programs.

The earlier days of television were primarily controlled by advertisers. They would fully sponsor most programs, in addition to having them produced. Just as television revenues exploded in the late 1950s, production costs were becoming very prohibitive. The cost of a full sponsorship for a prime-time hour rose from $33,000 in 1952 to $87,000 by 1960.

Many advertisers found themselves unable to justify the cost of advertising on network television, leading to the demise of the sponsorship system. At first there would be "shared" sponsorships, alternating each week or by segment.

As advertising agencies slowly relinquished control over programming to the networks, spots began to be sold. Spot advertising was placed anywhere on the station's schedule, based on time and size of the audience. In the mid-1960s, only 40% of all ads were 30-second spots. A decade later, 30s would represent 80% of all ads on television.

In time, advertising would become more sophisticated, requiring demographic information about the audience. It was no longer enough to know that "a lot of people were watching." Advertising on television at that time was fairly straightforward, recalls Albany broadcaster John Kelly: "In the old days, it didn't take a genius to put your new product on Sid Caesar, Milton Berle, Ed Sullivan, or Perry Como. Those shows got 80% of the audience back then." This would be the early beginnings of targeting specific messages at certain demographics, rather than delivering a mass message for anyone watching television.

Many second- and third-generation broadcasters believe that not only have broadcast licenses become a commodity, but also so has broadcast advertising. When they sold spots to their clients, they wanted to deliver results rather than simply relying on ratings. Jim Delmonico says he was also careful to maximize the exposure of each client's ad: "I would never run seven commercials for one client in the same show. We also wouldn't put two automobile dealers in the same break. Today, you'll see two or three. I've called managers and asked them why they do that, and they say they are having a tough time making payroll."

Segmentation in combination with the proliferation of stations during the 1980s and 1990s dramatically changed the broadcast advertising game. Sasha Gillman, former owner of WDST, believes that the migration toward single formats and stations dedicated to one genre of music—like classic rock, jazz or pop—has had a negative impact on radio: "Single formats really came into being when advertising agencies realized it was easier to measure audiences using that approach. It has really dulled radio tremendously." When Gillman was selling, she appreciated the diversity of advertisers she had to choose from because of the variety of different people WDST's broad-based eclectic format would attract.

As previously noted, radio came to depend on local advertising to sustain its financial health. The growth of cable television over the last 20 years, however, began to put pressure on local radio broadcasters in ways that local broadcast television never did. Compared with broadcast television, cable was more targeted and offered much less-expensive advertising rates. Former Katz Media executive Gordon Hastings would experience the encroachment of cable on his radio business first hand. When cable television started selling local television advertising in Oneonta, Cooperstown, Glens Falls, and Saratoga—Hastings' listening area—they were able to offer local businesses television commercials at radio rates. The spots aired as inserts on national cable networks like CNN or ESPN. One of Hastings' largest advertisers, a local Ford dealer, left his airwaves for cable: "Guess what? The Ford dealer didn't increase his advertising budget to accommodate both radio and television. We never had to compete with television before in small markets like that. It was occurring down the road in larger markets like Albany or further west. When local cable ad sales came in, it was like dropping a television station right into the local market. The advertiser dollar base was not large enough and didn't have enough elasticity to be able to accommodate that change."

Consolidation of Advertisers

Broadcasting would not be the only industry to consolidate its mom-and-pop businesses over the last 20 years. It was a phenomenon that would run through many other American industries as part of the overall trend toward deregulation. The impact it had on broadcasters changed the makeup of their traditional advertising pool, and in some cases, it would even shrink as a result. Malls sprung up, taking customers away from stores along "Main Street." Walter Maxwell reflects on what has occurred in hundreds of communities in New York: "We used to have seven local shoe stores in Kingston. Not all of them advertised with us, but there were seven. Now we have one, a Payless. The other shoe stores are out in the mall. They never spend a dime on local radio anymore. We've got one local pharmacy, the rest are Eckerd, CVS or Rite-Aid. Industry by industry disappeared, and as they went, so did the advertising."

On the other side of the state in Jamestown, Merrill Rosen has had the same experience. Many national brands have not found it necessary to rely on small market radio as part of their marketing mix. As a result, many small radio operators have been unable to drum up the financial support for local events they were once able to do, laments Rosen: "The local proprietors who would kick in the $150 for the local band to go to the Macy's Thanksgiving Day parade are gone. When you go to the local Wal-Mart, they don't even want to talk to you. It's a lot tougher than it was 20 years ago."

A Changing Audience in New York

There were also social forces far beyond the control of broadcasting, such as the shifting population trends of the 1980s and 1990s. As the U.S. economy transformed its industrial base into a service economy, many Northern states suffered huge job loses as a result. Upstate New York was particularly hard hit. The western tier of the state would be the eastern portion of what came to be known as the "rust belt" that ran into the Midwest. It's not hard to figure out that if the population and economy are in decline, advertising dollars, as well, are no longer going to be there to support the basic broadcast business model.

Amsterdam was once a major textile manufacturing center. It was known as the "Carpet Capital of America." Phil Spencer, owner of WCSS, watched its population decline from a peak of 35,000 in the 1960s to its present-day population of 18,000: "I couldn't afford the station today because there are no more stores here. Everything's been torn down because of urban renewal, but this town was once thriving." Buffalo, Rochester, and Syracuse, once central to America's industrial might, now play a smaller part in the overall American economy than they once did. "At one time, in the 1940s I believe, Buffalo was the ninth largest market in America. Today we're 47th. We've lost about 35,000 employees, and the population has just shrunk. I say to people here, if you can go into business and are successful in Buffalo, you can do it anywhere," comments Don Angelo, local sales manager at WGRZ-TV.

Most of those who left upstate New York were younger people looking for jobs. As a result, the population left behind is much older on average, a demographic not in high demand by advertisers. Walter Maxwell, referencing the official population figures for Ulster County, confirms this trend: "In 1970, 45% of the people were 24 or younger. By 1980 that dropped to 39%, and another 5% in 1990. The total population in the county increased from a 141,000 to 177,000, but that's all 65-plus."

In 1980, the CBS Television Network commanded 26% of the total viewing audience, according to David Poltrack, executive vice president, research and planning at Viacom, now the parent of CBS. Twenty years later it would take all the Viacom cable networks combined, including MTV, Nickelodeon, Comedy Central, and Country Music Television, plus the CBS Television Network, to reach the exact same share of the audience. Broadcast television currently holds just under a 50% share of the entire viewing audience. In Albany, John Kelly remembers advertisers used to buy "roadblocks" on the three local affiliates: "If you bought a spot on Channels 6, 10, and 13 between 6 p.m. and 6:10 p.m., which is all local news, you were guaranteed 100% of the television audience, now it's down to 38%."

Ironically enough, television broadcast rates have increased on average, even as the overall broadcast audiences have declined. Some advertisers feel shortchanged, saying they are paying more for less. However, industry insiders argue it is a fundamental case of supply and demand. "It defies logic," admits NYSBA president Joe Reilly, "But even with fewer viewers, broadcast is still a more efficient way to reach a mass audience than cable or satellite." As the economy expanded over the last two decades, more and more new national advertisers emerged to help offset "traditional advertisers" lost by the transformation of the American economy. Broadcast still delivers the largest audience possible, relative to other media, thus the intense demand for advertising on broadcast television and radio remains robust.

Consolidation of Broadcasting

A tidal wave of change would sweep away even more FCC regulations with the passage of the Telecommunications Act of 1996. Broadcasters have now had more than a decade to reflect on this legislation. Some say it has crushed the spirit of how business used to be done in broadcasting, while others believe it was necessary to remain competitive. Looking back, Senator Alfonse D'Amato offers the latter perspective, "On balance, it was not bad legislation, but the world of telecommunications is changing continuously. Consequently, all kinds of questions are going to continue to be raised."

Another lawmaker, the late Senator Jacob K. Javits, once told Bill O'Shaughnessy: "Bill, you either believe in the genius of the free-enterprise system . . . or you do not." O'Shaughnessy has defended the right of large corporations to speak freely via "issue" and corporate advertising, but at the same time he also holds out hope that some media conglomerates may begin to sell off some of their stations to someone who wants to become a "hometown" broadcaster. Eddie Fritts, president of NAB, also points out that unlike many other industries, deregulation has not exactly been across the board in broadcasting: "There has been consolidation in broadcasting, but unlike the airlines, truckers or the savings and loans, it has been limited in scope compared with those industries because it has been limited in terms of the size of each market."

Consolidation for the most part has not been viewed favorably by many broadcasters. Reluctantly, however, some will admit a course of action was necessary to survive in the highly competitive marketplace they now find themselves in. "If we didn't consolidate radio we would be in serious trouble today. They couldn't compete," says Reilly. The heart of the 1996 legislation was to free broadcasting from outdated regulatory constraints to allow it to compete on a more level playing field with other media. Over the last decade, the value of broadcast stock and even individual stations has risen dramatically. David Hinckley, the highly regarded critic-at-large for the *New York Daily News*, observes: "Consolidation hasn't been this horrible ogre that ruined radio. It hasn't. Radio in many ways is still thriving. The primary advantage of consolidation is that it has made radio much more of a major player than it used to be." Banding together, large concentrations of radio stations have been able to attract large flows of investment and advertisings dollars over the last decade in ways individual stations could never do before on their own.

Advertising efficiencies have been cited as a huge plus resulting from consolidation, particularly as radio has become more segmented. The buying process for advertisers has been dramatically streamlined, says former ABC Radio executive Dick Foreman, now a station broker: "For years, radio has been a business of fragmented audiences, too many mouths to feed and too complex for a buyer to buy. What we have now is a situation where a broadcast buyer for a major company looking to buy time in New York City no longer has to look at 75 different pitches from 75 different salespeople; now they have to review only five or six."

Foreman also points out that radio advertising was always relatively inexpensive compared with other media because of the internal competitiveness among radio stations, which put downward pressure on advertising rates. Now radio is able to derive more value from its airtime, focusing its energies solely on going head to head with newspapers and television, rather than beating up on itself.

The segmentation and consolidation of radio also fueled consolidation in the representation business. There was a time when "rep" firms would only sell advertising for one station in each market, but now they represent the competition as well. Jim Greenwald explains how that change occurred: "Let's assume for discussion's sake that we represented a single radio station in Rochester, New York, and let's say the rate in those days was a 15% commission. Then that station became part of a group of six stations. Then the owner of that group would turn to us and say, 'Now that you represent a bigger part of our business, we don't want to pay you a 15% commission anymore. We're now only going to pay you 10%.' Then we said, 'OK, you can pay us 10%, but we are going to have to start representing your competition too.' As a result, consolidation took place on both levels." Station owners and groups also increasingly demanded better marketing research, better programming advice, and other services from rep firms. Coupled with broadcast consolidation, rep firms like Katz Media and Interep were left with no other choice but to start buying out their competitors to achieve economies of scale for their services, sparking a wave of consolidation among rep firms. Jack Masla, Marv Roslin, Crystal, and Mort Bassett were among those reps who disappeared.

Basic operational efficiencies resulting from concentrating radio stations together was viewed as another positive benefit of consolidation. Over time, radio owners combined multiple stations into "clusters" to be managed by one or two general managers, rather than having a separate one at each station. Corporate ownership vastly enhanced the collective bargaining power of group owners as well. They could demand deep discounts from vendors who serviced the entire group, including office equipment suppliers, travel agencies, marketing research firms, and manufacturers of promotional items like T-shirts and mugs.

Maire Mason, currently vice president and general manager of WNEW, admits that consolidation helps significantly on a cost basis, but she is more skeptical when it comes to sharing personnel: "We now have one controller between two stations, and that really doesn't help me. We also have only one engineer to serve two stations. The personnel splits have been tough for me because there are a variety of other corporate priorities I am competing with."

Joe Reilly was recently asked to moderate a panel by the American Women in Radio and TV to discuss the current state of radio. To paint a picture of radio today, he opened up the panel by stating: "If this event had been held 10 years ago, there would have been 19 managers representing 25 stations. Those same stations are now represented by the five managers that sit here before you today." Bob Ausfeld is emblematic of that type of manager Reilly was talking about. He has had the distinction of sitting in the same seat while working for seven different companies since 1994, overseeing almost every station in the Albany market at one point or another. Currently he is regional vice president for Regent Communications in Albany.

As corporate owners started throwing their money around in the 1990s, many individual owners felt intimidated. Rather than take on a large corporation, many decided it was more prudent to take an offer they couldn't refuse. Former WBEN owner Larry Levite recalls that at the time he decided to sell, his options were pretty black and white: "Back in the mid-1990s, when I sold my station, you either had to be a buyer or a seller. I tried being a buyer and I just didn't have enough money, so I had to become a seller."

As with most mergers, duplicate positions are commonly eliminated, particularly senior positions and back-office functions. John Zach, an announcer at WBEN-AM, works for Entercom, which now owns WBEN. His station is among six others occupying office space all on the same floor. He describes the structure of the Entercom group in Buffalo: "There are only two general managers, one for the AMs, one for the FMs. Before, there were seven general managers. There were seven different switchboard operators. Seven different program directors. Each of these had 10, 20, 30 employees. They had separate studios, separate facilities, and separate buildings. They had property taxes to pay. All of that has been eliminated by one company owning all these stations under one roof." Some broadcasters would argue that there used to be five more sets of eyes looking out for the needs of the Buffalo community.

The rapid rate of mergers over the last two decades has also driven the ticket price of an individual station to stratospheric levels. Bob Ausfeld remembers when WGNA in Albany was purchased for $3.5 million in the 1980s. By the mid-1990s it was sold for almost $8 million. The high cost of local stations has made it prohibitive for a local group of investors or a single person to buy a station in their own community as they were once able to do. Just a few years ago WGNA was flipped again, this time for close to $20 million.

With the same exact pressure to deliver on the bottom line, Ausfeld says the higher valuations have to be paid for somehow: "When you have that kind of cost, it's still the same tower and it's still the same frequency and you can raise the rates to a point, but how do you make the bottom line? The bottom line is that staff gets laid off. You start using automation on weekends or you use voice tracking, prerecorded introductions, and segments voiced by an announcer. You just computerize everything." This reality also causes Ausfeld to worry about the opportunity to develop new talent in radio. Using voice tracking to spread just a few people around the country has severely cut back the stable of talent in the pipeline. Ausfeld believes that the departure of Howard Stern to satellite will be a wake-up call for broadcasters as they struggle to replace him from their thin talent bench.

With each new acquisition, layer upon layer of bureaucracy and the pressure to focus on the bottom line has put more and more distance between owners and individual members of the community they serve. As a long-time broadcaster and head of WPIX in New York City, Lev Pope is concerned about how today's owners can serve their communities as intimately as he once did: "I'm not saying that today's major market ownership is a bad thing at all, but the control has largely slipped away from the people who made it work so effectively, those who built these stations from scratch. Distant group owners may or may not have the same kind of interests in serving their community because there's more of an emphasis on the bottom line than there is on service to that community." Most senior management today in broadcasting is physically located hundreds or thousands of miles away from individual consumers. They are unable to attend Lions Club meetings, local charity events or meetings with civic leaders, as broadcasters once did before deregulation.

Ed Levine, another independent broadcaster serving central New York, notes that while there are plenty of corporate managers who do serve on boards of charities and other local organizations, he isn't precluded by bureaucratic red tape: "What it's coming down to, more and more, is that the manager doesn't have the ability to make decisions. Specifically looking at finances, they can't write a check. I can write a check." More broadcasters like Levine used to make decisions right on the spot about how they could help their community, whether it was to raise funds in the aftermath of a local tragedy or to organize a remote at a local charity event.

The concentration of ownership has also been blamed for what broadcasters refer to as "cookie-cutter" programming, generic content with local segments dropped in to give it some parochial flavor. While the homogenization of radio has helped to keep costs down in the short term, Joe Reilly is fearful that it will only end up hurting radio by sending listeners to satellite. However, David Hinckley thinks the programming differences after consolidation are more subtle: "I don't think there is a vastly different palate available to listeners than what they are used to. There is probably less diversity in the sense that a company that owns several radio stations in one town is probably going to look for that magic word *synergy*, where you have multiple stations that complement each other. Instead of an owner planning what his or her station would program, you have an owner programming what his or her five or six stations are going to do."

For all intents and purposes, New York City is the capital of the "blue states," but Hinckley thinks the corporate ownership of radio has more to do with why New York City doesn't have a country-western station. He recalls when Evergreen Broadcasting, now part of Clear Channel, bought WYNY and flipped it from a country format to a dance format in the mid-1990s. It ended up proving to be a very successful strategy. Hinckley interviewed Jimmy DeCastro, former head of Evergreen Media, sometime just after the switch. While country was a profitable format in New York City, DeCastro felt he needed to make a "splash" as a new owner in the number-one market. He felt he wouldn't make the same kind of splash with country as he did with dance. "I suspect if there was not the kind of consolidation that we've had and there were individual owners at each station, there might be a country-western station in New York City because there is an opportunity for someone to fill that niche, but in today's marketplace it doesn't seem to fit within the larger corporate plan," muses Hinckley.

Don Angelo cites the Lesniak family as one example of the effects of deregulation on programming in Buffalo. In the early 1960s, Dan and Nancy Lesniak used their life savings of $50,000 to buy WADV-FM in Buffalo. For over 30 years, they used their own radar and instincts to identify what their local audience wanted in terms of programming. It was an eclectic mix of jazz, Polish music, and other ethnic programs. They didn't make a killing, but they did make a living for themselves. In the 1990s, like many of their brothers and sisters in broadcasting, they were given an offer they couldn't refuse by a corporation, so they took it and retired. The new owners immediately changed the format to country-and-western, the kind of music you could listen to anywhere in the country, says Angelo. The local flavor and a small sense of belonging to a unique community was eliminated.

The guiding force of the wave of media mergers that swept through the 1990s was indeed the magic word *synergy*. On paper it made perfect sense for the television networks to buy up movie studios and for individual radio stations to be clustered into groups. However, the phenomenon of uniting all media on one digital platform is one of evolution, not revolution. The reality is that the stations with the smallest audience and smallest revenues at the bottom of a cluster are probably no more financially well off than when they were owned by individuals. Bob Ausfeld explains the financial realities of clusters: "When you do clusters, it's the top two radio stations in your cluster that you have your sales reps out selling all the time. They are the major priority in the budget, the ones who really bring in the dollars. Then we have the 'red-headed stepchild,' a really solid radio station, but it's kind of, like, third in line. It's the nature of salespeople out selling. They want to get the big dollars, and every once in a while they grab a few crumbs over here for the 'lost' radio station." For the most part, programming and marketing synergies have also failed to materialize. Typically, when one media outlet promotes something for its sister outlet, it gets nothing in return, doing nothing to help its own bottom line. As a result there is no incentive for cross-promotion unless it is mandated from above by senior management.

In the last couple of years, Wall Street investors and analysts, once champions of broadcast media, are now retreating. Ed Levine believes that the radio industry is not broken but has rather been unfairly beat up on by Wall Street: "There's nothing inherently wrong with the radio business at all. The radio business is mainstream America. Mainstream America's economy is not that good right now, and radio is reflective of that. We are just getting pulverized by the public markets right now because we went and promised 15% year-over-year growth in the late 1990s, and that's not sustainable." Many analysts have now come to realize that the double-digit growth experienced by broadcasters was primarily achieved through acquisition. Acquiring companies was the easy part. Most large broadcast corporations have been unable to execute on the promise of "synergies."

As Eric Straus reflects on the past, he believes that broadcasting needs a more balanced approach for the future: "We might have lost our way a little bit. We may have gotten a little too worried about the bottom line and not as worried about putting on a creative, enlightened radio station. There is an awful lot of monotony out there." Maire Mason concurs: "It's all about getting back to basics. They said AM was dead in the 1980s, right? It's vibrant today, with people screaming at each other. WABC-AM went to number one recently with a variety of conservative talk show hosts in a market that's 85% Democratic. I believe FM will find its way, too. We'll just have to be a little more innovative. We'll have to be a little more different."

With flat stock prices and growing difficulty managing these far-flung media empires, there are signs that some broadcast groups may start considering being broken up or selling off one or two of the least profitable stations in each cluster. The recent split of Viacom and CBS to boost its stock price provides an indication as to the new thinking now occurring in the corporate board rooms of large media companies. Who knows, maybe Bill O'Shaughnessy's dream of a new generation of local "hometown" broadcasters may yet one day come into being.

7

Impact of New Technology

"Technology is propelling us much faster than we may care to go. The critical element, whether talking about computers or broadcasting, is programming. The medium will certainly be there! We must make sure there always is a meaningful message."

— Dr. Marion Stephenson, former president of NBC Radio

The term "new media" is often used simultaneously with the Internet and is frequently applied to all forms of digital media. The phenomena of electronic media as a whole, including radio and television, is still "new media" compared with "print media," which has been in existence for centuries. It is the astonishing pace with which broadcasting has evolved over the lifetime of NYSBA that makes it seem a more mature medium than it really is.

Erica Farber, a long-time observer of the radio industry, points out that even the word *technology* didn't make its introduction into the daily lexicon of broadcasters all that long ago: "I think just the word *technology* is the impact. The meaning of that word has a far greater scope than it did 50 years ago. It wasn't part of our everyday jargon as broadcasters. I mean computers? Who had a computer on his or her desk . . . or a fax machine 25 years ago? No one had voice mail either. Technology in general has dramatically affected not only broadcasting but also how people function within business."

What sets broadcasting apart from the print media is its ability to disseminate information as soon as it's available, combined with the intimate manner in which it conveys information. For all the new technologies that have been introduced into broadcasting in its brief lifetime, the medium remains a familiar voice, a disseminator of information and an entertainer to the public.

Increased Productivity

As with other industries, there has always been a desire to speed up the production process in broadcasting to reduce costs, as well as to remain competitive. Taken for granted today, the computer has served as a workhorse behind the scenes, slashing the time required for basic back-office operations like payroll, shortening the sales cycle, and making business communications instantaneous. Larry Levite, former owner of WBEN-AM, embraced the computer early on: "We were not afraid to take a chance. We had a lot of firsts when I owned radio stations. We were the first station ever to have computers in New York State that I know of. I had a chief engineer who was into computers, and that was back when people didn't even know what a computer was. We were the first radio station to ever have the school snow closings done by computer."

Prior to the 1980s, disc jockeys would still write out the lineup for their songs by hand. The idea of using a computer database to organize songs was unimaginable. Bud Wertheimer was another early adopter of the computer. To give his DJs a more efficient way to mix their music, he had one of his engineers write a program using the computer language BASIC: "It allowed us to schedule music, hundreds of songs at a time, in different categories. We programmed basic rotations, so we had songs playing twice a day, even three times a day. We could do all kinds of things, like deciding if we didn't want two female vocals in a row, not having any groups in a row or songs from a particular year we didn't want played too close together." In today's world that level of content management has passed all the way down to the consumer in the form of Apple's iPod. The computer has found its way into almost every aspect of broadcast operations today, with some stations completely unattended, run by a computer alone.

The computer and all its accessories have undoubtedly made broadcasters more productive than they have ever been before, but some things have been lost in the process, says Jim Greenwald: "Before the age of computers, you did business in person or by a phone call. You had a Freiden or Monroe calculator to keep track of your books. We never had any of the sophisticated equipment you have today, so it was more of a personal business. Today so much is being done by wire, fax, and the computer."

Other broadcasters believe that the fast pace of business today has also negatively impacted creativity. There is no longer enough time to just "sleep on" a proposal before a voice mail or e-mail prompts a manager or reporter for a decision. The breakneck speed at which computers have been introduced into broadcast stations may have unknowingly truncated the "baking time" of the creative process before the best ideas have time to rise. Still others believe that the onslaught of information (particularly from e-mail correspondence) is creating an information overload, distracting workers from accomplishing even the most basic tasks.

As computers made the world of broadcasting move even faster, it was the satellite that made the world infinitely smaller. The basic technology for the commercial use of satellites was developed just after the Soviets launched their first satellite into space in 1957. Within a few years, active satellites were used to receive messages and then retransmit them on another frequency. In 1962, AT&T launched Telstar, the first satellite capable of relaying television pictures across the Atlantic. Despite its expense at the time, broadcasters quickly realized the benefits of transmitting video immediately. At the height of the Vietnam War, the networks sent video back from the frontlines via satellite to New York to be broadcast across the nation on the same day the footage was shot. Gone were the days of relying on the relative snail's pace of shipping film via airplanes.

In the 1970s, electronic newsgathering equipment (ENG) was introduced into the broadcast process, taking reporters out of the studio and into the field to share their stories live. As the cost of satellite transmissions declined and their quality improved in the 1980s, the networks began using satellites exclusively to distribute programming to their affiliates. It provided them with the greater flexibility of sending programs within different time zones and offered a greater choice of programming for local affiliates. Radio networks would also use satellites to distribute their programming, helping to fuel the growth of FM in the late 1970s and early 1980s.

Radio and television equipment also became more compact and thus more mobile, thanks to the transistor invented by Bell Labs in the late 1940s. It would not have a widespread effect in broadcasting until 20 years later when its price dropped, making it a more affordable option for broadcasters. The move away from tubes to transistors led to more compact design and construction, cooler operation, and extended use and lifespan of production equipment. Developed as an outgrowth of space research, printed circuit boards came into vogue in the late 1960s and early 1970s. They were more rugged and resistant to heat and humidity than transistors. Circuits helped make the production of broadcast equipment easier, faster, and cheaper than ever before.

The newsgathering and production process was also shortened when videotape replaced film. The expression "it ended up on the cutting-room floor" to describe footage that didn't make it to the final piece would no longer be taken literally but would remain in broadcasting's nomenclature. Bill Jaker, a PBS producer in Binghamton, believes the advent of tape had the greatest impact on how television was produced compared with any other new technology up until that time: "It really opened up so many possibilities. It just simplified a lot of things. Of course it was a lot easier to edit. All of a sudden, the quality of radio and TV became really more like the movies." Editing tape was much faster than processing film: Special effects could be incorporated more easily using tape, and the scheduling of programs was made more flexible. With the introduction of tape, the number of hours of live programming dramatically declined as well. Detractors and purists at the time felt actors would no longer perform with the same degree of intensity and focus they summoned up for live broadcasts. Bill Jaker concurs: "I think there was a certain directness and intimacy with the audience that you got on the live broadcasts."

Most television in its early days was shot live or on film. A small portion of programming used the Kinescope recording process, which produced images much grainer and fuzzier than film or live broadcasts. By the 1950s, a magnetic-tape recording process was being experimented with to deliver broadcast-quality images. The first practical videotape recording system (VTR) was introduced at the NAB convention in 1956 by Ampex. The VTR system was very costly. After four years on the market, fewer than 200 stations had bought one, primarily larger-market broadcasters.

On the radio side, reel-to-reel magnetic-tape recordings were beginning to replace disc records around this time. In the 1960s, a small plastic-enclosed, single-hub cartridge of tape was introduced. This new method of recording made fast-paced Top-40 stations easier to operate, eliminating the need to set up reels or fumbling to find the beginning of a song on a particular reel. The two-hub cassette was introduced by Philips in 1964 and was quickly adopted by consumers.

Improvements in Quality

Broadcasters constantly sought new technologies that helped improve the quality of their end product: programming. By degrees, they pursued their quest to make television's video images sharper and sharper, and radio's sound clearer and clearer.

Stereo technology helped FM in its struggle to find consumer acceptance, making it the dominant music medium. There were several clumsy attempts to achieve the high-quality sound of stereo. In the 1950s, a few broadcasters began experimenting with using both an AM station and an FM station to deliver stereo. The AM band was used for the right sound channel and FM for the left. There were several major drawbacks. First, since most listeners didn't have an FM receiver at that time, they received only half the signal. Secondly, the spectrum was being squandered because the same program was being sent out on two different wavelengths. By 1958, commercially produced stereo records became available, so this recorded music was now readily available to be broadcast in stereo. That same year NBC broadcast its famous "Bell Telephone Hour" stereophonically for its four owned-and-operated AM and FM stations. Additional experimentation over time would show that FM offered much better sound reproduction quality than AM. Teenagers hooked on rock and roll quickly caught on to this fact, helping fuel the rise of FM as the dominant band for music. By the mid-1970s, the majority of FM stations were broadcasting in stereo.

The impact of the introduction of color to television would be what stereo was to radio. By the fall of 1965, the three major networks began programming in color. NBC, led by David Sarnoff and his heirs, broadcast 95% of its prime-time schedule in color, CBS did half, and ABC just 40%. Consumer surveys at the time showed that color was associated with increased viewing, and more attention was paid to color commercials. All was not rosy in the early days of color. It was extremely expensive for stations to make the conversion to upgrade their equipment. Color cameras were three times as expensive as monochrome cameras, and it was estimated that the networks alone spent $30 to $40 million to convert to color. The audience, however, went crazy for color television. By the end of 1966, color television sets outsold black-and-white sets for the first time.

It's hard not to draw parallels between television's conversion to HDTV today with its conversion to color 40 years ago. Like color, HDTV has faced many of the same challenges, like getting television set manufacturers to agree on an industry standard, encouraging programmers to use the new technology, and getting consumers to experience the improved quality for themselves. Shell Storrier, former general manager of WKTV-TV, points to one important difference between color and HDTV: "I think the FCC is insisting that the broadcasters carry this new form of broadcasting. They didn't do it when color came along. Stations had the option of using color if they wanted to. Our station in Utica was one of the last to carry color." He believes that market forces should drive acceptance by broadcasters: "When the sales of color sets went up and the price of color equipment went down, we did get into color." The upgrade to digital, like color, carries a hefty price tag. Storrier estimates that a small station will need to spend between $5 or $6 million for the upgrade. Broadcasting in HDTV requires stations to invest in new transmitters, cameras, videotape recorders, towers, antennas, and even new sets for local news.

HDTV has been billed as the biggest innovation since color in terms of clarity and crispness of the picture it will offer. The official deadline for conversation is December 2008, when the analog signal is slated to be "shut off." In 1997 Congress passed legislation permitting broadcasters to use both the analog and digital systems until 85% of the national audience owns HDTV receivers, helping spread out the investment for the upgrade. Beyond developing a better picture, the congressional drive to upgrade to digital lies in lawmakers' hopes to generate a new source of funding for the government by selling the analog frequencies to entrepreneurs for alternative uses other than broadcast. According to Joe Reilly, roughly two-thirds of television stations in New York have already upgraded to digital.

Even with the popularity of color television, it still took 17 years before the majority of American households bought a color set to replace their black-and-white set. Unlike color, there hasn't exactly been a run on HDTV sets in retail stores. NAB president Eddie Fritts says the biggest challenge for broadcasters today is not only their own transition to digital but also helping to make consumers aware of the benefits of digital: "I think the main challenge for broadcasters universally is the transition from analog to digital both on television and on radio. As that occurs, television will require a significant transition, which will, in essence, change every television set in America. In television it has to change dramatically, so the net of that is helping consumers with this transition." The falling price of HDTV sets should begin to help spur greater consumer acceptance, with models now available for under $1,000.

Proliferation of Programming Choices

The bulk of the technologies adopted by television prior to the 1970s involved improving the quality of the broadcast or speeding up the various processes involved in its production. The rise of cable, the remote control, and the VCR in the 1970s would be technologies that began to give consumers more choice and more control over their viewing experience. This would be the beginning of the long-term trend of "personalized programming."

Radio had its rivalry between AM and FM, and television would have its own between VHF and UHF. In the early 1950s, the FCC began issuing licenses for UHF in hopes of providing a universal television service and greater diversity of programming choices. Due to poor receiver design, UHF ended up having much less coverage than VHF. This would be its Achilles heel, stunting its growth through much of its existence. The FCC also failed to issue the necessary rules and guidelines to put UHF on equal footing with VHF. As with FM, most people couldn't receive UHF because their televisions did not have a special receiver capable of receiving the UHF signal. As television grew, the networks preferred being affiliated with VHF stations to achieve wider coverage, and of course the ad dollars came along with such an affiliation. Lacking network affiliation, the term *independent* was often used interchangeably with UHF. In time, as the syndicated programming market began to blossom, UHF would achieve moderate success, offering reruns of network shows as previously described.

Cable began to find its way into American homes when a little-known subsidiary of Time-Life announced plans to use the satellite Satcom I transponder to deliver movies to participating cable system head ends nationwide. It was called Home Box Office or HBO. A year later, Atlanta media mogul Ted Turner had grander visions for his UHF station in Atlanta when he announced he was going to make the programming from his station available to all cable systems. He called it a "super-station."

Long before the remote-control, handheld device, people used commercial breaks as an opportunity to grab a snack from the fridge or go to the bathroom. Generally speaking, they were also less inclined to change stations, which meant having to get off the couch to change the channel. Prior to the late 1970s, there wasn't a whole lot of reason to "channel surf" anyway, because most people still only had a few channels to choose from. The remote control or "clicker" combined with the rise of cable changed all that.

The VCR also began making its way into American homes by the late 1970s, gaining a firm foothold in households across America a decade later. The first Betamax machines went on sale in February 1976 for the whopping price of $1,300. While the VCR gave viewers the ability to watch their favorite shows when they wanted to, most Americans ended up using their VCRs for movie rentals.

There would be an ill-fated attempt in 1980 to create the country's first Direct Broadcast Satellite (DBS) system to reach rural areas, and inner city locations inadequately served by cable. The Satellite Television Corp (STC), a subsidiary of COMSAT, applied to the FCC to design and launch the country's first DBS system. Ahead of its time and starved of unique programming, none of the original DBS applicants survived, but they did provide a window into the future.

Impact of Cable Television

The impact of cable television on broadcast television would not be as dramatic as the impact broadcast television first had on radio, but over time cable has undoubtedly slowly eaten away at the dominance of the broadcast networks. Beginning in the late 1940s, some communities in rural areas with poor off-the-air reception banded together to establish community antennas (CATV) wired to homes so they could receive broadcast television. Cable, in its earliest incarnation as CATV, grew very slowly. By 1952, only 70 systems were serving 14,000 subscribers, each paying a monthly fee of around $5.

Broadcasters initially welcomed cable because it extended their signal into areas that were unable to receive it. Unsure of cable's potential, some broadcasters like Harmon Broadcasting in Utica began investing in it, says Shell Storrier: "In 1963 we got into cable because we didn't know if cable was going to help us or hurt us." A pioneer in helping bring rock and roll to radio in Buffalo, as well as building WKBW-TV from scratch, Al Anscombe would also jump into cable. While visiting a television station in Scranton, Pennsylvania, he had his first encounter with cable when he discovered that the station doubled as a cable operation: "There was this enormous room with only three guys working in it. When I got through wandering around, we went out to lunch with the manager and I asked him, 'I don't understand what's going on in that other room there.' He says to me, 'That's cable. It's the thing of the future.'" Anscombe told the manager that *cable* was a dirty word up in Buffalo. Some broadcasters around this time viewed cable as a something of a "parasite," generating revenue from broadcast programming without providing any compensation to broadcasters for the right to re-air their programming.

Inspired by what he saw in Pennsylvania, Anscombe went back home to western New York and started approaching towns around Amherst about starting up a cable service: "I put a brochure together about how cable works, how we would string it to telephone poles and attach a wire to people's homes." He told the town council in Amherst they wouldn't have to invest a thing. He would also pay a small stipend of 50 cents a hookup for the use of roadways and back lots. "I told them to figure out the potential; estimate the number of homes in the area and we'll go down past something like 60% of the homes with cable." Anscombe did the math for them, showing the town that it stood to gain a windfall of approximately $100,000 if it granted him a license to bring in cable.

The town ended up giving him a license for 10 years, and he started rolling out the cable in the early 1980s. Back then, he admits, cable operators didn't have to work too hard for their revenue: "I could send a bill out on the last day of the month, and on the third day, I would already have 90% of the money collected. It just rolled in. It was small change, around $5 or $6 a household. Some people would write a check for three months and just send it in." He would eventually sell an 80% stake in his company to John Rigas of Adelphia. Rigas, now in his 80s, was sentenced in June 2005 to a long prison term following the collapse of his personal fortune and his cable empire based in Coudersport, Pennsylvania.

Looking toward the future, Don West, the prescient former editor of *Broadcasting & Cable* (who was also once the assistant to Dr. Frank Stanton, the former president of CBS), laments the growing power of cable and broadcast's reluctance to upgrade to digital: "I think the worst thing of all for broadcasters was the increasing dependence on cable as the primary distribution mechanism. You now have cable and satellite sending or distributing 85% of all the signals in the country. The broadcaster is on the verge of being squeezed out of over-the-air medium distribution. Although the broadcasters have been involved in the digital transition, they've never really been in favor of it as an industry."

The Rise of FM

Despite the extremely slow acceptance of FM, its impact would have one of the most profound affects in the development and growth of radio since the advent of television. Gordon Hasting refers to FM's emergence in the late 1970s as the "Second Renaissance" in radio. As a technology it was superior to AM because it delivered sound in higher fidelity, and its short-range frequency enabled FM stations to stay on the air all night long. Nearly half of all AM stations in 1960 were restricted to daytime operation so that they wouldn't interfere with higher-powered stations at night when AM signals could travel farther.

Like many other technologies, many different variables had to come together before FM would take off. In 1952 there were 616 FM stations on the air throughout the United States. That number would drop to 530 five years later, just as television was exploding. FM's primary obstacle was that most people did not have a separate FM receiver at this time, therefore they couldn't listen to the frequency. There was also no legislation mandating that radios be made with FM receivers. AM radio was extremely entrenched. In fact, many FM stations were owned by AM operators, so they simply ran the exact same programming on their FM band. Without unique programming, AM owners didn't exactly give consumers a reason to rush out and buy an FM receiver.

Since no one was listening to FM, the industry turned to storecasting in the late 1940s to generate some revenue from their FM transmitters. Storecasting was the process by which FM operators would send background music to stores, cutting out the talk by using a special tone. In 1955 the FCC ruled that broadcasters could only storecast using multiplexing, a process of sending out two simultaneous signals, one for stores and one for the general public.

Prior to 1960, the financial backbone of FM was background music, explains Bud Wertheimer: "All FM broadcasters at that time were multiplex, Muzak-type operators. We used it for Muzak, and then we'd use the second channel for in-store broadcasting, the commercials you hear in the stores. Basically we had this normal FM station, and unbeknownst to the public there was music and commercials being piggybacked on that signal." Two major Muzak competitors came to dominate this service, Amalgamated Music Enterprises, run by Wertheimer's father, Albert "Al" Wertheimer, and Starcast America, run out of Philadelphia, the forerunner to the cable giant, Comcast.

While many FM stations fell on hard times during the 1950s, Wertheimer and his father would be busy snapping them up to expand their Muzak business: "We were already on the air with those stations, so we had to buy them just to keep our Muzak customers happy. Here you had the FM broadcasters going broke, and the Muzak operators were in the cities making millions of dollars a year in the private music station business, so we had to keep those stations alive."

FM's fortunes started being reversed with the passage of three important pieces of legislation in Congress, says Wertheimer: "All-channel legislation directed that no radio could be built without being able to receive *both* AM and FM. There was also the stereophonic rule and the dual polarization rule." Before all-channel legislation, Wertheimer remembers that getting an FM radio installed in a car cost about $200. Now it was mandatory to have FM as part of all car radios. People no longer had to look at FM as a separate technology; there were now more channels to choose from on the radio dial. A new standard of stereo broadcasting was also decided on after many tough battles. Stereo would help distinguish the quality of FM's sound from AM. "Once stereo was brought in, it meant you had two channels of music, a left and a right. It gave FM a huge advantage over AM radio. It sounded far better," explains Wertheimer.

Dual polarization would be the most important of the three pieces of legislation in Wertheimer's opinion: "Everyone started putting vertical stubs on their antennas, so they could have two signals going out, one horizontal and one vertical. They would meet, basically "dual polarize," and the signal would fill out, enabling almost any radio, car radios in particular, to pick up the signal." Before dual polarization, signals were sent out only horizontally, creating some "dark spots" because the signal only had one level of polarity in it. The new legislation permitted broadcasters to add additional wattage to each plane, helping to fill in big holes in the FM signal, adding more coverage as well as delivering better reception.

By the early 1960s applications for FM stations outpaced those going dark. The AM spectrum was becoming so crowded that the only way to get a new station on the air was to use the FM band. As the decade wore on, FM would be the fastest-growing broadcast service. The pendulum would swing in FM's favor by the late 1970s. Walter Maxwell explains that FM was finally able to beat out AM because of music: "AM had the majority of the audience back then. It didn't have to worry about FM, because AM was the real moneymaker. Then everyone became interested in the quality of the music AM couldn't deliver on, but FM could. As a result, FM appealed to the younger audiences." Also around this time

FM stations began giving away FM converters as prizes to help expand their listenership.

In the early 1970s, Jim Greenwald, then head of Katz Radio, understood that the FM band was about to start singing a sweeter tune. To develop its potential he hired Gordon Hastings away from RRR FM, an FM rep firm, as director of new business. At the time Hastings was hired, Katz Radio represented only old-line AM stations. His task was clear: to represent as many FM stations as he could sign up. He first helped AM owners of FM stations better develop their FM properties. As Hastings looks back, it was a tough sell: "People called FM 'elevator music,' and there were a lot of other pejorative things said about it." Confident about FM's future, he would go market to market making his pitch, presenting Katz's latest FM marketing research. His efforts paid off handsomely. In 1972 Katz Radio represented only 60 stations. Just four years later they grew to over 200 stations, representing 80% of the leading FM stations.

There were many other broadcasters in New York who believed in FM's potential. Frank Lorenz remembers his legendary father talking about the future of radio: "He saw the future of FM radio, and this was only in 1957. He was sitting around the dining room table talking about the new sound spectrum of the future." George "Hound Dog" Lorenz's vision would be realized when he put WBLK-FM on the air in 1964.

Bill Brown Jr. of WBTA-AM also tried his luck with FM in the late 1970s, putting WBTF-FM on the air. "At that time it was the first modern country-music station in western New York. Of course that format would become very popular in later years," he recalls. While FM was just starting to hit its stride at this time, WBTF struggled. Brown could only assume that in the rural area he was serving, farmers just weren't ready for FM because most of them probably didn't have an FM receiver in their pickup truck or tractor.

There is no doubt that technology was a significant factor in the rise of FM and the decline of AM, but many broadcasters believe programming played a more crucial role. Ralph Guild of Interep says FM stations had nothing to lose, so they were willing to take more programming risks: "It was the little daytimers and the low-power FMs that created most of the new formats in the 1960s and 1970s because they didn't have the audience that the big AMs had, so they had to come up with creative ideas to get their niche." Bob Bruno was working at WNEW-AM at the time of FM's rise and agrees that programming fueled FM's rising star: "I've always believed in the power of content. I don't think people are as band conscious as they are content conscious. If you provide the right content on whatever band, I think you can carve out an audience for yourself."

Bob Ausfeld views the growth of FM as an evolution of radio. It was a combination of factors coming together at the same time that lead to FM's success:

"FM started being built into all radios, into cars, and then all of a sudden you could buy little AM/FM radios at the corner drugstores. The kids wanted to listen to the music; they didn't want to listen to all the chatter on the AMs. It was a wake-up call for radio." Ausfeld also looks back at that era as a resurgence for radio. While the AMs started losing their audience, FM attracted a whole new audience from a younger demographic.

In 1980 Nancy Widmann's and FM's destiny would be inextricably linked. She became the first female executive at CBS Radio when she was named vice president and general manager of WCBS-FM. The station was hardly successful compared with the other formidable stations in the CBS stable at the time. She recalls: "When I took over CBS-FM it was losing money. Talk about being at the right place at the right time." FM was just beginning to stir in New York, she says. She vividly remembers the excitement of her first ratings book: "When we got the first book that we could sell, everything just moved from there. Over the next five or six years, it was just pure excitement. I mean the world was changing."

Widmann eventually moved on to become president of CBS Radio during the reign of the infamous Larry Tisch. Widely known and admired for his philanthropy in the New York area, Mr. Tisch was viewed as a "white knight," protecting CBS from various corporate raiders in the mid-1980s. His company, Lowes Corporation, gained controlling interest in the stock of CBS, paving the way for him to become chief executive officer and chairman of the company. To most CBS employees, Tisch turned out to be anything but a savior for CBS.

While most of the CBS divisions were left bruised and battered by Tisch's relentless cost-cutting tactics, Widmann decided to take the offensive, showing him why he should invest more in FM. "One of the first things I did as president of CBS Radio was to take Larry down to CBS-FM: It was this tiny, little radio station in the corner of the 17th floor." She called him up and asked him if she could give him a tour of the station. Widmann says it was an eye-opener for him because he was so used to seeing huge empty sound stages in television, which he deemed as lost business opportunities. The 'tiny, little FM station' on the 17th floor, however, was enormously profitable: "I took him down there and I walked him around. Everybody was on their best behavior of course, and Ron Lundy was on the air. When I was taking Larry Tisch around, Ron Lundy put on the song 'Hats Off to Larry.' I thought I was going to kill him." Larry didn't catch the joke, but he quickly caught on to the potential of FM. He turned to Widmann and said: "This has got to be the most profitable square inch in all of CBS!" Soon after, he gave his full blessing to Widmann to buy more FM stations. By the late 1980s, FM stations dominated radio, collectively serving about three-quarters of the radio audience.

AM Evolves

Many AM stations took it on the chin when FM starting throwing its weight around, but others chose to evolve and go with the flow. "I think some full-service AM stations like WOR managed to keep music integrated into their stations on a limited basis and then started to expand into talk and news information components. Some of them still to this day dominate their market," says Bob Bruno.

AM would also remain a mainstay in many small markets, according to Bill Brown Jr.: "FM didn't hurt a small market station like WBTA because you can't get school closings, local weather, and accident reports on FM. You have to listen to the local station for that. It probably hurt us in taking away our audience for music because FM was a better sound and less talk." When Brown owned WBTA he estimated that three out of four radios in his 60,000-person listening area, directly between Rochester and Buffalo, were tuned into WBTA in the morning. Sports, talk, and news would eventually become the dominate formats in AM, making it a huge moneymaker once again.

As the FM wave rolled along, one of the most significant changes it left in its wake was the concept of "segmentation." Rather than program to attract the widest possible audience, broadcasters began to identify distinct demographic groups like teens, urban, or women, programming to each group's specific tastes. As previously noted by Ralph Guild, Warren Bodow says FM pursued a niche strategy just to make themselves known: "FM divided up the market into such small pieces that in order to survive, stations had to identify themselves with a particular demographic that advertisers would want to buy into. Instead of the mass medium of broadcasting, it became a medium of 'narrowcasting.'" Bodow also believes that FM's success with segmentation was a forerunner to the concept of cable networks targeting specific demographics and genres of content.

Long before FM came into full bloom, even before radio networks began to regularly use satellite to distribute their programming, the ABC Radio Network experimented with its own version of segmentation. In 1967, Wally Schwartz was brought in as president of the ABC Radio Network to help shore up its sagging fortunes. He was charged with the task of implementing a strategy of creating multiple radio networks. The basic concept was based on multiplying the number of ABC's affiliates in each market by maximizing the use of its AT&T lines. "It was a major undertaking because it was so new. A lot of people just turned up their noses at the idea and said there was no way it would ever work. They were wrong," recalls Schwartz.

In the days before satellites, the key to reducing distribution costs was how to best utilize the number of hours a network paid for its landline service from

AT&T. Schwartz explains how the feeds were disseminated in a typical hour: "We did the information feed at the top of the hour, the FM feed at 50 minutes past the hour, the entertainment feed at 30 minutes at the hour, and the contemporary feed at 55 past." Schwartz now planned on creating four different affiliates in each market for ABC using that same single feed. Each station was based on a different format like music, news, or sports, so they would only take programming from the feed that applied to their respective format. It was an unconventional idea at the time and helped breathe new life into ABC Radio, says Schwartz: "At the time it was humongous. We had a five-year plan, and I think, by the third or fourth year, we broke even. Every year after that we were profitable, and it's been profitable ever since. I think that was probably the biggest single accomplishment I contributed to broadcasting."

Satellite Radio

AM and FM are no longer mere rivals, but are now united to stave off the emerging threat from satellite radio. A technology once used to simply distribute radio programs to broadcast stations around the country is now delivering programming directly to consumers. Joe Reilly expresses little concern about Sirius or XM, the leading players in satellite radio, at this point in time: "They've got 6 million listening to hundreds of channels. We've got 175 million." Enabling people to search through those hundreds of different music channels broadcast in digital quality is exactly how satellite radio hopes to lure subscribers. Proponents of satellite radio also point out that music offerings like classical or jazz fill in the gaps in local broadcast programming where such genres of music aren't available in many markets. They have also started taking the battle onto broadcast radio's turf, signing on big names like Howard Stern, Bob Edwards of NPR, and Opie and Anthony.

Broadcasters are quick to point out that satellite radio has one huge disadvantage: It can't offer local programming. When Don Angelo of WGRZ-TV in Buffalo bought his new car, it came with the XM service. He admits he now listens only to broadcast radio for the local news: "The only reason I listen to one local radio station, WBEN, is to get some local news. Then I'm done and I switch right over to XM to listen to some jazz or the comedy channel."

Satellite radio, currently a subscription service, also touts the fact that it's commercial-free. This is not entirely true, however. Only 65 of Sirius's 120 channels are 100% commercial-free, and only XM's music channels are "100% commercial-free." XM also hiked its monthly subscription rate from $10 to $13 in 2005. Sirius also charges $13 a month. A recent survey by J. P. Morgan of 1,600 consumers (both satellite subscribers and nonsubscribers) showed that commercial-free programming is the biggest driver for demand of satellite radio. While satellite radio still reaches a very small percentage of the total available audience, its growth curve is very steep, and that has kept the attention of investors. Both satellite radio providers are under intense pressure to build revenues to service their massive debt loads. Many analysts believe it will take years before either company turns a profit. Satellite radio's detractors also point to "churn" as its Achilles' heel. Many satellite radio subscribers seem reluctant to "re-up" beyond the introductory offer they receive from auto manufacturers.

Ralph Guild cautions that the emergence of satellite radio is more significant than most broadcasters are willing to give credit to at the present time. He is hopeful competition from satellite will only make broadcasting even better: "I think satellite is going to force broadcasters to rethink a lot of the things they are currently doing today, such as programming that perhaps may not survive in a more competitive environment where there are far more alternatives. I think it will make the radio industry stronger in the long run and bring more new listeners on-board. Satellite could even generate new formats that terrestrial broadcasters can jump into."

Local programming aside, terrestrial radio is counting on High Definition (HD) Radio as its weapon of choice to fend off satellite radio. The new technology will enable a stand-alone radio station to send out multiple signals, offering even more targeted programs. Consumers, however, will need to buy a special HD radio to receive the digital signals. Jim Boyle, an analyst at Wachovia, predicts there will be more HD radios in 2012 than satellite radios.

In the near term, broadcast radio is just beginning to unleash a well-coordinated public relations campaign about the benefits of local broadcast radio. NYSBA has lent a significant hand to this effort, recently awarding $10,000 to Crawford Broadcasting's station's WLGZ-AM and WRCI-FM in Rochester for the best "pro-radio" spot to be broadcast throughout the State of New York starting in the summer of 2005. WVOX-AM in Westchester was already airing spots of its own: "Real . . . live . . . authentic . . . AM and FM radio! It's the real deal! . . . Nothing . . . not television, not the Internet . . . and certainly not any distant 'star wars' satellites can diminish the essential value, the relevance, and the immediacy of local hometown community radio. . . ." The winning NYSBA spot features a satellite bill collector asking a radio listener to pay for what he or she has always taken for granted: free radio. NYSBA has also put the wheels in motion to turn it into a national spot, sending copies of the spot to each state broadcasters association with an individualized tag for each state.

If anything, satellite radio, podcasting, streaming, and, soon, cellphones offering radio programming have demonstrated that there will be even more radio in the future, not less. Cellphone manufacturers Nokia and Motorola will introduce cellphones with radio services in 2005, and Spirit has announced a partnership with Sirius to offer radio content to its subscribers. The challenge for terrestrial broadcasters is not simply about survival but rather identifying the new role they will play in the vastly expanded world of radio. A local community station will no longer be limited to a broadcast signal as its sole means of distribution. It will be liberated from a strict 24/7 schedule as well, using various digital forms unaware of space or time. Local programming will no longer be limited to one channel, but will be broken down into several different local channels offered by the same station, or by offering individual programs on demand via podcasts or downloads on the Internet. A true local community radio station will also begin to delve deeper into the power of its local community, helping its citizens create audio content on their own, to be shared with their neighbors in an infinite array of capacities.

The Innovative Mindset

There have been seismic shifts and small rumbles of technological change that have shaped broadcasting from its inception and will continue to do so. Technology has also impacted the individual careers of broadcasters, as well as their day-to-day decisions. There are two approaches to dealing with change: Resist it or adapt to it. John Zach attributes his long, successful career in radio to using the latter approach: "Looking back, I have never been resistant to any kind of change. I didn't fight computers; I became proficient at them. I didn't fight the introduction of the cart machine or the introduction of the CD player. I had lots of colleagues say, 'I don't want this crap, I want my old reel-to-reel.' Any kind of change that comes along, many people choose to fight it. I embraced all these changes and I think being accepting of change is a key to really hanging in."

New technologies are being introduced more quickly than ever before. "Now technology changes are occurring every 20 minutes and just as you master it, you find yourself back in the old days," quips John Kelly. There is almost no choice but to adapt to technological change. It's almost as if the fast pace of innovation is now becoming institutionalized in broadcasting. Just as new technologies establish new formulas or methods, their fresh tracks are being wiped away by the winds of change. In the early days of the business, it seemed as though new technologies used to be introduced less frequently than they are today. Broadcasters have always been constantly absorbing innovations whether it was tape, color, or satellite to make their programming even better. Over the years some have fought to resist change, while others like John Kelly believe adapting was the better approach: "One of the things that helped me in my career was I never fell in love with anything in business. As long as some end goal was accomplished, whether it was a faster or cheaper method, I tried it." Change is not something to be feared but to be understood. More often than not, change manifests itself in a subtle manner. It's just a matter of whether you choose to see it coming or not.

There are a slew of emerging technologies now bubbling up and beginning to shape and mold yet another new role for broadcasting. On the radio side, thousands of Internet radio stations have sprung up in cyberspace offering a plethora of programming choices and formats. The phenomena of Apple's iPod has sparked a new way to listen to radio on demand, anytime listeners want, called "podcasting." Technologies to improve the quality of radio's sound were once enough to gain a competitive advantage, as with the battle between FM and AM. Today's listeners not only demand better sound quality but also more control over their programming choices just as streaming on the Internet, satellite radio, and podcasting now offer them.

Broadcast television is still a $90 billion industry. It is in no way an elephant ready to keel over, but there is no doubt it has more flies to swat at in the way of new technologies than every before. Its total share of the audience continues to shrink, but broadcast TV still commands the most lucrative adverting rates in the entire media landscape because of its ability to deliver the largest audience relative to all other media.

The DVD player, personal video recorders, video on demand, and broadband are merely the hipper cousins of cable, the remote control, and the VCR. They have continued the tradition of giving consumers more control over their viewing experience. Broadcasters are accustomed to almost complete control over their scheduling, commercials and promotions. They will now have to become used to millions of consumers who now want to have their say in the creative process.

Gearing Up for the Future

No longer is it enough to teach students the basics of journalism to prepare them for entering the broadcast industry. Dr. David Rubin, dean of the prestigious Newhouse School at Syracuse University, says technology has had a lot to do with how students are now trained for journalism. "We've really had to stay a half step behind the industry, watching where the technology is leading," he says. The curriculum at the Newhouse School is now almost a mix of academic theory combined with vocational training: "It is possible many of our students will be a 'one-man band,' where you have to be not only the camera person but the reporter as well. We've had to add the necessary skills to function as a one-man band into the course work." Despite all that training, Dr. Rubin is most concerned about the industry's ability to hang on to these fresh recruits: "My greatest concern is that they leave us with a real sense of idealism and the desire to do well and practice journalism as we've taught them to practice it. I worry that after two or three years they won't stick around because of the low pay and high pressure in the business."

The change brought on by technology today is mind boggling. It has changed how broadcasters look at their competitors, how they gather news, how they choose programming, and even how they make the decision to expand into new distribution channels like cable or the Internet. It's hard not to wonder where all this change is headed. Larry Taishoff, former publisher and son of the founder of *Broadcasting & Cable*, says his senior editor Don West saw the end result long ago: "He was the first one I ever recall using the term 'information age' in an editorial. After that everyone started using it. He was serious about it, and also serious about what he calls the 'black box.' One day there will be a black box where you can get all different kinds of information and entertainment." From a technology point of view, the idea of a "black box" is already coming to pass, as cable operators now offer phone service, video programming, and broadband access to the Internet. Microsoft has gone so far as to introduce new software, its "Media Center," enabling consumers to easily move content and programming back and forth between their PC and television.

There is also the question as to whether all this innovation is necessarily a good thing. The changes are welcome as long as consumers keep getting a greater choice of quality programming, says Dennis Swanson: "The end result is the viewer gets a better product. When I was a kid you had four or five signals coming into your home; now you have 300 or 400 channels. The consumer has become the beneficiary of the technology, and I think the technology makes the product even more viable." Technologies like satellites, smaller cameras, and ENG trucks have also been able to take people to places they never would have been able to experience for themselves. Computer-generated graphics have provided broadcasters with an additional visual element to help better convey information in their stories.

There is some concern, however, that the focus on technology has not necessarily made programming better. For the most part, many of the technologies like cable, satellite, broadband or video on demand are merely auxiliary distribution channels that still need to be programmed just as broadcasting always has been. Broadcasters Foundation president Gordon Hastings reminds us that people watch programming, not technology: "In 1978, I remember people saying, 'Well, cable's got a 40 share and that's as far as it's going to go because the only people who buy cable are the ones who live out in the woods or behind a hill somewhere and can't get over-the-air TV.' They never understood that people don't watch delivery systems, they watch programming. They will go wherever the programming is, and they don't care how it gets into their television sets."

From his perspective, Dean Rubin of the Newhouse School at Syracuse believes all the new technologies that have been introduced into broadcasting have had a disappointing effect on the quality of journalism. He often wonders if all the money spent on new technologies might not have been better invested in journalism instead: "Clearly, the answer to that is 'Yes.' In a way, the need to invest in new technology draws resources away from where it could be more directly applied to the journalism. I think that's unfortunate." On the other hand, the rise of the Internet has made information more transparent than ever before and is bringing more and more people into the newsgathering process every day.

Sometimes unfairly, radio has been singled out for using technology to streamline its operations. It is often criticized for the use of voice-tracking, pre-recording segments to localize programs. Detractors believe it has made radio programming homogenous, taking the true flavor out of local radio. Broadcasters must remember that technology is just a tool. Erica Farber explains: "I would submit that when voice tracking is done well, you wouldn't even know it's voice tracking. The stations that do a crappy job of voice tracking probably sound crappy to begin with. It's not the technology, it's the people employing the technology."

What will always remain constant and the guiding force in broadcasting is the ability to listen to local communities and to serve in a way that is meaningful to them despite whatever the next technology happens to be. Good writing, solid interviewing, and sharing a well-told story are timeless, whether to entertain or inform. Just as technology provides consumers with infinite choices, it will also provide them with the tools to slice away the weeds of gossip, rants, and tawdry entertainment as they seek out quality information and entertainment to help them live a fuller life. Radio in particular, even in the emerging digital world, still retains the unique ability to uplift and enlighten. For all the technological advances introduced over the last two decades and those yet to be devised or imagined, radio with its mobility and flexibility is still the medium closest to the people.

8

The Next 50 Years

> "Don't ever do anything that will hurt your reputation, because in the end that is all you really have in life."
>
> —Thomas S. Murphy, founder, Capital Cities Broadcasting

Predictions from long ago: The scene, a family living room: "It's the year 2000 and we have all been magically transported and deposited into the 'average' New York household. . . . There's a live-in computer! There, in what looks like the family room, just across from the fireplace wall, is a console with a panel of color-coded buttons. Above the console are two 36-inch screens flanked on each side by two smaller 19-inch screens. On each side of the two smaller screens are speakers about 8-inches square. As you look around, you notice that these speakers are inconspicuously spaced on all the walls of the room and the adjoining rooms.

"On questioning, our hosts of just a couple decades ago tell us that the computer service to which they subscribe (at a cost of $200 per month!) supplies a variety of services by way of a small dish, which is located on the roof of their home. They explain that the services allow them to order direct from the supermarket and do their banking and stock transactions, and also select from 200 or so other entertainment, communication, and informational choices that can be assigned, at the push of a button, to any of the display screens or speaker/headphone outlets." NYSBA published these predictions 25 years ago in the December 1980 issue of "Newsbreak," about the future of media for a time that has now already passed us by. Many of their predictions would come true, although not precisely on schedule, and some are still in the works.

The thrust of the article was concerned with the role of broadcasting in an environment that has become our daily reality. The article goes on: "Whatever happened to broadcasting? We wonder and are told that it still exists in this futuristic world. Our mythical hosts explain that there is a smaller antenna on their roof, one that brings them local radio and television service. From these sources, they receive local news, weather, and traffic information that affects their daily lives, informational programs concerning the social, governmental, business, and commerce of the area in which they live. . . . Oh, and by the way, they say, it remains today as it has been since its beginning, a *free* broadcasting service."

Those were predictions, prognostications, but of some things we are certain. As cable matures and the Internet comes into its own, broadcasting will survive as it always has, by evolving and responding to the changing needs of the people. Bill O'Shaughnessy reminds us: "I am a great believer that radio is like Lazarus in the Bible. You can't kill it. Television didn't kill it. The Internet didn't do it. I don't think this satellite radio is going to touch it either. Radio is still the medium closest to the people, even in this high-tech, speeded-up, electronic day and age. It is the medium of the poor, the lonely, the misbegotten, the misunderstood, the disenfranchised, and the hurting in our society. Therein lies its potential."

The majority of New York's broadcasters realize, however, that it will not be business as usual in the coming years. There will be even more competition, the audience will continue to disintegrate into niches, consumers will come to expect that all programming be on demand, and that news coverage will offer a wide rainbow of different perspectives. This is the new "family living room" in which broadcast finds itself as it struggles to redefine its long-term direction. Randy Bongarten, president of Emmis Television and also a former president of NBC Radio, along with several other broadcasters, believes that the future of the industry lies in its local roots: "I think broadcasting has a terrific future. You just have to be prepared to deal with change. There's no question there is a lot of change going on right now. There are a lot of challenges. There is a lot of uncertainty out there, but I believe in the basic value of what broadcasters bring to the public and to advertisers. At the end of the day, despite all the competitive media that has grown up and continues to sprout up, television and radio are the most powerful local advertising mediums in the world." However, over the next 20 years, some futurists predict the very concept of television, radio, the computer, and the phone as we know it will disappear from our collective consciousness.

Infinite Competitors

When the New York State Broadcasters Association was founded 50 years ago, competition among broadcasters was something of an anomaly in most New York markets. Some cities were still devoid of a television station and many could only boast a radio station or two. If anything, the print media had the most to lose with the rise of broadcasting, defending its deeply entrenched mo-

Fig. 73. The controversial talk show legend Don Imus gets "support" from WNBC's Bob Sherman. Arriving in New York City in 1971, Imus turned morning radio on its head. He unleashed his clever sarcasm on guests and told people what he really felt, rather than resort to the "happy-go-lucky" morning format that was the mainstay of radio for decades.

Fig. 74. Edythe Meserand was one of New York City's first woman broadcast news executives. She began her 50-year career at NBC in 1926, the same year WJZ and WEAF joined forces to form the National Broadcasting Company. In 1935 she joined WOR, staying there in a variety of news and publicity posts until 1977. There she helped build one of the first modern radio newsrooms in the country during the outbreak of World War II.

Fig. 75. The self-proclaimed "King of All Media," Howard Stern, speaks on a panel at a NYSBA Executive Conference along with Randy Bongarten (left), former NBC Radio chief and current Emmis Television president, and Don Weeks (right), current morning man on WGY Radio in Schenectady.

Fig. 76. Pictured left to right are NYSBA president Joe Reilly; Ed McLaughlin, former ABC Radio chief, who discovered Rush Limbaugh; and Bill Stakelin, the newly appointed chief executive officer of Regent Communications.

Fig. 77. Two thumbs up for Polito Vega, broadcasting salsa and other Latino sounds in New York City for more than 45 years! Carey Davis, vice president and general manager of La Mega, WSKQ-FM 97.9, is on the right.

Fig. 78. Former Governor Mario M. Cuomo makes a special NYSBA tribute to the legendary broadcaster William B. Williams for his many years of continuous entertainment. His career would span 40 years, before he died in 1986, 30 of them as host of WNEW's "Make Believe Ballroom."

Fig. 79. In 1959, while working at WINS in New York, Bruce Morrow adopted the moniker "Cousin Brucie." There are few DJs more closely associated with rock and roll of the 1950s and 1960s than Cousin Brucie. His 40-year career has passed through WINS, WABC, WNBC, and WCBS-FM. He recently signed on with satellite broadcaster Sirius. He is pictured here with his wife, Jody.

Fig. 80. Scott Shannon is regarded as one of the most influential radio programmers of the last 20 years. His "Morning Zoo" concept vaulted Z-100 to the top of the ratings in the early 1980s. Currently he is teamed with Todd Pettengill on WPLJ's "Scott and Todd."

Fig. 81. WBTA's "mobile unit" is everywhere apparent, keeping citizens informed and connected in Batavia and other communities in western New York. Pictured here is a remote for the "Miss Silver Belle" promotion during the Christmas season sometime in the mid-1970s.

Fig. 82. "The Bob and Ray Show" had New York laughing for over 30 years on NBC, CBS, the Mutual Broadcasting System, and New York stations WINS, WOR, and WHN. They were known for developing offbeat characters and parodying popular television and radio programs. Bob Elliott (left) and Ray Goulding (right) are pictured here talking to an intern in the WOR studio.

Fig. 83. WMCA's "The Good Guys" became the most popular radio lineup in New York City in the 1960s. They made appearances together, dressed alike, and even had the same haircut! Some of the original "Good Guys" are pictured here. Left to right: Joe O'Brien, Harry Harrison, Jack Spector, Dan Daniel, Gary Stevens, and Dean Anthony.

Fig. 84. WNBC's Jack Cafferty and Sue Simmons broadcasting live from the deck of the USS *Intrepid* in 1985. Simmons was recently inducted into the NYSBA Hall of Fame in recognition of her 25 years as an anchor at WNBC-TV. Her long-time co-anchor Chuck Scarborough, a 30-year veteran of WNBC, was also inducted.

Fig. 85. "What time is it?", Buffalo Bob Smith would ask the "peanut gallery" at the beginning of each "Howdy Doody Show." Smith got his start in radio in his hometown of Buffalo. Martin Stone, Smith's agent, would convince him to move his children's program, "Triple B Ranch," to the new medium of television in 1947. It would become one of the most enduring children's television shows of all time.

Fig. 86. Geraldo Rivera with Al Vicente (left) of WGNA in Albany and Vicente's wife, Elsa (right). Rivera was the first Puerto Rican television news reporter in New York City. He was hired by Al Primo in the 1970s as part of his "Eyewitness News" format which would make WABC's newscasts more reflective of the people they were serving.

Fig. 87. "The Big Three" network news anchors need little introduction as icons of their respective networks' evening news broadcasts over the last 20 years. Since the departure of Tom Brokaw in 2004, then Dan Rather in 2005, and the late Peter Jennings's unfortunate death from lung cancer, many believe the era of the "larger than life" network news anchor has now passed into history.

Fig. 88. A young Gabe Pressman questions the then Lieutenant Governor Malcolm Wilson. Pressman has been reporting the news in New York City for over 50 years, spending 40 of them at WNBC-TV. He is still actively reporting and hosts a weekly public affairs show on Sunday mornings called "News Forum."

Fig. 89. Buffalo's dominant television news team for over 25 years, pictured from left to right, with their respective years of service at WKBW-TV: anchor Irv Weinstein, 1964–1998; sports anchor Rick Azar, 1958–1989; and weather anchor Tom Jolls, 1965–1999.

Fig. 90. Phil Beuth (left), then an executive at WTEN, is pictured here greeting game show host Dennis James (center) and former WTEN announcer and Hollywood star Ted Knight (right) in 1961. Knight was returning to where his career began, to help out with a WTEN telethon.

nopoly on local news and information. Television would give radio a scare, but it quickly got back in the saddle as a local medium focused on news and music. "It's certainly more complicated for us than it used to be," observes Joe Reilly. He wonders aloud: "What new technology could take people away from broadcasting or what new form of content could take them away?" Television broadcasting has been battling cable for the last 30 years, and it's overall command of the television audience has indeed been diminished.

Satellite radio is an emerging interloper in radio, but additional competition is also being generated within broadcast radio itself. Dennis Webster, a long-time announcer at WJTN in Jamestown, understands that veteran broadcasters like himself need to rethink their approach to broadcasting to make sure they aren't drowned out: "The number of just terrestrial-based signals that are now available in our community compared to 10 or 20 years ago is much greater. Whether it comes via satellite or traditional terrestrial radio, choices for listeners and the number of signals that will divide up the advertising pool is going to increase." The FCC has also recently approved the development of low-powered radio stations, those of the 50- to 100-watt variety, to help fill in "the gaps" of audiences they believe are currently underserved by both commercial and public broadcasters.

Alan Chartock isn't all that concerned about satellite radio. He is already watching out for other new technologies on the horizon that may adversely affect radio: "We don't know what the future of broadcasting holds. We just don't know. Satellite radio is up there, poised to potentially do tremendous damage to the established stations. There are people who think that in 20 years you won't find a tower anywhere. We don't happen to agree with that. We know there's technology that would like to do to satellite radio what it's planning to do to everyone else, which is streaming radio from your computer." What Chartock is referring to is the emerging phenomenon of "podcasting," using Apple's wildly popular iPod to listen to your favorite radio broadcasts anytime and anywhere you want, as well as skipping over commercials. It is to radio what the Personal Video Recorder (PVR) is to television. Internet radio is another emerging competitor as it stumbles through its adolescent stages. As a pioneer in rock and roll, broadcast television, and cable, Al Anscombe says he would have been comfortable taking a chance on the Internet: "I wouldn't be afraid to get into it, although my age is against me." He's now in his 80s.

The world of television is about to explode beyond media mogul John Malone's vision of a 500-channel universe. Forget cable or satellite, says Metromedia's Stu Subotnick, a flood of choices will soon be delivered via broadband: "There are going to be a lot of alternative programming choices coming into the home through a lot of different mediums. Obviously you have cable, you have satellite, but as broadband starts to come to the home, in one form or another, you're going to get new providers of content. Clearly, television is going to have a lot more competition, and the personal computer in the home itself with broadband access creates competition that never existed before." Over the next few years, telecommunications providers will get into the video distribution game using IPTV or Internet Television Protocol. Telecommunications companies like SBC, Verizon, and BellSouth will use their communications networks to deliver television programs directly to consumers' homes, much the same way they do now with voice data and information over the Internet. Access to television shows and other original video content will no longer be limited to network schedules. Instead they will now be made available to consumers on demand.

All this new competition is supposed to create more choice for consumers, and many believe that's a good thing, but it's not without its consequences. "People don't spend as much time with television anymore because there are so many alternative things for them to do. The world has changed so much," observes Phil Beuth. Broadcasters not only compete with other mediums but also for the very time and attention of consumers, who feel compelled by today's societal conventions to jam-pack their already busy schedules.

The proliferation of network news programs, cable news networks, news websites, and now blogs are challenging the underpinnings of traditional journalism. John Kelly believes that information distributed on the Internet is increasingly blurring the line between reality and fact: "One of the things I fear most is that with so many different voices out there, a great deal of what they have to say may not be factual. Radio and television used to rely on the journalistic approach, in which facts would be vetted and stories would have some validity."

Some in the industry regard bloggers (those who post daily diaries, rants, or articles on the web) as "trophy hunters," waiting to pounce on established journalists if there's even a whiff of a misquoted fact. Others believe that the phenomenon of blogs will keep professional journalists on their toes, providing even more transparency in the newsgathering process. Lawrence Taishoff, former publisher of *Broadcasting & Cable*, believes that the tidal wave of information available today has washed away the trust Americans once held for both broadcast and print journalists: "We have been rather naive in the past. We're seeing it for what it is now. We trusted the news media. You cannot, except for certain areas, trust the news media anymore."

Not only has competition blurred the line between fact and fiction, it has also muddied the waters in terms of the audience broadcasters are trying to reach. "Radio has become much more of a niche business, and I don't think any individual radio station today can have any significant impact. Radio is very narrowly focused now," comments former radio station owner, R. Peter Straus. He believes the challenge for broadcasters now is to first figure out whom they want to target and then to "go after" them. Determining who your target audience is and defining who your competitors are will only become more difficult, he warns. "It gets more and more complicated as there are more and more different impacts on any one soul," said Straus, who once headed the Voice of America in the Carter administration.

For the most part, broadcasters used to define themselves by the geographical community they were licensed to serve. Some believe that audiences are now better defined in metaphysical or psychographic terms, by their values, interests or lifestyles. If a businessman or businesswoman is traveling on the other side of the country, should they be given the opportunity to tune in to their local broadcast at home or should they be left no option but to watch the local broadcast in the given market in which they are traveling? This is one of countless questions broadcasters must answer in the coming years.

It has been almost a decade since the passage of the Telecommunications Act of 1996, which launched an era of unprecedented competition in the media and communications marketplace. The spirit of the bill was to allow the natural forces of market competition to determine how content providers, like broadcasters, would develop programming for consumers. Some broadcasters like Paul Dunn believe that more regulation is needed once again to make broadcasters more accountable for the special access they have to the public's airwaves: "I used to get into big arguments with broadcasters because I thought things like the Fairness Doctrine were important. With the expansion of ownership, I think issues like that should be raised." Other broadcasters feel they are still being forced to compete on an unlevel playing field because they are held to special rules, unlike cable, satellite radio, and the Internet, which have a free hand in how they create content. In 2003, the U.S. Senate blocked the FCC's efforts to further relax ownership rules. After a public outcry to slow the pace of deregulation, the FCC was barred from enacting a new rule to allow one company to own television stations that reach 45% of the national audience, up from 35%. Maybe the people really do know best, but only time will tell.

Media on Demand

With relatively few changes, the broadcast model has worked like a clock for the last 50 years. A programming schedule is developed and tweaked when necessary to attract the largest possible audience and then access to that audience is "sold" to advertisers. Simple enough. Viewers and listeners now desire the same degree of control over their television and radio consumption as they do on the Internet. This emerging behavior is no passing fad but a fundamental shift that will radically change how broadcasters manage their businesses.

There has been a shift from "mass media" toward "mass personalization" over the last two decades as consumers desire to have content tailored to their individual tastes. Bob Bruno places this trend in a larger societal context: "There's been a shift in the culture in terms of perspective. It has shifted from 'me as an individual fitting into a community' to more of 'me as the center of the community' and 'everything relating to me.'" Broadcasters have traditionally developed broad program concepts to attract the widest audience possible, but the emerging media marketplace now requires multiple programming concepts to attract a comparably sized audience that just *one* broadcast program used to attract alone. The cookie-cutter, one-size-fits-all formula no longer works in every instance.

To really delve into the intricacies of tomorrow's media behaviors, one need not look further than the media behaviors of today's youth. John Kelly frequently shares a story about a conversation he once had with his 10-year-old granddaughter about the future of local television. "I asked her what her favorite channel was and she responded, 'Channels 33 and 34.' In Albany that happens to be Disney and Nickelodeon. I was shocked. I asked her, 'I meant your favorite local station.' She asked me, 'What is a local station?' If you don't have a kid on your board of directors, you're gone," advises Kelly. Dick Novik has shared a similar experience as he watches his teenagers listen to their iPods instead of radio. He is concerned that technology might be getting ahead of the broadcast industry: "That's the concern I have, that we have been very slow in converting analog to digital both on the radio and TV side. I think we've got to get with that program very quickly before we lose these kids forever."

USC Annenburg's Internet Project, an annual study on the effects of the Internet on media behavior, have shown that the growth of Internet usage, particularly among the young, has in fact come at the expense of time spent with television and radio in particular. Interestingly, there is also evidence that the heaviest users of the Internet also watch more television than those who use the Internet less frequently. It is also not uncommon for people to be using two or even three different media at the same time. This behavior has been described as "multitasking." Andrew Heyward, president of CBS News, has referred to teenagers as "information impressionists," describing their tendency to piece together a story from a variety of different news sources rather than just one or two as their parents do. Recognizing this growing behavior, Ernie Anastos has recently added a local newspaper to his radio holdings in the Albany-Saratoga region: "I combined the stations with print. We started a local newspaper up there, the *Star* newspaper. I worked on that idea because it's a multimedia industry these days. You have to a little bit of everything."

Despite the evolving media behavior of consumers, it can never be forgotten that people buy entertainment, not technology. Cable television started taking off only when it began to provide compelling programming that couldn't be found on broadcast television. Satellite radio unarguably gives consumers a far greater selection of music and unprecedented control over how and when they listen to that music. Local radio broadcasters, however, see satellite's lack of local programming as a competitive advantage to be exploited.

Unlike previous technologies introduced into the broadcast domain, Personal Video Recorders, Video On Demand, and podcasting give consumers unprecedented control over their consumption of programming. They aren't merely a form of distribution like cable or satellite. They don't necessarily improve the production quality of programming as FM once did in radio or as HDTV is now doing for television. People can now "time shift" and watch programs when it is convenient for them with all the functionality of a DVD player, like the ability to rewind, pause, and fast-forward. The PVR has enabled Bill McKibben to watch even more news now: "I'm PVRing the local and national news at 6 and 6:30 p.m., which I never thought I would do. When I first got a PVR, it never occurred to me to do that, but now I skip around and look at all the various broadcasts. I'm even thinking of going back to what I used to do when I was in the television business, watch all three broadcasts, but I used to have to use three different television screens!" McKibben is not alone. Several studies have demonstrated that television usage increases with the introduction of a PVR into the home-viewing experience.

One of the most interesting phenomenon, especially among younger generations, is the willingness of consumers to pay more and more for programming. Phil Beuth never thought he would see the day: "I see people paying for television. Right now, I myself pay over $100 a month to get television, $67 for satellite, and $35 for cable. I just put in a $15,000 home theater that I could never dream I would have before. I never would imagine I would be paying as much as I now do for television."

DVD sales are now one of the primary revenue streams in Hollywood as box office sales continue to decline. Long-time editor of *Broadcasting & Cable* Don West makes his own prediction about the growing trend toward paying for content: "I think it's very likely that the major networks—NBC, ABC, and CBS—will become cable ventures in the next 10 years. They will get the same coverage they get now, but they won't have an affiliate cutting down their clearances, so they can get 100% of their inventory and start getting money for it. Broadcasters have been pursuing a dual-revenue stream for a long time. Eventually they will not be able to compete with other media that do have multiple streams."

Jim Champlin believes that one of those secondary revenue streams for broadcasters lies in the untapped potential of the Internet: "As a radio or television station, you can present a website that has a large amount of information you can't put on the air because of limited airtime such as community events, school closings, etc. There are all sorts of things you can do on the Internet that stations aren't taking advantage of right now." The Internet can also help broadcasters respond to the "on demand" media behaviors of consumers, providing them with local information anytime they want. Champlin warns that broadcasters can no longer afford to overlook the Internet: "They need to understand that they are now in the communications business, not the broadcasting business. I think they have been a little myopic in their thinking. They are reluctant to understand that communications of the future are going to involve the Internet, and you'd better be part of it."

Fostering Localism

The most effective antidote to meeting the rising challenges of the digital media world may lie in broadcasting's local roots. NAB president Eddie Fritts outlines his vision for the future of broadcasting: "By and large, broadcasters built their franchises on localism and that's something no other industry has done. It is important for us as an industry to make sure we continue our local franchise. If, however, we abandon that franchise of localism, then I think we are no different from any other communications medium, and we will not have the ability to attract the mass audiences we have now." Even in the age of the Internet, radio is still the most mobile and immediate method of distributing breaking news to a mass audience. Albany broadcaster Jim Morrell is not naive about the obstacles radio will face as new entrants come into the marketplace, but he believes radio will always be guided by localism: "Now with some of the computer processes you have today, along with the Internet, it is certainly conceivable that there's going to be some transitions, but we're going to have to adjust to it. I think radio is going to survive very nicely for those people who are going to take advantage of the local community aspect of a radio station. It'll be different, but it'll still be the same as well."

Day by day, media outlets are becoming more and more defined by the audience they serve and by the type of content they deliver, rather than by their means of distribution. Broadcasters used to be one of only a few voices in local communities, but now they need to figure out how to make themselves heard among a chorus of other content providers and distribution mechanisms. Don Angelo fears the broadcast networks will no longer need their affiliates because they will have their own direct entrance ramp onto the information superhighway: "Local television stations better figure out real quick what they're going to do for programming. I think the ones that figure out that they need to supply local news and local programming will survive because people will come back to them just for that type of unique fare."

The vast majority of people attracted to broadcasting in its early days saw it as a way to serve their local community. They ingratiated themselves into the fabric of the community, joining the Elks Club and the Kiwanis and sitting on the boards of local charities so they could better understand the needs of their neighbors. Some broadcasters believe that cherished bond with local communities is now evaporating. Adrienne Gaines believes satellite radio and iPods are the least of broadcasters' worries today: "I really think one of our biggest challenges is finding a way to maintain and enhance our bond with our communities. I think a lot of local radio stations take that for granted, especially since the FCC pulled back requirements for community affairs." It is true that "old-time" broadcasters were once obligated by a stack of community service requirements from the FCC, but many of them probably wouldn't have acted any differently because they understood it was good for business. The Wall Street buzzword thrown around today to describe this once revered strategy is "superserving" the community.

There are some lone broadcasters who still serve their communities the old-fashioned way. Paul Dunn describes WBRV in Booneville as broadcasters just doing their job: "It's a typical old-line local radio station where you can hear everything from obituaries to help-wanted ads to swap shops . . . but it really serves its community." Ironically enough, the tried-and-true methods of exemplary broadcasters like Bill O'Shaughnessy may be coming back into vogue, says John Kelly: "O'Shaughnessy, for all his flamboyance and interest in national issues, has always been a local broadcaster, and now that's where the future of this business is once again headed."

Coming Full Circle

The cycle of broadcasting may be coming full circle in more ways than just getting back to basics in terms of better serving local communities. Executives and owners with broadcasting principles coursing through their veins are slowly coming back into gatekeeper positions. They are taking over from the corporate titans who orchestrated the swell of wealth experienced by the industry over the last decade, says Bob Ausfeld: "Ten years ago we had 'money' people who wanted to be broadcasters. When you have money people who become broadcasters, all they want is money back. Now, there has been a trend over the past three years of broadcasters taking over companies. They want to make money but are once again running their stations like broadcasters."

Despite its imperfections, the consolidation of broadcasting wasn't all bad. It helped bring business fundamentals to a "mom and pop" industry and made many of them wealthier than they could have ever imagined. It seems as though the pendulum is beginning to swing back in the other direction, as many in the industry are coming to realize that real growth will come from getting back in touch with local communities rather than from snatching up more properties.

Unfortunately, broadcast stocks, once the darlings of Wall Street, have taken a beating over the last few years as investors review the highly leveraged balance sheets of broadcast companies. More than just hopeful sentiments, Don Angelo believes some large broadcasting companies may start to divest some of their stations: "Depending on the economy, because they're so highly leveraged, these big groups may get squeezed to the point where they're no longer profitable, and they're going to have to start breaking up."

Aside from dire economic predictions, large broadcast empires may also begin seeking ways to weed out their weaker properties. Ed Levine predicts the weakest stations in each cluster will be the first to go: "In the next five years you're going to see some of the big companies like Clear Channel throwing out their fourth and fifth FM stations in a market. They aren't profitable, which makes them time-consuming, so you're going to see some stations start changing hands."

If these scenarios were in fact to play out, most broadcasters hope those who truly love the business and aren't simply looking for a good return alone will once again enter the ownership ranks. They also argue that individual owners would have closer ties to local communities rather than the "absentee owners" who reside halfway across the country.

Developing the Next Generation of New York Broadcasters

Delivering on the promise of localism and meeting the challenges of a highly competitive media landscape will require an investment in the very foundation of the industry—its people. While the business fundamentals introduced in the industry over the last two decades have made it more financially healthy, there is concern that broadcasting is losing sight of its core values. "Hopefully it will stay the same and remain a people business. Despite everything that's happened over the last 80 years, that's the thing that has made this industry what it is—the people. We don't see a lot of young talent today because I believe it has become a business-oriented industry almost exclusively," remarks Don Angelo. There is a balance that needs to be achieved between profits and serving the public good, warns Dennis Swanson: "I always get worried about a business where the employees seek a higher-quality product than the owners sometimes do. I realize profits have to be made. They become more and more difficult in the competitive environment we find ourselves in, but I think we have to remember we are operating on public airwaves and we have a responsibility to serve our communities."

Bill Grimes would spend the formative years of his career at CBS before leaving to eventually become president of ESPN during the 1980s. He remembers the culture there as having "hero bosses," managers who took the time to mentor and train those coming up through the ranks: "They looked at the concept of training and motivating new people, preparing the next generation of managers at CBS as a key responsibility." CBS, at one point, even created the "CBS School of Management" to provide junior executives with formal management training. Grimes fears, in an age when managers now oversee several clusters rather than just a station or two, that there is little time left to help guide the next generation along. However, Nancy Widmann has been pleased by her daughter's training experience at the nation's largest radio conglomerate, Clear Channel: "I have to tell you that my daughter got the most extraordinary training at Clear Channel. I was stunned by the way they trained her. They're making an investment in account executives. We had training programs inside our radio station, but they were really limited." With the proliferation of media outlets, there is also concern about the depth of the talent available to fill the ranks without compromising the quality of programming.

Other broadcasters also ponder whether aspiring broadcasters today are getting into the business for the right reasons. The future quality of broadcasting also rests with their individual long-term career goals, observes John Zach: "Some of the younger people are coming into it for the wrong reasons. I see it every day. They want to start in radio, but as soon as they can, they gravitate toward television. Not because they're really interested in becoming good writers, researchers, gatherers of news or investigative reporters, it's because they want the recognition, the glamour. If they get the recognition, it's going to make them a lot of money." It should be noted that the industry today also helps promote this type of approach toward managing one's career, offering far less job stability than in years past and often callously referring to employees as "headcounts."

The business side of broadcasting has often faced a greater challenge in recruiting young people than on the programming side. For the most part, young adults are attracted to the bright lights and glamour on the creative side of broadcasting rather than the nuts and bolts of selling airtime. Sexy or not, sales is the lifeblood of broadcasting. Nick Verbitsky says the industry needs to face the music on how to attract good people to sales: "I talk to kids all the time about careers. When you mention going into sales in radio or even television, it's not even on their radar. What I'm finding is that more and more jobs are being eliminated. I mean things are tight at a lot of stations. You can't save your way to prosperity in any business. We've got to invest in the radio business, and we've got to bring young people into this industry to keep this going."

Timeless Lessons

Many of the broadcasters who dedicated their entire careers or lives, in some cases, to building television and radio stations in the State of New York are now passing into history. Those now entering the business are full of youthful exuberance and think they have it all figured out. Keela Rodgers remembers when her husband was starting out: "Younger people *always* know better. When Jim started out he had *all* the answers." The breadth of knowledge and the depth of the insights possessed by New York's broadcast legends are a priceless resource from which the next generation of broadcasters can draw upon. The technology may change, the dynamics of the audience's behavior may evolve, new revenue streams come and go, but it is the "essence" of broadcasting, of serving local communities, that will help the next generation of New York's broadcasters navigate a complicated future.

Before a sale is made or a story is run, respect is the key ingredient on the path to living a fulfilling life and to becoming a respected broadcaster. "What I can pass along to young people is to treat broadcasting with respect. Treat the advertisers and the audience with the respect they deserve. Don't be expedient. Say what you mean. Program to the highest level, not to the lowest level, and that will pay great rewards for you, not just for your company, but for yourself," eloquently states Jim Duffy, the former ABC Network chief. It is a given to have respect for oneself and for others. In broadcasting, it is also important to have respect for all those who have walked the pathways before, building the proud legacy of radio and television in New York State. An old boss of Ernie Anastos once told him: "If you're working hard and not succeeding, someone will succeed after you. If you're not working hard and succeeding, somebody worked hard *before* you."

Advice as old as time, but not always heeded, is to just be honest in everything you do, whether it's sales, promotions, or reporting. Outspoken Pat Tocatlian was always known for being a straight shooter in upstate New York: "Well, you can be really nice and sweet, and kind of weasel around to get what you want, or you can be like I am. I tell people what I really think." Of course, she advises to always be respectful of other's beliefs and interests, but over time she has discovered that being direct can prevent a lot of misunderstandings, as well as save time and money.

Anyone seeking a career in broadcasting who does not possess a passion for it will most likely never be truly successful or certainly will never have any fun doing it. Dick Foreman reflects on the philosophy that guided him through his career: "I have been fortunate to toil in the fields of my passion." As previously noted, many young adults entering the business today often have misguided goals like becoming famous or making a lot of money. "I don't think anyone ever made a lot of money without being passionate about what they did. You gotta be on the bus before you can ride," advises Joe Reilly.

Adrienne Gaines has had her share of interns over the years. She's had some good ones and some bad ones. She has always been able to spot the ones who will become successful because they step up to the plate, asking to do more than their fair share and seeking to learn everything they can about broadcasting.

The land of television is filled with countless long-forgotten television programs and business deals. Those that leap from the pages of history were a result of someone who took a risk, a chance. Mediocrity may help achieve the status quo, but it will never help make a mark in the annals of broadcasting. Leavitt Pope encourages tomorrow's managers to go with their gut and not to be afraid of failure: "You have to be willing to take a chance. If you don't take a chance in this business, you're lost. You can do focus groups sometimes, but you have to learn to go with your gut. Just take a shot. Failure is only a bad thing if you keep making the same mistake."

Most people are afraid of sales because of the fear of rejection. Ironically, there are probably few people in all of broadcasting who don't use some sort of sales technique to best perform their jobs. Reporters "sell" people on doing interviews, or producers "sell" their news directors on a new segment idea. No, there isn't always money on the line, but broadcasters across the board constantly put their ideas out there, setting themselves up for possible rejection. Their secret is to insulate themselves with their conviction in the idea they are selling. Warren Bodow believes that understanding sales is crucial to understanding the business as a whole: "Selling, getting rejected, and learning how to push back are invaluable in helping people learn the real values of their medium. In order to know how to work the inside, you need to know how to relate to the outside."

There is tremendous pressure on today's young managers in broadcasting to focus on the bottom line. As has already been discussed, many broadcasting businesses are now part of enormous conglomerates that must answer to the scrutiny of Wall Street analysts, whether they appreciate the intricacies of broadcasting or not. Jim Champlin reminds the next generation that doing good is good for business: "No one should ever get too taken by the concerns of the bottom line. If you concern yourself only with the bottom line, you're going to forget about people, particularly about serving your community. Ultimately you're going to forget about your bottom line because you're not going to be able to deliver it."

Steve Baboulis warns that broadcasters must also guard against complacency: "You should always keep your ear to the ground to make sure you are in tune with what your viewers are telling you. There are some things you must report as a local broadcaster, and there are also some things that are discretionary, items your viewers will tell you they want to see. Striking the balance on all those factors is really going to make local broadcasting remain relevant forever." He uses the example of his station's morning news program. At one time it never had a local morning show, but by listening to its viewers and through its research, the station noticed a lifestyle change that warranted it. Today, like many broadcasters, the station has two full hours of local news programming every morning.

Broadcasting is a people business, a fun business. It is also a business that has the difficult task of showing a community its face in the mirror every day, whether they like what they see or not. As Alan Chartock puts it: "It's incredible fun. One of these days, we're all going to be under a marble slab somewhere, and either our life is going to have meant something or not. I believe what we do means a great deal."

The venerable and shrewd Sumner Redstone, chief executive officer of Viacom, has recently declared the "age of the conglomerate is over." Real financial growth comes from serving people and fostering creativity in both programming and sales. Smaller media entities are more adept at staying closer to the people. After all, who is better served—by a general manager overseeing one station or a general manager overseeing a dozen?

The tentacles of bureaucracy often smother the heart of broadcasting: creativity. Churning out mediocre programs to meet a profit target will slowly turn away listeners and viewers, compromising profits in the long term. Many analysts have now come to agree that the dramatic rise in value of broadcasting over the last 20 years has been mostly attributed to financial schemes under the guise of deregulation, mergers, and consolidations, tactics that have now exhausted their usefulness. The job of Wall Street analysts is to serve investors. The job of broadcasters is to serve an audience. They are two entirely different agendas that must be balanced to ensure the continued development of financially healthy companies designed to serve the *greater* good.

The competitive landscape moving forward will be dictated by how well a media entity serves its audience by genuinely listening to its needs and observing its evolving tastes and behaviors. Emerging digital technologies should not be viewed as threats to broadcasting but rather as opportunities to get even closer to the people. Radio, television, newspapers, magazines, film, the Internet, and other digital platforms on the rise are no longer mutually exclusive. They are merely different "touch points" to reach out to citizens in an even more personalized ways.

When some people think of broadcasting, they may conjure up images of transmission towers or a radio receiver. Others may think of their favorite television shows or remembrances of watching television anchors as they described turning points in history. The word *broadcast* is defined as "widely published, disseminated, or scattered." To be certain, it is all of those things, but at its very core, the essence of broadcasting is about listening and serving. The next generation of New York broadcasters must not become distracted by arbitrary financial targets, the latest "whiz-bang" technology or passing consumer fads.

The mantra "to serve," "to listen," and "to innovate," which has served the profession so well for the first 50 years, shall be the guideposts that will continue to secure broadcasting's place in the future of the Empire State.

Appendix

Past Presidents

Michael R. Hanna*	(two terms)	1955–57
E. R. Vadeboncoeur*		1957–58
William Doerr*		1958–59
Robert Leder		1959–60
George R. Dunham*		1960–61
Paul Adanti*		1961–62
Sam J. Slate*		1962–63
Merl L. Galusha*		1963–64
R. Peter Straus		1964–65
Perry S. Samuels		1965–66
Robert A. Dreyer*		1966–67
Robert K. King		1967–68
Walter A. Schwartz		1968–69
C. Glover Delaney*	(two terms)	1969–71
	(President Emeritus)	1974–75
Robert E. Klose*		1971–72
Richard L. Beesemyer		1972–73
William O'Shaughnessy		1973–74
Leslie G. Arries Jr.*		1974–75
Philip Spencer*		1975–76
Leavitt J. Pope		1976–77
Robert M. Peebles*		1977–78
Tony C. Malara		1978–79
Martin F. Beck		1979–80
Neil E. Derrough		1980–81
William W. Irwin		1981–82
Donald F. Snyder		1982–83
Jack G. Thayer*	(January–April)	1984
Arthur M. Angstreich	(May–December)	1984
Richard D. Novik		1985

Past Chairpersons

Laurence A. Levite	1986
Walter C. Maxwell	1987
James E. Champlin	1988
Patricia C. Tocatlian	1989
Donald D. Perry	1990

Rod Calarco		1991
Cathy Creany		1992
John F. Kelly		1993
Arnold Klinsky		1994
Warren G. Bodow		1995
Michael Eigner		1996
Maire Mason	(two terms)	1997–98
Gary Nielsen		1999
William Cloutier	(January–April)	2000
Dennis Swanson	(two terms)	2000–2001
Eric P. Straus		2002
Bill Ransom		2003
Ed Levine		2004
Stephen Baboulis		2005

*Deceased

New Yorker of the Year Award Recipients

The Honorable Mario M. Cuomo Governor, New York State	1985
Thomas S. Murphy Chairman and CEO, Capital Cities/ABC, Inc.	1986
Eugene Lang Founder, "I Have a Dream" Foundation	1987
Rudolph Giuliani U.S. Attorney, Southern District of New York	1988
The Honorable Saul Weprin Chairman, Assembly Ways and Means Committee	1989
The Honorable David N. Dinkins Mayor, City of New York	1990
New York State Operation Desert Storm Troops	1991
The Honorable Daniel Patrick Moynihan United States Senator from New York	1993
Matilda Raffa Cuomo First Lady, New York State	1994
Robert C. Wright President and CEO, NBC	1997

Libby Pataki First Lady, New York State	1998
Ivan Seidenberg Chairman and CEO, Bell Atlantic/Verizon	1999
Senator Joseph Bruno New York State Senate Majority Leader	2000
George Steinbrenner Principal Owner, New York Yankees	2001
New York City Fire Department The 300+ firemen who lost their lives at the World Trade Center	2002
Regis Philbin Co-host, "Live with Regis and Kelly"	2003
Jim Boeheim Head Coach, Men's Basketball, Syracuse University	2004
Jeanine F. Pirro District Attorney, Westchester County, New York	2005

Delaney-Cuneen Award Winners

Robert M. Peebles	1976
Richard Hughes	1977
Phil Beuth	1979
Arthur Harrison	1980
Martin F. Beck	1981
Edward McLaughlin	1982
Leslie G. Arries	1983
Tony C. Malara	1984
Arthur M. Angstreich	1985
Leavitt J. Pope	1987
Ralph Guild	1988
John W. Tabner	1989
Maurie Webster	1990
James Delmonico	1991
Shell Storrier	1992
Vincent DeLuca	1993
Richard D. Novik	1995
Lawrence P. Sweeney	1996

Broadcaster of the Year Award Winners

John F. Kelly	1997
Mel Karmazin	1998
Tim Russert	1999
Regis Philbin	2000
Roone Arledge	2001
Dick Ebersol	2002
Lowry Mays	2003
Dan Rather	2004
Peter Jennings	2005

Carol M. Reilly Memorial Award Winners

Maire Mason	2001
Sarah Hughes	2002
Lieutenant Governor Mary Donohue	2003
Joanna Bull	2004
Marylou Whitney	2005

The Broadcast Beat

Don Imus once observed: "In the hierarchy of the newspaper and print business, writing about radio and television is one step up from *delivering* the damn thing!"

The I-Man's friendly jibe aside, the broadcasting profession in the Empire State has been fortunate that its doings and deliberations were covered by all these gifted and able journalists during NYSBA's first 50 years.

Cindy Adams, *The New York Post*
Val Adams, *New York Daily News*
Jack Allen, *Buffalo Courier-Express*
Ken Auletta, *The New Yorker*
Jim Baker, *Buffalo Courier-Express*
Jane Barton, *Variety*
P. J. Bednarski, *Broadcasting & Cable*
Valerie Block, *Crain's New York Business*
James Brady, *Ad Age*
Les Brown, *Variety*
Adam Buckman, *The New York Post*
Reed Bunzel, *Radio Ink*
Jim Carnegie, *Radio Business Report*
Kevin Casey, *Talkers Magazine*
John Crosby, *Herald Tribune*
Fred Danzig, *Ad Age*
Gary Deeb, *The Buffalo News*
Jerry DelColliano, *Inside Radio*
Fred Dicker, *The New York Post*
Bob Doll, "Small Market Radio Newsletter"
John Eggerton, *Broadcasting & Cable*
Erica Farber, *Radio & Records*
Don Fitzpatrick, *ShopTalk*
Matthew Flamm, *Crain's New York Business*
Scott Fybush, *NorthEast Radio Watch*
Kay Gardella, *New York Daily News*
Kevin Goldman, *New York Magazine*
Jack Gould, *The New York Times*
Doug Hall, *Billboard* and "The Hall Report"
Doug Halonen, *Television Week*
Michael Harrison, *Talkers Magazine*
David Hinckley, *New York Daily News*
Richard Huff, *The New York Post*

Ed James, *Broadcasting & Cable*
Harry Jessell, *Broadcasting & Cable*
Richard Johnson, *The New York Post*
Steve Knoll, *Variety*
Mary Ann Lauricella, *The Buffalo News*
Mona Lipschitz, *Talkers Magazine*
Jack Loftus, *Variety*
John Mainelli, *The New York Post*
Jim Mann, *The Gallagher Report*
Carl Marcucci, *Radio Business Report*
Carole Marks, *Talkers Magazine*
Kim McAvoy, *Broadcasting & Cable*
Mark McGuire, *Albany Times-Union*
Paul McLane, *Radio World*
Mark Miller, *Broadcasting & Cable*
Jay Mitchell, "Small Market Radio Newsletter"
Jack Messmer, *Radio Business Report*
Jack O'Brian, *The Journal-American*
John J. O'Connor, *The New York Times*
Barbara Pinckney, *Albany's Business Review*
Alex Philipidus, *Suburban Business Journals*
Tracy Primeau-Lewis, *The Legislative Gazette*
Eric Rhodes, *Radio Ink*
J. Max Robins, *Broadcasting & Cable*
J. Don Schlearth, *Buffalo Courier-Express*
Dave Seyler, "Radio Business Report"
Norm Shaw, *Westchester Business Journal*
Jeff Simon, *The Buffalo News*
Liz Smith, *The New York Post*
Allan Sniffen, *New York Radio Message Board*
Michael Starr, *The New York Post*
Larry Taishoff, *Broadcasting & Cable*
Sol Taishoff, *Broadcasting & Cable*
Tom Taylor, *Inside Radio*
Don Tranter, *The Buffalo News*
Neal Travis, *The New York Post*
Tony Violanti, *The Buffalo News*
Don West, *Broadcasting & Cable*
Robert Windeler, *The New York Times*
Len Zeidenberg, *Broadcasting & Cable*

ABOUT THE AUTHOR

Stephen Warley has written extensively about broadcasting and the development of digital media. As general manager of TVSpy.com, a website dedicated to broadcast television, he created a column, "Next Generation TV," analyzing new content, business, and technology opportunities in television.

His first book, *Vault Career Guide to Journalism & Information Media*, was published in 2005. He completed his MBA in media management and finance at Fordham Business School in 2004. As part of his MBA, he co-authored a research study analyzing the digital media strategies of the Top-25 media companies. It was published in the summer 2005 edition of Booz Allen's *Strategy + Business*.

Previously, he has worked as a project manager for ThirdAge Media and as a segment producer at CNBC. He has also produced and provided production support for various CBS broadcasts, including *CBS News Sunday Morning, The Early Show*, CBS Sports' coverage of the XVIII Winter Olympic Games in Nagano, Japan, and CBS News' special coverage of the 9/11 attacks, *America Under Attack*. He graduated magna cum laude with a BA in history from Providence College in 1996.

Name Index

Boldface numbers refer to numbered
photographs listed on the page after
the table of contents.

Herman, Scott, **54**
Heyward, Andrew, 88, 200
Hinckley, David, 69, 121, 169, 172–73
Horne, Lena, 146
Hosking, Bob, **15**
Hughes, Richard "Dick," 24, 140
Hughes, Sarah, 26
Hundt, Reed, 55
Huntley, Chet, 126

I

Imus, Don, 141, 145, 158, **73**
Ito, Judge, 41

J

Jackson, Hal, 96
Jackson, Janet, 52, 159
Jacobsen, Steven, 88
Jacon, Mary Anne, 23, **4**
Jagger, Mick, 152
Jaker, Bill, 116, 122, 178
James, Dennis, **90**
Jankowski, Gene, 133
Jansing, Chris, 134
Javits, Jacob K., 19, 139, 169
Jay, Bobby, 141
Jennings, Jason, 11
Jennings, Peter, **87**
Jolls, Tom, **87**
Judis, Bernice "Tudie," 2

K

Kanze, Peter, 116–17
Karmazin, Mel, 101
Kasem, Kasey, 100
Kaufman, Murray "The K," 151
Keesee, Fred, 4
Kehelle, John, 135
Keith, Hastings, 82
Kelly, John, 8, 23, 42–43, 98, 112, 115, 119, 166, 168, 190, 198, 200, 203, **16**
Kemp, Jack, **30**
Kennedy, John F., 134, 138, **48**
Kennerknecht, Gary, 15
King, Bob, 1–2, 23

King, Guy, 149
King, Larry, 19, 121, 144, 158, **24**
King, Martin Luther, 78, **38**
King, Roger, 6, **9**
Kirchhofer, Alan, 102
Kirchhofer, Alfred, 103
Klavan, Gene, 145, 157–58, **65**
Klein, Elliot, 14
Klestine, Fred, 152
Klinsky, Arnold, **31**
Klose, Robert "Bob," 23, 28
Kluge, John, 99–100
Knight, Ted, **90**
Knox, Seymour, 104
Koch, Ed, 19, 143, **28**
Kuralt, Charles, 134

L

Labunski, Steve, 149
Laird, Melvin, 81
Landers, Bob, 145
Landsman, Dick, 22
Langston, Andrew, 66, 78, 92, 109, **31, 59**
LaRosa, Julie and Rory, **43**
Law, Bob, 141
Lawrence, Dick, 146
Lazare, Jack, 145
Lehrman, Lew, 19, 143
Leone, Lew, **57**
Lesniak, Dan, 173
Lesniak, Nancy, 173
Levine, Ed, 23, 54, 59–60, 77, 94–95, 100, 112, 161–63, 172, 174, 204
Levite, Larry, 20–21, 86, 143, 144, 171, 176, **30**
Ley, Martha, 79
Liberace, **67**
Lieberman, Linda Arnold, 156
Lillis, Barry, 76
Limbaugh, Rush, 19, 47, 121, 142–45, **68**
Little Richard, 148
Loevinger, Lee, 46
Lombardo, Phil, 75, 96
Lorenz, Frank, 119, 147–49, 185, **30**
Lorenz, George "Hound Dog," 111, 146–48, 152–53, 185, **70**

O

O'Boyle, Maureen, 19, 121
O'Brien, Joe, 149–50, **83**
O'Connor, John (Cardinal), 19
Ogilvie, David, 109–10
O'Grady, James, Jr., 14
O'Hara, Marty, 145
Ohrenstein, Manfred "Fred," 44
Opie and Anthony, 188
O'Reilly, Bill, 19
Orzio, Nicholas, 74
Osgood, Charles, 19, 121, 134
O'Shaughnessy, David, 66
O'Shaughnessy, Matthew, 66
O'Shaughnessy, William "Bill," 6–7, 15, 18, 20–21, 23–24, 28, 51, 66, 69, 73–75, 81, 83, 89, 160, 163, 169, 174, 196, 203, **10, 18**
Owen, Mitch, 103–04

P

Paar, Jack, 157
Pacheco, Johnny, 155
Page, Jimmy, 152
Paley, William S., 82–83, 99, 132–33, **62**
Palumbo, Nancy, 50
Pappas, Ike, 145
Parish, Joe, **59**
Parson, Pat, **7**
Pascucci, Mike, 96
Pataki, George E., 9, 34–35, 42, **29**
Pattison, Bob, 88
Patton, John, 156
Pauley, Jane, 19, 121
Peebles, Robert "Bob," 7, 20–21, 23–24, 28
Pettengill, Todd, 158
Philbin, Regis, 19
Poltrack, David, 168
Pope, Leavitt, 19, 86, 101–02, 131, 140, 172, 207, **10, 49**
Povich, Maury, 19
Powers, Bill, 35
Pressman, Gabe, **88**
Presley, Elvis, 147, 159, **70**
Primo, Al, 18, 62–63, 128–30
Purtan, Dick, 149

Q

Quaal, Ward, 47

R

Ransom, Bill, **61**
Raphael, Sally Jesse, **22**
Rappleyea, Clarence "Rapp," 44
Rather, Dan, 19, 121, **4, 87**
Rayburn, Gene, 157–58
Reagan, Ronald, 46–47, 51–52, 61, 128
Reasoner, Harry, 126
Redstone, Sumner, 208
Reed, B. Mitchel, 149
Reed, Fred, Jr., 78
Reid, Ogden Rogers, 19, 83
Reilly, Carol, 24, 26, 98, **2**
Reilly, Joseph "Joe," 3, 5, 6–13, 15–16, 19–21, 23, 25–28, 31, 34–36, 39, 41, 43, 49, 60, 66, 75, 107, 168, 171, 172, 180, 188, 197, 207, **7, 8, 18, 58, 76**
Rene, Henri, 146
Reynolds, Joey, 146
Rich, Mike, 145
Rigas, John, 190
Rio, John "Mr. Leonard," 158
Riordan, John, 80
Rivera, Geraldo, 19, 121, 130, **86**
Rivera, Isaias, 88
Rizzuto, Phil, **63**
Robinson, Jackie, 61
Robinson, Rachel, 61
Rockefeller, Nelson A., 19, 30, 38, 50, 131, 140, 164, **11, 26**
Rodgers, Jim, 53, 64, 71–72, 85, 92, 111–13, 138–39, 160, 206
Rodgers, Keela, 53, 64–65, 85, 92, 112, 206
Rose, Charley, 141
Rose, Susan, 59
Roselli, Jim, 76, 116
Rosen, Merrill, 70, 76, 133, 167
Rosenblatt, Albert, 40
Roslin, Marv, 170
Roth, Paula, 49
Rowan, Steve, 135
Rozelle, Pete, 156
Rubin, David, 53, 191–92

Subject Index

Black music, 152
Blizzard of 1977, 84–85
Blogs, proliferation of, 198
Bohack's, 136–37
Books on tape, 65
"Breakfast Club," 122
Break line of pay, 129
Broadband, 191—02
Broadcast advertising
    evolution of, 164–66
    New York State Assembly efforts to tax,
        33–34
Broadcasters
    accidental, 61–63
    availability to community, 85–86
    defending rights of, 27–56
    insurance for, 13–14
Broadcasters Foundation, 18, 68, 96
Broadcast Indecency Act (2004), 159
Broadcasting
    business side of, 205–06
    competitiveness in, 2–3
    consolidation of, 169–74, 204
    cycle of, 203–04
    distinguishing between print media
        and, 175
    evolution of, 162
    as family business, 63–66
    future quality of, 205
    life passion of, 58–61
    New York's relative importance in, 2
    targeting potential of, 108
    trials and triumphs of building, 92–96
    women in, 78–79
    workshops to expand knowledge in,
        11–13
Broadcasting Magazine, 82–83
Broadcast journalism, role of, 126–27
Broadcast licenses, 162–64
    commoditization of, 52
    renewal of, 55
Broadcast personalities, 146
Broadcast sales, 107–08
    strategies for, 112–14
Broadcast stocks, 204
Broadcast television
    impact of cable television on, 181–93

value of stations, 104–05
Buffalo, University of, 87
Buffalo Evening News, 102–03
Buffalo Spree, 86
Bumpers, 116

C

Cable television, 126
    growth of, 166
    impact of, 181–83
    proliferation of, 198
"Call-in" radio talk show, 141
"Call-on-Albany" Day, 44
Calls on Congress, 43–45
Cameras in the courtroom, 38–42
Capital Cities/ABC, 98
    Walt Disney Company's acquisition of,
        98
Capital Cities (CapCities) Broadcasting,
    103
    founding of, 66, 97, 163, 195
    management of, 6, 52, 117–18
    sale of ABC to, 142
    strategy for growth, 97
Cash flow funding, 104–05
CBS
    affiliations sought with, 99
    free speech defense and, 83
    in-house syndication arm of, 45
    management of, 120
    news broadcasts on, 131–32
    spin-off of in-house syndication arm,
        45
    spot advertising on, 107
CBS Broadcast Center, 88
CBS Broadcast Group, 133
CBS News, 88
    management of, 88, 91
CBS Pentagon correspondent, 135
CBS Radio, 79, 186
    advertising on, 110
    formats on, 122
    management of, 2, 118, 186
CBS School of Management, 205
CBS Television, 105, 106, 168
    affiliate swaps and, 105–06

Electronic newsgathering equipment (ENG), 177
Emergency Alert System (EAS), 42–43, 83
Emergency Broadcast System (EBS), 23
  effectiveness of, 42–43
Emmis Television, 16, 196
Employee ownership programs, 119
English language, 79
Entercom, 171
Entrepreneurialism, 91
Equal Employment Opportunity (EEO) programs, 14, 45
ESPN, 166, 205
Essex Weight Loss Center, 110
Evergreen Broadcasting, 173
Exclusivity, 113
"Eyewitness News" format, 18, 128–29, 130, 138

F

Fairchild Publications, 97
Fairness Doctrine, 46–48, 51, 67, 138
Fan clubs, 148
Federal Communications Commission (FCC)
  approval of low-powered radio stations, 197
  control over political programming and obscenity, 53
  deregulation activities by, 44
  docket 80/90, 53–54
  Equal Employment Opportunities (EEO) requirements of, 14
  Equal Time Amendment, 47
  Fairness Doctrine, 13, 46–47, 51, 67, 81, 82, 138, 199
  Financial Interest and Syndication Rules (Fin-Syn Rules), 45–46
  HDTV and, 179
  Inspection Checklist, 17
  length of safe harbor period, 159
  outreach requirements, 15–16
  ownership rules under, 93, 97, 162–63, 199
  Prime Time Access Rule, 45
  storecasting and, 183
  transfer of licenses, 45

Federal deregulation, 51–53
Films
  guidelines for valuing, 33
  videotape replacement of, 177–78
First Amendment rights, 13, 40, 46, 80–83
"First Team News," 135
FM
  growth of, 177
  rise of, 123, 183–84
Fort Orange Club, 6–7
Fourth branch of government, 80–83
FOX, 88, 126
"Fred Friendly Roundtable," 12
Free speech, right to, under First Amendment, 80–83
Frequency programs, 115

G

Galaxy Communications (Syracuse), 59, 162
General Electric, 61, 106–07
Gideon Putnam Hotel, 20
Glen Falls, 166
"Global Black Experience," 141–42
Good Humor Ice Cream Company, 108
Goodwill, stirring, in community, 74–77
Government intrusion into content, 160
Granite Broadcasting, 65
Graphics, computer-generated, 192
"Great Idea Exchange," 11
Great Northeast Blackout, coverage of, 53

H

Handshake deals, 111–12
Happy talk, 137
Harmon Broadcasting (Utica), 182
HDTV, 179, 180
  Federal Communications Commission (FCC) and, 179
Hearing, listening versus, 122
Herald-Tribune, 19, 73
Herald Tribune Radio Network, 73–74
Heritage programming, 79–80
High Definition (HD) Radio, 189
Hillbilly music, 153
Hispanics in broadcasting, 80

New York State Franchise Tax Return, 33

New York State Lottery, 50

New York State Radio and Television Broadcasters Association. *See* New York State Broadcasters Association (NYSBA)

New York State's Civil Rights Law, 38

New York State Tax Commission, 33

New York State Wagering and Racing Systems, 50

The New York Times, 37, 62, 65, 82

Nickelodeon, 168, 200

"Nightline," 133

Non-Commercial Sustaining Announcement (NCSA) program, 16–17

Nonentertainment programming, 126–27

Normandy Broadcasting (Glen Falls), 25

Norton Simon conglomerate, 108

O

Obituary announcements, 70–71, 114

Off-network shows, 125
  creation of new market for, 45

Oldies format, 153–54

On-demand media behaviors, 202

Oneonta, 166

The Oneonta Star, 135

"Operation Good Neighbor," 77

"The Oprah Winfrey Show," 68

Otesaga Hotel (Cooperstown), 20

Ownership, trials and triumphs of, 92–96

P

Pamal Broadcasting (Albany), 17, 98

Payless, 167

PBS station (New York), 35

The Pentagon Papers, publication of, 82

Performers Royalty Bill, 43

Personalized programming, trend of, 180

Personal touch, 111

Personal video recorders (PVRs), 191, 197, 201

Philips cassettes, 178

Phone drives, 115

Play-by-play broadcasts, 156

Podcasting, 189, 191, 197, 201

Positioning, concept of, 11

Prime Time Access Rule, 45

Printed circuit boards, 177

Print media, distinguishing between broadcasting and, 175

Productivity, increased, 176–77

Profit sharing, 119

Programming
  cookie-cutter, 124, 172–73
  developing, for television, 124–26
  effects of deregulation on, 173
  heritage, 79–80
  homogenized, 53
  innovative news, 128–34
  live local, 125
  nonentertainment, 126–27
  personalized, 181
  proliferation of choices of, 180

Project Literacy, 75–76

Project SMART (Stop Marketing Alcohol on Radio and Television), 49

Promotions, 115–17, 151–52

Pryor Cashman Sherman & Flynn, 31

Public broadcasters, protecting New York's, 35–36

Public service announcements (PSAs), 16–17, 50, 75, 88

"Puppet Playhouse," 73

Q

Quality, improvements in, 178–79

Quarter-hour maintenance, 123–24

Quinnipiac University (Hamden), 47

R

Radio, 121–22
  cellphones offering programming, 189
  creation of multiple networks, 187
  formats on, 122–24, 146, 147, 149–54, 166
  on the Internet, 191
  as niche business, 198–99
  satellite, 159, 188–90, 196, 197
  talk, 47, 141–45
  urban, 96

WSNY Radio (Schenectady), 5
WSYR-TV (Syracuse), 4, 53, 136
WTEN-TV (Albany), 37, 97, 134
WTLB Radio (Utica), 13, 67, 78, 127
WTNH-TV (New Haven, CT), 137
WTRY (Albany), 26, 98
WUFO Radio (Buffalo), 154–55
WUTR-TV (Utica), 15
WVIP Radio (Westchester), 73, 74
WVOR (Rochester), 104
WVOX Radio (New Rochelle), 28, 69, 74, 89, 189
WWNY-TV (Watertown), 84, 85
WWOL Radio (Buffalo), 149, 152
WWOM Radio (Albany), 6
WWRL (New York City), 10, 15, 66, 109, 141, 155

WWSC Radio (Glens Falls), 25
WXLO, 4
WXRA Radio (Buffalo), 147
WXRL Radio, 153
WXXI Public Broadcasting (Rochester), 35
WXYR Radio (Buffalo), 64
WYNY Radio (New York City), 173

X

XM (satellite radio), 188

Y

Young Broadcasting, 160

For additional copies of this
book and for more information about

NYSBA

please write:

**New York State
Broadcasters Association
1805 Western Avenue
Albany, NY 12203**

or call:

518-456-8888

or visit our website:
www.nysbroadcastersassn.org